THE
ONE
AND
ONLY

CHIC HARLEY - AMERICA'S GREAT ATHLETE

TODD C. WESSELL

Peppertree Press
Sarasota, Florida

Part of the proceeds from book sales will go toward

CHIC HARLEY MEMORIAL TRIBUTE.

www.chicharley.com

For information regarding permission,
call 941-922-2662 or contact us at our website:
www.peppertreepublishing.com or write to:
the Peppertree Press, LLC.
Attention: Publisher
1269 First Street, Suite 7
Sarasota, Florida 34236

ISBN: 978-1-936051-32-8

Library of Congress Number: 2009904923

Printed in the U.S.A.

Printed May 2009

Paperback edition printed July 2009

TO DAD, NANA AND THE FAMILY

In one of the greatest tributes ever afforded an Ohio State student/athlete, the school's famed marching band broke with tradition on November 20, 1948 by changing the name OHIO to read CHIC. Never before had such an honor been given to anyone associated with the school. The occasion was Chic's triumphant return to Ohio State following years of struggling with mental illness.

TABLE OF CONTENTS

Chic in famous punting pose which nearly 30 years later was etched on facade of the University Theater across from Ohio State campus.

FOREWORD

To many today, the name Chic Harley means nothing other than something to do with a young lady on a motorcycle. To some, it triggers a wisp of recollection linked with puzzlement and a blurred sense of sorrow. To others, feelings of wonder and pride percolate.

Nine decades after he played his last college football game and thirty-five years since his death, only a handful of people still alive really knew this remarkable man, who led such an astonishing life, and the profound effect he had on American sport, in particular, football.

In his day, Chic was not only considered by many as the best football player in the country, but one of its greatest all-around athletes. People from all corners of the nation heard of his blazing speed, his magical ability to pass and punt, and his knack for hitting a baseball. He was not only considered a natural-born athlete, but a natural leader because of his unassuming, magnetic personality and special athletic skills. Throughout the first half of the twentieth century, his fame remained widespread, despite the tragedy of mental illness that by the 1930s had completely engulfed him. Over time, as his friends and those who had witnessed his amazing feats died off and the stigma of schizophrenia hardened the hearts of many, memories of Chic Harley gradually clouded over much of what really was. The once fore-gone conclusion that the horseshoe-shaped Ohio Stadium would be named in his honor faded away, possibly in part because of salacious, untrue rumors that he had contracted venereal disease.

Suggestions that an appropriate memorial be erected on the Ohio State University campus to recognize his contribution to the school and community drifted into the abyss. To most, Chic Harley had become an aberration—a glimmer of the past that somehow could not be defined. Time had created a vacuum, which served as a spawning ground for half-truths, fabrications, and inaccuracies, despite many good intentions. This book will dispel most of those untruths and sharpen the focus on who he was and what he was like as a human being, as documented by never before seen records and through the eyes of those who knew him.

Charles "Chic" Harley was a great American athlete. But he was also a great man who was loved by many friends, admirers, and family members—a handful of who still live today.

Beginning in the late 1940s, with the arrival of new medicines and treatments, Chic Harley's mental condition—once thought hopeless—began to slowly improve. He no longer was confined to the mental wards of the Danville, Illinois, Veterans Hospital, where he had resided since 1938. He could now travel north to Chicago to spend time with his sister, Ruth, and her large family, and on occasion, to Columbus to watch a football game or attend a team reunion. During those journeys to Ruth's suburban home in Des Plaines, Chic would spend from a few weeks to a few months enjoying his sister's hospitality, sharing time with his nephew Richard and Mary Jane and their six young children. Chic would regularly make the treks on the major holidays like Easter, Thanksgiving, and Christmas, and various other times during the year when no special reason existed for him to travel north other than to be with loved ones.

Those were great times. We would visit and do everything we could to strike up a conversation with our Uncle Chic. Occasionally, he'd let out a belly laugh, which would last but a few seconds before he caught himself and settled back into his usual quietness. Uncle Chic always seemed to be smiling. He was genuinely interested in his surroundings and current events and enjoyed reading the newspaper. He was immaculate in his appearance, usually wearing a nicely pressed suit and dress shoes that would scream out a shine. His white hair was always neatly trimmed. And when standing, his hands were usually tucked into his pants pockets, accentuating his shy demeanor. If prodded, Uncle Chic would answer a question with a one- or two-word answer. Every time someone would enter a room, he would reach out to shake the person's hand, always flashing a welcoming smile. It never ceased to amaze me that his handshake was always firm and strong, despite his advanced years. Not once do I recall a negative word spoken by or against Chic.

The two people who knew Chic the best in those years were Ruth and Richard. Ruth lived up to the promise she made to her dying mother, Mattie, in 1947 to do everything she could to take care of her brother. She constantly worried about his health and well-being. Finding room for Chic in her cramped home, nurturing him, feeding him, and pouring out her love to him was all part of keeping her word.

After Ruth died, Richard stepped up to fulfill the wishes of his mother and grandmother. While Dad always told his children that Uncle Chic was a great football player, Dad always stressed that Uncle Chic was a better human being.

The full and accurate story of Chic Harley had to be told before it was too late and replaced with guessing fueled by rumor that comes with the passing of time. He was much more than just a great athlete. His story is one that embraces the human emotions of love, kindness, compassion, tragedy, deception, and admiration. Other stories have been written about Chic Harley. None, until now, have told the full and complete saga as seen by those who really knew him, shared a dinner table with him, enjoyed his company on vacations and during holidays, sang with him, and could truly call him their friend and their uncle.

Time, like the continuous lapping of waves against the beach, has a way of washing away the footprints of life. No one or nothing is to blame. It's the way this world of ours functions unless someone or something intervenes.

The One And Only is the result of a 35-year quest to make sure that the footprints laid down by America's Great Athlete, Chic Harley, do not disappear. It's a biography that takes the reader on the trail of the Harley family's journey from Virginia to Ohio to Illinois then back to Ohio. It describes in full documented detail the great ups and downs of a man whose star has not yet completely faded from the memories of all who have heard his name.

When asked by his nephew Richard Wessell which sport he liked the most, Chic thought for a moment and answered "golf" because he enjoyed the serenity that the game brought to him.

ACKNOWLEDGEMENTS

My first recollections of the possibility for a book being written someday about Charles William "Chic" Harley date back to somewhere in the early 1960s, when my dad, Richard Wessell, would often talk about his dream project. In those days, we'd frequently see Uncle Chic at my grandmother's house visiting with his sister, Ruth, for extended stays, having traveled north from the Veterans Administration Hospital in Danville, where he lived for many years.

It was clearly evident that Dad was proud of his uncle. Dad, of course, was well aware of Chic's greatness as a football player and the high esteem he received from Columbus and the Ohio State community. But the roots of Dad's awareness burrowed well below the surface. Underneath, his real love and fascination with Uncle Chic was with his personality and demeanor and the way he carried himself through a life of majestic ups and treacherous downs—always humble, always reserved, never boastful. That's what endeared Dad the most to his famous uncle. What Chic accomplished as a young man before Dad was born only intensified his interest in his mother's youngest brother. Through personal observation and experience, Richard Wessell's life as an only child evolved to embrace many of the same winsome characteristics Uncle Chic possessed.

As for development of this book, I believe that those individuals who tirelessly devoted themselves to unearthing and spreading the story sensed from the beginning that they were involved in something special. A man whom they knew little or nothing about came alive as the weeks passed into months and years. While only a precious few who were involved actually knew Chic, everyone nurtured his or her own personal connection with him, giving even more credence to the belief that his story must be told.

The debt of gratitude I owe all of these individuals is immeasurable. The devotion they gave brought these pages, and we hope, Chic Harley, to life for everyone to learn about and enjoy.

Sometime around fall 1912 as Chic Harley's fame began to spread, Mattie Harley began cutting out newspaper clippings of her son's athletic performances. At first, the articles were small accounts mainly of football games. With each high school contest came lengthier stories about his running, passing, and kicking. When Harley finally reached Ohio State University in 1915, the number of reports had become a torrent. Mattie saved everything she could, carefully gluing them in a large scarlet-colored family album. Emblazoned on its front was a large white "O," signifying Ohio State University. Eventually, hundreds of articles, photos, and letters detailing the athletic life of Chic from the period of 1912 to the 1930s filled the album. This formed the foundation of *The One and Only*. When Mattie died, she passed the book down to Ruth. When Ruth passed away, she gave it to her son, Richard, for safekeeping. Now, the children of Richard and Mary Jane Wessell bear the responsibility of maintaining this treasured family record.

A great deal of gratitude for this book is owed to Russ Finneran, an Ohio State graduate whose father and uncle knew and loved Chic. Russ remains passionate about the prospect of Ohio Stadium one day being renamed Harley Stadium. His frequent visits to the Ohio State Archives unearthed precious material used in this book, and he remains one of Chic's biggest cheerleaders.

Early on, I received considerable help tracking down information from the Cook County Circuit Court Clerk's Archive Office as well as the Staley Manufacturing Company in Decatur, Illinois, for which Harley played all of his professional football games. The Cook County Clerk's Office provided tremendous help tracking down Harley birth and death certificates. At Ohio State, Bertha Ihnat, manuscripts assistant of the Archives Office, displayed great patience fulfilling our many requests for information. Also, in Columbus, Chris Lewie, an author and OSU alum, provided us with leads and information, as did Tom Pearcy, grandson of John Wilce, from his suburban Chicago home.

We also want to thank Connie Paul, daughter of Louise Havens, and her nephew Michael Paul for spending time with us telling stories of Chic and Louise and showing us the Varsity "O" pin he gave her in 1919, signifying their close relationship.

Former Ohio State Athletic Director Andy Geiger was very gracious during a visit to his office in 2004, where he explained that the creation of the famed Ohio State "Ring of Fame" in the horseshoe stadium was the idea of my dad. We also want to acknowledge the encouragement we received from Ohio State Associate Vice President of University Development John Meyer during a 2008 visit to the college campus.

A big part of this book involves the nearly four decades of Chic's life when he lived at the Veterans Administration Hospital in Danville, Illinois. Approximately one thousand pages of medical records, hospital reports, and personal letters, available only to close family relatives, were obtained through the hard work of Alice Horstman, assistant to U.S. Rep. Henry Hyde of Illinois's 6th Congressional District.

A very special thank you goes out to Tony Tomlinson, an engaging family man we just happened to stumble upon during one of our endless searches for Chic Harley clues. Unbeknownst to us at the time, Tony's passion was genealogy. When he heard about our journey to learn more about the Harley family, he leaped to the challenge by offering his services free of charge. Tony spent hundreds of hours pouring over ancient records in search of signs to help unravel the mystery of where the Harley family came from and what circumstances helped shape Chic's parents and Chic himself. Tony turned out to be one in a million.

The efforts of my brothers and sisters, all of who knew and loved Uncle Chic, are also very much appreciated. The recollections of Bob, Rick, Kiki, Shelby, and Steve provided rare insight into the subject of the book that can only be provided by close family and friends.

Once the initial draft of the book was written, five close friends agreed to read the manuscript and provide me the valuable input I needed to move forward. Without their help, I'm afraid *The One and Only* would have fallen woefully short of its potential. Those five individuals are: Mike Poulos, a high school pal and accomplished newspaper movie critic who had to endure my constant verbal updates on the project; Mary Alice Wenzl, a fellow worker and talented travel writer who cheerfully helped out in so many ways, as she copied and filed thousands of records, attended meetings, and poured over first drafts, always willing to help make the project become reality; Karen Kozenczak, an author in her own right who developed a strong sentimental attachment to Chic; good friend and avid reader Steve Tolan; and Dick Barton, the owner of a Chicago public relations company, who, like the author, is a newspaper reporter at heart.

In preparing the book for publishing and distribution, a team of Chic Harley enthusiasts was brought together for the common goal of getting the word out. Their yeoman efforts were and continue to be focused and professional. Those team members are: Barton, Wenzl, Ron Friedman, Michelle Friedman, Christopher Schulp, and Bob Ibach.

Spending dozens of hours pouring over the manuscript and taking on the all-important task of editing was Diana Cook, who did a great job. Diana was referred to me by award-winning travel writer Mary Bergin. The task of publishing the book is Julie Ann Howell's from The Peppertree Press, headquartered in Sarasota, Florida.

Finally, words cannot adequately express the appreciation and love I have for my close-knit family that had to endure the long nights and weekends I spent away from home piecing together *The One and Only*. My wife, Carolyn, never complained and was always encouraging, even to the point of presenting me with a birthday gift of an Oxford American Thesaurus that stayed by my side through the whole process. As for my four children, their strong interest in the book and in the life of their great-great uncle is something that will remain with me for the rest of my life. My son, Tom, put his great graphic design talents to work creating the cover of this book. My youngest offspring, Danny, an aspiring photographer, did a great job snapping the photo of me you see at the back of *The One and Only*. And my daughters, Erin and Katie, were always ready and willing to gobble up and comment on the latest installment of Uncle Chic as it rolled off my Apple computer.

CHAPTER 1
Always in Our Hearts

On Thanksgiving Day, 1973, Charles William Harley, then seventy-nine years old, played in his last football game.

Yellow, green, and bright orange leaves covered the playing field at Woodlawn Park, a square-shaped Chicago suburban neighborhood setting that was outfitted with a gray metal swing set, two basketball hoops, and a merry-go-round. Local kids particularly liked the merry-go-round, where white-knuckled members of their group would grasp the steel railings and hold on for their lives while someone would devilishly pull and push the whirling device to make it go faster.

For the last four years of his long life, Uncle Chic would spend his Thanksgiving holidays at the three-level, three-bedroom home of his nephew, Richard Wessell, in Des Plaines, Illinois, a thriving suburb about twenty miles northwest of downtown Chicago. Chic greatly enjoyed the many treks he would make to Des Plaines throughout the year, especially for Thanksgiving, where he would join Richard and Mary Jane's large family of six children and their scrawny-haired schnauzer named Wendy. At dinnertime, everyone would gather around the large dining room table, where candles lit up the room and a huge browned turkey awaited its final destination.

The family visits were a far cry from what Chic experienced in the Danville, Illinois, Veterans Administration Hospital, where he had lived since 1938. The Wessell household with its come and go, hurry up, noisy blend of chaos and love, reminiscent of many homes that are filled with adolescents and young adults, had no resemblance to the blandness and regimentation of the government-run VA Hospital of downstate Illinois. Whenever Richard and Mary Jane invited Chic to their home, he leaped at the opportunity, first securing permission from his caretakers, then catching a train for the three-hour trip north to Chicago. There, on his own, he would transfer to another rail line for the short hop to Des Plaines.

Following the death in 1969 of Chic's sister Ruth, Richard, her only child, took over the responsibility of keeping watch over his uncle. The switch from mother to son was only natural. For most of her life, Ruth had taken care of her older brother, providing him with the attention and affection he desperately needed during a lifetime that otherwise was filled with much loneliness and despair. Of the eight children of Charles and Mattie Harley, two died at young ages, leaving six who enjoyed long lives. And of those six, it was Ruth more than any other who dedicated herself to the care of Chic, who, by age 28, had become ravaged by mental illness.

During the troubling years of the Great Depression, Richard, then a boy, lived with Uncle Chic and the extended Harley and Wessell clans on the north side of Chicago. It was there that his mother and other family members would tell stories of how Uncle Chic fifteen years earlier had lit up the gridirons of Midwest college campuses performing superhuman feats of speed, strength, and grace. Despite a shy personality laced with low self-esteem, Chic's fame during his high school, college, and short professional football careers from 1912 to 1921 had spread far and wide across America. The family stories Richard heard during those days about his famed uncle helped form a bond between the two that remained unbroken. When the call came to take care of Uncle Chic after the death of Ruth, Richard did not flinch.

On his many getaways to Richard and Mary Jane's home, Chic would eat meals with the family, he had his own bedroom, he spent days watching television and taking short walks in the neighborhood, and he often participated in playing table games. He would accompany the family on journeys to local grocery and department stores and even on vacations to Wisconsin. On New Year's Day 1972, while with the family in Lake Geneva, Wisconsin, Chic spent the day watching college football games on TV. At one point in the lobby of the hotel, as snow fluttered to the earth and stinging winds howled outside, guests gathered around a piano with Chic to play tunes and serenade him. His face lit up as bright as the logs in a roaring fireplace just a few feet away.

While always reluctant to engage in lengthy conversation, Uncle Chic nevertheless made it known that he liked to munch on chocolate candy, loved very hot black coffee, and never turned down an invitation to sip on a cold beer.

On the Woodlawn Park gridiron in late autumn 1973, Chic Harley one last time felt the joy of the game that he had dominated more than fifty years earlier. Given the role of "quarterback" on that chilly fall day, Chic held firmly onto the football as family members danced around their uncle, with each encouraging him to run or pass. Smiling broadly, shuffling his feet, and turning left and right, he eventually tossed the ball underhanded. It fell to the ground with a thump only a few feet away.

In everyone's mind, Uncle Chic had scored another touchdown.

Charles William "Chic" Harley at about the age of 1 following the cutting-off of his long curls.

Birth certificate shows that "Charley Harley" was born on September 15, 1894 in Chicago to Mattie and Charley Harley.

CHAPTER 2
Arriving in Ohio

Farming in eighteenth-century Virginia was backbreaking, but for many, it was the only way of life they knew. A man needed strength and determination to till the soil, plant seedlings—corn, tobacco, beans—in spring, hover over the crops in summer, and harvest them in the fall. Long days under the southern sky could be mercilessly hot. Turning over clods of earth sent dust skyward, stinging the eyes and filtering onto lips and into nostrils and mouths. Only rain and nightfall provided relief.

Even when the sun set over the Blue Ridge Mountains, John G. Harley and his wife, Nancy, found little rest. Their young and growing family required more nurturing and attention with each new arrival. Life wasn't easy, but they coped, improvised, and lived the best they could.

Born on May 9, 1754, in Ireland, John Harley was just twenty-one years old when the battles of Lexington and Concord ignited the Revolutionary War. If he favored his new nation's cause for liberty, there is no record that he took those passions to the battlefield. He was a farmer.

The first Harleys were part of a large migration of Scotch-Irish to America. Willing to undergo hardships and face danger, these were hardworking, tough-minded people who pushed themselves relentlessly just for the chance to see the next day. They were intelligent, proud, and provident, and they attracted others of like character to the frontier.

After the war, a major policy of national expansion and benevolence toward those who had fought began to take shape. Cash-strapped but land-rich, the new nation had found a way to compensate the heroes of America's struggle for freedom by offering them the one thing that was in plentiful supply: land. It proved to be a godsend for citizens who yearned for a better life and more opportunity. Veterans healthy and daring enough could move west, far from the familiar grueling surroundings of Shenandoah County in north central Virginia and into a new territory ripe with excitement, potential prosperity, and room for them to spread their wings.

Before the passage of the Northwest Ordinance in 1787, the Commonwealth of Virginia had given up most of its claims to western lands except for a large chunk north of the Ohio River between the Miami River on the west and the Scioto River on the east. Known as the Virginia Military District, it consisted of roughly 6 million acres of forest and prime farmland and encompassed what later became twenty-three Ohio counties, including Ross and Franklin. In Ross County, the city of Chillicothe would spring up in 1798; in Franklin County, the city of Columbus would follow in 1812. Virginia veterans could procure this land, the amount and location depending on rank and length of service.

When the Virginia Military District finally opened for settlement in 1794, it's likely that John and Nancy Harley had been married for only about a year, having wed in Nancy's hometown of Carlisle, Pennsylvania, possibly at the First Presbyterian Church. The church, one of the oldest in the region, dated back to 1734, when Scotch-Irish began settling in Cumberland County. The year Nancy was born, 1774, local patriots met in this church to elect delegates to the First Continental Congress. Perhaps its most illustrious member was James Wilson, a signer of the Declaration of Independence, an author of Pennsylvania's constitution, and a Supreme Court justice. President George Washington worshiped there on October 5, 1794, while on his way to the western part of the state during the Whiskey Rebellion.

Two years after their marriage, Sarah, their first child, was born in 1795, followed by Catherine in 1801, John G. Jr. in 1802, Barbary Ette in 1807, Michael in 1808, Robert in 1810, Mary in 1812, and Martha in 1817. All were born in Virginia, except Martha, who was born in Ross County, Ohio. By 1801, John had made up his mind that his and his family's future lay in the wide open spaces of the West, which to many by now meant Ohio. That year, he and Nancy agreed that they would work toward finding land somewhere north of the Ohio River, where the cost of living was cheap and the opportunities were many. John had already acquired two tracts of land totaling 420 acres along the Scioto River on the eastern border of the Military District in Ross County. Originally owned by two veterans of the Revolutionary War, the land was described as "beginning at a large white oak, sugar tree and buckeye." The survey document, paid for by John Harley, that formalized the sale was signed by President Thomas Jefferson and Secretary of State James Madison. Sometime before 1806, Harley disposed of that property for some unknown reason. Nevertheless, he and Nancy still wanted to settle in Ohio. After several hard and dangerous trips back and forth from Virginia, where Nancy remained with the children, John Harley finally pulled up stakes in 1812. He led Nancy and their seven children—likely accompanied by many others seeking a new life—over the hills and mountains of western Virginia, out of the Shenandoah Valley forever, toward their new home in the wilderness.

The long and arduous trip probably occurred in the spring and summer to avoid harsh winter weather. The family's fragile wagon, loaded down with all their worldly possessions, traveled over dusty and dangerous roads. At times, John and his oldest son, John Jr., would have to rip through thick brush that had grown over the narrow trails with sharp steel knives and muscle. Other hazards slowed their progress: swirling streams, tree stumps, large boulders, and the elements. It wasn't easy, but they persevered. Occasionally, they came upon a hamlet where the few people around provided respite with conversation and opportunities to barter for food and tools.

By now, more and more Virginians were arriving in Ohio, particularly in Ross County and its growing city of Chillicothe. The first cabins had been erected by white men in the Scioto Valley and Ross County around 1796. Before long, the town showed signs of prosperity with several stores, a tavern, a mechanical shop, and an industrious populace. The Indians who remained—mostly Shawnee—hadn't forgotten the treatment they received by the white men who pushed them off the land. In 1803, Ohio officially became a state, and Chillicothe, its first capital. Under the Northwest Ordinance, slavery was not permitted.

By the time the Harley family arrived, the population of Chillicothe was about 1,500. Within a few years, several new banks would be up and running, and the town would be the site of a prisoner of war camp, at Camp Bull, for British soldiers captured during the War of 1812. In 1816, the state capital moved from Chillicothe to Columbus, about fifty miles north, where development nineteenth-century style was flourishing.

By the early 1820s, word had spread from the nation's capital to Ohio and adjoining states that a proposal first put forward by Presidents Washington and Jefferson might not be that far from reality. The War of 1812 had put a halt to development of a series of canals linking Ohio and the Ohio River Valley with the rest of the country to the east. But with the end of hostilities, interest in canals took off again. Work on the first and one of the most famous American canals, the Ohio and Erie, began in 1825. Thousands of laborers, many Irish immigrants, poured into Ohio to dig through mud, rock, and forests and over creeks and streams on a massive public works project to link Lake Erie on the north to the Ohio River on the south. It was agreed that two major routes would be chiseled out connecting the lake with the river. One would follow the general topography of the Miami River from Lake Erie and the Toledo region in the west, heading south. In the eastern part of the state, the canals would follow the Scioto River Valley, stretching from Cleveland to Portsmouth and the Ohio River. Laborers were paid thirty cents a day and given a jigger of whiskey. Later, the wage was increased to fifteen dollars a month, an appealing sum to thousands who flocked to the area in search of steady work. Many local farmers jumped at the opportunity. The canals were to be at least twenty-six to forty feet wide and four feet deep so the mule-drawn flat-bottomed boats carrying their crops and people could glide along the waterway at the speed of three miles per hour. It was remarkably inexpensive and fast-paced compared with the overland alternative.

On July 3, 1827, the first boat on the Ohio and Erie Canal traveled thirty-seven miles from Akron to Cleveland through forty-one locks and over three aqueducts, creaking under a huge cargo of ten tons of goods. Everyone realized quickly that this new form of transportation would transform their counties and state into profitable centers of commerce. By 1831, workers had dug their way to the city of Newark, eventually making their way to Columbus and on to Chillicothe. An 11.6-mile feeder canal connecting Columbus to the Ohio and Erie Canal opened in 1832.

The canals brought exciting opportunity to Ohio. By 1840, it had become the third most prosperous state in the country. By 1850, its population had zoomed to almost 2 million. The crops produced by farmers like Harley in Ross County, once available only to locals, could now be transported to new, faraway markets like Pittsburgh and New York and Canada. The canals also paved the way for trade in the South, such as in New Orleans and ports beyond.

For the Harley family, the canals opened up opportunities beyond farming, and new and exciting enterprises that offered steady income and took them to places like Columbus,

Granville, and Zanesville. John G. Harley Jr. was the first of the children to become a canal boatman, followed by his younger brothers Michael and Robert. Michael, like his father, was a farmer, but by 1870, and now more than sixty years old, he was listing his occupation as "canal boatman." Forty-one years earlier, on July 15, 1829, Michael Harley had married Elizabeth Emmons. Their oldest daughter, Elizabeth Jane, born in 1831, continued to live at home in Chillicothe into her thirties. In 1862, a major family upheaval occurred when Elizabeth Jane revealed to her parents and her two sisters, Ellen and Sally, also living at home, that she was pregnant with her first child. Records do not identify the father, other than to say he was from Massachusetts. So at age twenty-eight, without a husband but with a loving family, Elizabeth Jane gave birth to a healthy young boy on December 2, 1862, in Ross County, Ohio, near Chillicothe, whom she named Charles William Harley. For the next six years, Elizabeth Jane, with the help of her mother and father and sisters, raised her young son. Almost six years later, on September 22, 1868, Elizabeth married Stephen Farrell, who was divorced and originally from New Jersey. According to the 1880 census, their household by then consisted of Charles, age 18; his stepsisters, Lina, 10, and Sarah, 8; their mother, Elizabeth Jane; and Stephen, a machinist by occupation.

How, when, and under what circumstances Charles Harley met Mattie Trunnell in the early 1880s is unknown. Both had roots in central Ohio. Her paternal grandfather, Frances Trunnell, was born around 1818 in Maryland, and married Elizabeth Allwine, a young woman four years younger than he from Perry County, Ohio, on November 11, 1838. One of their nine children, David M., served in the Union Army during the Civil War and married Caroline Hertz on April 17, 1866. Born in Ohio in 1845, Caroline was the daughter of German immigrants. Tragedy struck the Trunnell household when Caroline and her youngest daughter, Carrie, died mysteriously in 1871, leaving her two other daughters without a mother and David without a wife. One of the surviving daughters, Mattie, was three years old. Unprepared to care for two young girls, David sent Mattie to live with Caroline's sister, Lizzie Hertz Glass, who a few years earlier had moved to an apartment in Columbus from New York City after her husband died. Mattie grew up with Lizzie's own daughter, Carrie, attending school while Lizzie worked in a bindery shop. Mattie rarely saw her father, who eventually became a carpenter in Cleveland, where his brother Albert lived and worked as a painter.

However Charles and Mattie met, in all likelihood, once the ice was broken, the couple discovered that they had much in common beyond being natives of central Ohio. Mattie's childhood, like Charles's, was unconventional and probably stressful and lonely at times. Charles, born out of wedlock, never knew his father, although his mother married and did all she could to fill that vacuum. But now their childhoods were behind them. Mattie, the more outgoing, was tall, lanky, and athletic, and instantly drew attention with her wide, attractive smile. Charles was more reserved, tending to keep his thoughts and words to himself.

Charles William Harley and Martha "Mattie" Trunnell were married on May 7, 1885, in Columbus. Two months later, Mattie gave birth to their first child, Walter, to be followed over the next fourteen years by Marie, William, Irene, Helen, Charles Jr. (Chic), Ralph, and Ruth. It was a mighty large family—even by late nineteenth-century standards—with Mattie at the center, raising and caring for the children, while Charles followed in his stepfather's footsteps by becoming a machinist. He took a liking to the Linotype, a marvelous new machine that replaced the laborious method of typesetting by hand. It used liquefied lead to form letters and then placed those letters in perfect position to form rows of type and then columns of type that were positioned on heavy lead plates and wrapped around printing press cylinders. The process enabled newspapers to churn out copies at blazing speed and media companies to easily and affordably publish numerous daily editions in an era that predated the invention of radio by several decades.

By 1893, after ten years of married life in Columbus and five children, Charles and Mattie decided to move to Chicago, where employment opportunities were more plentiful. Like millions of Americans at that time, many from Midwestern states like Ohio, the Harleys were victims of economic depression. The Panic of 1893 was the worst economic crisis ever to hit the United States up to that point, sparking runs on banks and huge numbers of home foreclosures. More than 15,000 companies went bankrupt, and 500 banks failed, hitting hard all industrial cities and triggering labor strikes and unrest.

With the economy in such dire straits, Charles Harley, by then a veteran Linotype operator who eventually would work for most of the Columbus and Chicago daily newspapers, moved Mattie and the kids to the "City of the Big Shoulders." He quickly found employment at one of the big city papers, where he worked in a huge room filled with the clickety-clack of a dozen or more gleaming Linotypes. With Charles securely employed and the family settled in a south side neighborhood, the Harleys' sixth child came into the world.

Charles William Harley, who almost from the beginning was called Chic and was almost never referred to as a "junior," was born at his family's home on Indiana Avenue on September 15, 1894. He was small and chubby, with only a few strands of hair and features typical of newborns. Within a few months, his hair would begin to grow and curl upward behind his neck, prompting oohs and aahs from Mattie and sisters Irene, Marie, and little Helen. Though small, Chic was healthy and happy, as were his mother, father, brothers, and sisters. The only time Chic's health suffered was when he experienced convulsions at age three. How they were brought on is a mystery. That occurred in the same eventful year, 1897, when his sister Helen suddenly became ill and died at age four of meningitis. Four months after Helen's death, a brother,

Ralph, was born, though he, too, would die young, at age thirteen, of typhoid.

The last of the Harleys' eight children, Ruth, was born on April 7, 1899, in Chicago. Chic was four and a half years old. Ruth's arrival marked the beginning of a lifelong loving brother-sister relationship that never faltered over the next sixty-eight years. It was the kind of endearing bond that sustained them both through the best and worst of times.

Chic (right) with youngest sister Ruth and unidentified boy outside backyard tent in Chicago.

Chic striking a menacing baseball pose.

*Harley (bottom second from left) with his 1914 East High
School basketball teammates.*

CHAPTER 3
Coming of Age

Chicago in 1893 was like a breath of fresh air for Charles and Mattie Harley. The rugged near south side neighborhood they moved to was aflutter with activity with the World's Columbian Exposition taking place only a mile or so away, along the lakefront at Jackson Park. The family had arrived in this growing, anything goes kind of city only a few months before the fair opened on May 1. More by chance than design, the Harleys were smack in the midst of the world's celebration of the four hundredth anniversary of Columbus's discovery of America.

The fair was a showcase of American ingenuity and strength at a time when the nation was beginning to flex its international muscles. It featured buildings by renowned architects, along with the debut of such consumer goods as Shredded Wheat and Juicy Fruit gum. It was also the beginning of a new holiday in the United States, Columbus Day, and what was to become a daily ritual for schoolchildren: recitation of the Pledge of Allegiance. In the months before Chicago was chosen over New York as the site of the fair, a war of words was fought over which of the two cities would host the event. New Yorkers were aghast that a backwoods town like Chicago could even be considered a finalist. They started calling Chicago "The Windy City." They did so not because they admired its lovely breezes off Lake Michigan, but because they had grown sick and tired of what they considered the city's overzealous bragging in trying to win over the fair's selection committee.

People in Chicago always seemed to be on the go, and why not? Its location in the heart of America made it the crossroads of the country. Rail and shipping lines from the East converged to spread goods, culture, and influence westward. The clunking of horses' hoofs pulling railcars filled busy streets lined with smart-looking houses and shops. Only a few years earlier, cars had replaced the slower, less efficient omnibus, which carried as many as twenty people crammed into a small covered wagon over the city's bumpy streets. A smaller trailer aligned on a single rail made the ride much smoother and eased the stress on horses. By the last decade of nineteenth-century Chicago, elegant sailing ships and smoke-belching steamboats were moving up and down the shoreline on a daily basis. Despite the languishing economy, most Chicagoans had jobs. The World's Fair gave them a new sense of pride and hope at a time when most people still vividly remembered the calamitous Great Chicago Fire of 1871. Life was relatively comfortable, if not particularly prosperous, and people had hope in the future.

Still, there were times when things seemed bleak. The shaky economic conditions had a profound effect on many people in the city, in particular, a small town just to the south that had been founded only a few years earlier. Aptly called Pullman, the town had been created by George M. Pullman as a place where employees of his railcar manufacturing plant could live, shop, go to the library, and satisfy every other daily need. When business slowed in 1894, Pullman cut employees' wages, but not their rents. It was a recipe for unrest that eventually grew into violence. Threats of a strike were finally carried out on May 11. By late June, switchmen started refusing to reroute trains carrying Pullman cars, resulting in many firings. Within days, the nation's rail center with its twenty-four train lines was paralyzed. President Grover Cleveland ordered federal troops to intervene, and on July 3, they entered the city. A day later, outraged strikers set off fireworks and tipped over railcars. Blockades were set up, and rioting by as many as 6,000 strikers intensified when, on July 7, a huge fire engulfed seven buildings at the World's Fair. The black billowing smoke was clearly visible to much of Chicago, the Harleys included. While it's believed that no member of the Harley family worked at the Pullman factory or was involved in the strike, they, like everyone else in Chicago, were riveted by the event. That same day, National Guardsmen fired into the crowd of rioters, killing at least four people and wounding at least twenty. By early August, the ferocity of the strike was easing by the sheer strength of the 14,000 federal and state troops, deputy marshals, and policemen. In the end, the Pullman employees did not get their rents lowered, but the strike showed the power of unified labor as well as the willingness of the U.S. government to intervene on behalf of business when confronted by strikers whose actions threatened the delivery of vital goods and mail.

Charles and Mattie Harley felt they had no choice but to move from Columbus to Chicago. The national recession had hit central Ohio particularly hard. The Linotype jobs Charles had counted on at any one of Columbus's three daily newspapers fizzled out. Like so many others, the Harleys had a large family to feed and bills to pay. Heartsick, a bit frightened, but also excited with anticipation, the couple decided to move to the great city 350 miles to the northwest and leave behind the only home they, and previous Harleys and Trunnells dating back a century, had known—Columbus.

For most of the Harleys' first twelve years in Chicago, Charles managed to find work as a Linotype operator, as he had in Columbus. In the mid-1890s, Chicago was home to about a dozen daily newspapers, all fierce competitors that clawed and sometimes even beat their way to capture a bigger share of the burgeoning advertising and circulation market. Thousands of immigrants and fortune seekers flocked to Chicago on a daily basis. They needed to know where to rent apartments, buy food, and apply for jobs. The only source of that information was a local newspaper, and in Chicago, there were plenty to choose from. Because of his experience, Charles eventually found Linotype jobs, even though it might take ten interviews to land one. In between, he worked as a clerk at one of several post office branches scattered throughout the city.

In their first dozen years in Chicago, the Harleys lived in various locations, starting on the south side, then moving to Western Avenue on the west side of town. Years later, they settled in the northwest neighborhood of Logan Square.

The year 1897 brought great personal tragedy to the Harleys when their fifth child, Helen, died at the age of four. Until that spring, she had been a healthy and happy child. Then Mattie, who was pregnant at the time, and Charles noticed that Helen's normally sunny disposition was quickly changing. She became irritable, feverish, and lethargic. A visit to the doctor brought the devastating diagnosis of cerebral meningitis, an inflammation of the thin membranes that cover the brain and the spinal cord, usually caused by bacteria or viral infection. For a young child like Helen, meningitis meant that death was knocking on the door. Treatments such as penicillin and other antibiotics were decades from discovery.

Helen died in the early morning of April 7, 1897. She had just turned four years old nine days earlier. The death of one so young had to be devastating to the entire family, even for Chic, who was still six months shy of his third birthday and had little conception of what had happened, except that he would never again see the sister who was closest to him in age.

Exactly four months after Helen's death, Mattie gave birth to a boy they named Ralph, the couple's fourth son. And exactly two years after Helen's death, on April 7, 1899, Ruth, Charles and Mattie's last child, was born. Six of the surviving seven children lived long lives. Ralph died at age eleven on July 3, 1909, thirty-three days after being stricken with typhoid fever.

Economic heartache continued to plague the country after the turn of the century. In 1906, with job prospects drying up once again for Charles, the Harleys were seriously contemplating moving back to Columbus. Walter, the oldest, was now twenty-one and, like his father twenty years earlier, an aspiring machinist. Chic was almost twelve, and high school was on the horizon.

Two thousand miles away in the city of San Francisco, the lives of the Harley family and millions of other Americans changed for the worse when at 5:18 A.M. on April 18, the earth quaked so violently that it sent nearly 3,000 people to their deaths. One of the worst natural disasters in American history, it transmitted a strong economic ripple around the world, including in Chicago. Fires that the earthquake sparked in subsequent days caused the most damage by far. Approximately 25,000 buildings in 500 city blocks were destroyed. The mayor authorized vigilantes to shoot looters on site; some 500 were killed. Nearly 140 insurance companies paid claims totaling as much as $300 million (many billions in today's money), causing the international financial system to raise interest rates and consequently discourage loans. Within a year, credit was so tight that an economic panic, similar to the one that hit the country in 1893, had set in. For the Harleys, again, the time had come to survive the recession by following the jobs.

By mid-1907, Mattie, Charles, and their seven children were back in Columbus, Ohio. The family settled into a large, ordinary-looking two-story house at Kelton Avenue and Mound Street on the city's east side. A covered porch ran across the front of the house. Above the porch were four large bedroom windows below a sloping roof and attic. The neighborhood was anything but quiet. All day long, interurban trains rumbled along Mound Street, ferrying commuters back and forth to downtown Columbus, two miles to the west. Before long, the family decided to move again to where Charles would be closer to his work at the daily newspapers. They chose a house at 1251 Mooberry, which, unlike their previous residence, was tucked away in a peaceful neighborhood surrounded by woods. Years later, after the woods had been cleared out, the East Freeway ran past the house, carrying tens of thousands of trucks and cars every day.

Chic first enrolled in Ohio Avenue Grade School, then transferred to Main Street School. About two blocks away from Main Street School was Franklin Park, where children played baseball, football, marbles, and a game called "rough and tumble," a fun activity similar to football. As Columbus sports columnist Russ Needham remembered years later, "The number of kids on a side depended on how many showed up."

Growing up in Chicago, Chic had played marbles with his neighborhood friends. Whoever lagged his marble nearest to the horizontal line scratched across the top of the circle started first—something everyone strived for. Chic was good at earning first shot honors. In fact, when it came to marbles or any other type of competition, the boys always knew that Chic was the toughest competitor. Chic carried these talents and others with him when the family returned to Columbus.

Years later, at age eighty, Mattie remembered her youngest son as very normal, very "clumsy," and very shy, except when it came to sports. "It was everything from marbles to baseball and football that he loved," she said. "You would never have thought he was clumsy, but he was, except on the football field," said his brother Walter.

As a preteen, Chic loved to visit the Main Street firehouse, where his Uncle Charles Edmonds worked. He gave Chic the nickname "Noisy" "because he'd come and prowl around, but not say much." One day, Uncle Charles surprised Chic with the gift of a pet raccoon. "He loved it, and it followed him everywhere," recalled Mattie. "Once the animal strayed, and a saloon keeper put him in the window. Chic recognized it. The proprietor let him have it when the raccoon rushed to Chic, and he whispered in its ear."

Chic enrolled in East High School in late summer 1911. More introverted than ever, he probably avoided school activities his freshman year with the possible exception of intramural sports. As a student, he was at best average. Being outdoors, running, playing, and competing were his passions, not bookwork. While he loved his parents and brothers and sisters, the one family member he was particularly close to was Ruth. As young children, a bond had grown between them that would last their lifetimes. Even though Chic was four and a half years older, the two naturally drifted to each other. Ruth, athletic herself, could play baseball, and she was a fast runner. During summers, they would pitch a tent in the backyard and camp out with other neighborhood kids. People recalled that Ruth often wore loose-fitting dresses with her hair in pigtails and that Chic liked to wear long-sleeved shirts and snug-fitting caps, which were popular with the boys then.

Football in Columbus at this time was beginning to attract attention. While the town's university, Ohio State, fielded a football team, along with a whole host of other intercollegiate and intramural sports, athletics at Columbus's five high schools (North, South, East, West, and Aquinas) were more popular than the university's. Ohio State was a curious place to many Columbus residents, being situated north of the downtown area, which many citizens of Columbus knew very little about, other than much of the campus land tended to flood in the spring when the Olentangy River overflowed. Until 1906, many regarded football as a sport for roughnecks who feasted on brutal competition. Rules were loosely adhered to, and the successful team almost always won by relying on muscle and brawn rather than skill and intelligence.

That all began to change when college authorities that included not only coaches, but faculty members, deans, and presidents started calling for a major overhaul in rules. The growing number of serious injuries and deaths gained the attention of President Theodore Roosevelt, who declared that football must change from a gladiator-like spectacle to a real sport. Otherwise, the government would step in to force changes or even put an end to the game. In 1910, a series of revisions that led to modern-day football were adopted. They set the stage for players of all shapes, sizes, and levels of talent and strength to compete. No longer was the game reserved for those players who could drive into the line the hardest or had the meanest dispositions or the biggest bodies. It was now a game of deception, speed, brains, strength, and grace that opened up opportunities to many who had so much to offer.

By the time Chic's sophomore year arrived, encouragement from friends helped him to decide to try out for the football team. Everyone knew he had the talent. The only question was whether he had the courage to compete on an organized, interscholastic level against the best players in Columbus and possibly the state of Ohio. There was also concern on Chic's part about his size. He was slender, weighed only 130 pounds, and stood about five feet, six inches tall. That was small, even for a sophomore. When he was prodded about trying out for the East High School squad, Chic expressed strong reservations because most of the players were much bigger than he.

The coach of the East High School Black and Orange football team, later nicknamed the Tigers, was Frank Gullum. He was hired in 1910 to try to rebuild a program that had spent the previous five seasons languishing and unable to dent the armor of crosstown rival North High School. Gullum was a capable coach who motivated players with stern instruction, rather than just fear. At games, Gullum wore a derby hat, a neatly pressed suit, and a high white-collared shirt. His hair was always neatly trimmed, and he was always clean-shaven, accentuating a large chin and pleasant-looking face.

From the moment Chic stepped out on the East High practice field in September 1912, Gullum knew someone special was in his midst. Before long, the diminutive Chic was "making monkeys" out of teammates bigger and more outgoing, like 200-pound Joe Mulbarger, Al "Husky" Thurman, the Courtney brothers—Hap and Harold, and John Vorys. Kids in Chic's neighborhood flocked to East High in the late afternoons not to watch games, but to watch Chic in practice. One of those neighborhood boys, Russ Needham, noticed that fewer and fewer kids were hanging around Franklin Park playing "rough and tumble." Investigating why, he discovered that they had pedaled their bicycles to East High, where "kids by the hundreds used to stand around watching East practice just to watch this marvel of football."

By the time the season began, Gullum had recognized Chic's talent not only as an athlete, but as a leader who could inspire by example, rather than words. Gullum named him the starting quarterback of the team, a rare promotion for a second-year student. At most schools, the quarterback, also known as the pivot man, had the most important offensive job on the team. How important depended on the talent of the player and the willingness of the coach to utilize that player's skills. Besides the quarterback, each offensive unit had a center, two tackles, two guards, two ends, two halfbacks, and a fullback. The quarterback was the chief play caller, either receiving the ball from the center or instructing one of the players behind him in the backfield that it was coming to him. If the quarterback received the ball, he usually had the option of either running with the ball or, if he could pass, hurling it to one of his ends who had scampered downfield toward the opposing team's goal line. Throwing the ball those days was rare, mainly because few could do it with precision due to the fact that the ball was bigger and rounder than in modern days, making it harder to get a good grip.

Gullum knew from the beginning that Harley was one of those extraordinary players who not only was as fast as lightning, but could throw the bulky oval like it was a baseball. When he ran with the ball, Chic had a knack for darting around and through opposing players, all of who were trying to grab him. He was unusually strong for his size and almost unstoppable once he got into the open. Gullum also soon discovered that Chic could punt the ball forty or fifty yards with ease, could accurately drop-kick field goals over the uprights from forty yards out, and regularly booted extra points under pressure after touchdowns. On defense, his swiftness and natural abilities led Gullum to assign him to safety, where he was free to roam the outer reaches of the defensive zone, where he could use his blazing speed to hunt down and tackle opposing ball-carrying players. He was the cleanest of players and, with few exceptions during his three years of varsity play, rarely was injured.

In his first game at East, Chic started out well, but failed to score in a 16-0 win over Mount Vernon. He successfully completed a pass that set up the team's first touchdown of the day. The following week, on October 13, 1912, East lost to Delaware High School 13-7. It was one of only three losses Chic experienced in his twenty-four-game high school career. In this battle, a newspaper account said one reason Chic was unable to get on track was because "everyone was telling him what to do."

Against Doane High School the following week, East won by shutout, 13-0. Chic, now gaining confidence, tossed a touchdown pass to Hap Courtney. The second touchdown was scored when Chic, looking to pass, only to find no one open, tucked the ball under his right arm and ran into the end zone.

In East's fourth contest on November 3, Newark proved to be too tough, winning 15-7. It is not known whether Chic played or scored. It was in the Orange and Black's fifth game of the season that Harley tore out from his cocoon and into the athletic limelight. Against Athens High School, he scored three touchdowns on runs of sixty, forty, and forty yards for East's 40-6 victory.

Following a 7-7 tie with Springfield the following week, the season finale took place on Saturday, November 24. It was the annual showdown against archrival North High School, staged on Ohio State University's Ohio Field. East had lost to North in the previous five contests. That losing streak met an abrupt end when Chic ran for two touchdowns, both on fifty-five-yard gallops, for a triumphant final score of 20-3.

By the end of the 1912 season, Chic Harley, who had emerged seemingly out of nowhere, was being heralded as one of the best quarterbacks in the city. He scored at least thirty points from scrimmage that year and an unrecorded number of extra points or field goals.

As good as 1912 was, it was nothing compared to his next two seasons. Besides football, he also was excelling on the high school baseball and track teams. He became close friends with the Courtneys, Mulbarger, Thurman, Vorys, and many others who naturally admired his athletic prowess, but also found him appealing in many other ways. In the summer, his gang of friends set up a boxing ring in the haymow of a barn owned by the parents of a neighborhood chum. Every day, Chic, Vorys, and a group of boxing enthusiasts would spar in the loft surrounded by large bales of hay. During one match, Harley landed a roundhouse square that sent Vorys flying backward, crashing through one of the barn doors. Dazed, the future congressman brushed himself off none the worse for wear, and their friendship remained intact for the next fifty years.

In track, Chic was considered one of the best high school runners in Ohio, regularly competing and winning in 50-, 100-, 220-, and 440-yard runs as well as low hurdles competitions.

In the summer of 1913, with one year of varsity football under his belt, Chic was jolted by his parents' announcement that they had decided to move back to Chicago. Whatever prompted Mattie and Charles to make the decision this time, moving back and forth between Chicago and Columbus was becoming something of a family ritual as job opportunities for Charles ebbed and flowed with the economy. Chic was adamant that he did not want to leave Columbus. He was comfortable at East High School, enjoyed his group of close friends, and was excelling in football, baseball, basketball, and track. He also was picking up the game of golf and had a job as a lifeguard at Franklin Park. (He was a strong swimmer, too.) His life was safe, enjoyable, and fulfilling, and he did not want it to change. He refused to go back to Chicago.

Furthermore, one girl, in particular, had caught his eye: Louise Havens, a pretty, outgoing neighborhood girl who was popular, enjoyed sports, and attended East High School. She had a pleasant, round face and short, dark brown hair and was two years younger than Chic. It's possible that they met in school, and, both having last names that began with the letters "Ha," it's plausible that they sat next to each other in class or at school assemblies.

Louise's brother, William, had been a standout end on the East football team a few years before Chic. She probably watched him play and had been introduced to the sport by the time Chic signed on with the team in 1912.

In later years, some of Chic's friends remembered that on rare occasions, he took a high school girl out on a date, but nothing ever came of those brief encounters. "He took my sister, Neoma [*sic*], out once," recalled Harry Bliss, a lifelong friend and later college teammate of Chic's. "He hardly talked to her. He was very shy. But after that, he went with Louise Havens. He fell in love with her. They knew each other in high school, and they were very close."

"He kept company with the same girl all during high school and college days," a medical report said years later, adding that they planned to get married. Circumstances that had yet to appear proved to be beyond the control of either one, making marriage impossible.

Coach Gullum had all the confidence in the world that his 1913 East High School team would perform even better than his 5, 2, and 1 squad of 1912. All signs pointed to a great season, primarily because most of the top players were returning, such as center Vorys, the Courtney brothers, the two "Tubbys"—Lind at one of the tackle positions, and Touer at a guard slot. But without question, the main reason that Gullum and the rest of East High were certain that something special was about to be unleashed as late September approached was that Chic Harley would return for his second season.

As difficult as it must have been to leave their youngest son behind, Mattie, Charles, and the rest of the family left for Chicago in the summer of 1913. Chic stayed in Columbus with friends who were willing to take him in. Mattie worried deeply about leaving Chic, but eventually succumbed to the pleadings of her son, his many friends, coaches who were desperate to keep him on their rosters, and even East Principal John D. Harlor. For the next two years, Chic had a warm bed, regular square meals, and a welcome mat at the homes of Joe Mulbarger, his bulky, floppy-haired teammate whom he shared punting duties with, the Vorys family, and even Principal Harlor, whose son, Allen, played on the football team. Team captain John Vorys made it his mission not to let Harley get away. On a few occasions, perhaps because the Mulbargers or Voryses were out of town, Chic had to find a different place to stay. During his senior year, he took a room for a while in a building behind the high school. To help Chic financially with rent and other expenses, a candy sale was held each Friday, at which teachers and students bought "prodigious quantities."

Right from the beginning of the 1913 football season, East, led by the likable and introverted Chic, dominated Ohio high school football. In its first game, at Indianola Park in Columbus, East clobbered West High School 32-6, with Chic scoring three touchdowns and kicking one extra point.

A story headlined "Chic Harley Is Bear on Offense" went on to say:

To Chic Harley must be given a great deal of credit for that 32 to 6 victory. The little quarter who was the marvel of all football students who attended the game, and there were many there, too, shone above the other men on the field as a blue diamond would if surrounded by so much coal. His open field running was marvelous. Time and again he circled the ends for 15 and 20 yards dragging a West player by either leg. Of course, the whole credit for victory must not be given to Harley for his mates helped him a great deal with splendid interference, but minus Harley the East machine would be an automobile without a carburetor.

Chic was just getting started in a spectacular season that few, if anyone in American football, could equal.

The following week, on October 5, East and Harley trounced London High School 59-0, with Chic again scoring three touchdowns and kicking one extra point.

"East High, or rather Harley High, as it has been dubbed by local football followers, had a regular Sunday school picnic sort of a game with London's inexperienced crew of gridiron players

Saturday morning at Indianola Park," wrote the *Dispatch*. The instant Chic touched the opening kickoff, he was off to the races, scampering ninety yards through the entire London team for a touchdown. The clock had ticked away only twenty seconds.

Two weeks later, Chic displayed not only his raw running and passing talents, but his kicking ability in an 86-6 creaming of South High School on Ohio State University's Ohio Field. He personally scored three touchdowns on runs from scrimmage, and set up several other scores with his rifle-like passing. After the first half, he was used sparingly, with the exception of kicking points after touchdowns. All told, Chic booted eight extra points that day. South High supporters expressed happiness that at least their team had been able to put six points on the scoreboard. The lone touchdown came on a fumble by East in the end zone in the third quarter.

It was more of the same a week later, on Saturday, October 26, when the Orange and Black shut out Mt. Vernon High School 62-0. While Chic scored only one touchdown in this contest, his open field running and hurling were credited with setting up nearly all of the team's other TDs. In this game, as in the previous week's bout with South, Chic kicked eight extra points.

A week later, Chic suffered one of the few injuries of his football career in a game against Newark High School at Indianola Park. Near the end of the contest, which East won 40-0, Chic and a Newark player were knocked silly after their heads collided at midfield while going after a pass. The Newark player required three stitches, and Chic bled profusely for a while. Harley's injury was not expected to keep him out of the lineup for the following week's important game, the annual showdown with North High School. Before the collision, Harley had scored four touchdowns against Newark and belted the same number of extra points.

The battle against longtime rival North was billed as the biggest game of the year in Columbus. A record-breaking crowd of 6,500 was expected to fill Ohio Field's bleachers for the 2 P.M. contest the next week. (If Ohio State attracted 4,000 fans, it was considered a good crowd.)

Coach Gullum was confident that his team could defeat North for the second year in a row, and he was not shy about expressing his thoughts. "The game ought to be easy for East," he said with an air of superiority. North coach John Swain felt otherwise, saying, "With an even break in luck, we will win."

Rain was predicted, which meant a wet, muddy field. Swain and his gridders squealed their delight with the forecast, which they believed would slow down the dangerous Harley. Several graduates of North High, who by then were playing football for prominent college teams throughout the nation, returned to Columbus with offers to help Swain. Whitey Foss, a North graduate and former football great at Ohio State, showed up at a practice session five days before the big game.

"Every Ohio State student knows Foss never lacked pep. He always had it and also the ability to impact it on others," reported the *Dispatch*. Throughout the entire week, students, teachers, and parents at both schools were transfixed on the upcoming game. East held a huge rally on Monday night.

"Quarter Harley of East will not be able to pull off the sensational stuff which has made him the most talked of high school player in the city," predicted one sportswriter. On game day, under the headline "North Jubilant Over Heavy Field," the Dispatch wrote that "North adherents believe that the heavy going would make it impossible for Chic Harley, East's speedy merchant, to get away with any of his spectacular end runs and that North's superior weight in the line would enable Swain's men to gain by old-fashioned football." Another writer, realizing the raw skill of Harley and his almost single-handed ability to determine the outcome of a football game, said, "For those who have not seen Chic Harley in action, it will be worth the price of admission to see this little fellow going at top speed, for with North as the opposing team, he will no doubt extend himself to the limit, something which his friends say he has not done this year."

Sunday's paper reported the amazing news: "East Shoves North Entirely Off the Road." Led by Harley, who unselfishly used himself as a decoy and set up scoring chances by throwing and running the team into positions to score, East pummeled its crosstown rival 47-0. As one sportswriter described the game:

By a clean, admirable victory yesterday afternoon on Ohio Field . . . the youngster proved that he is without a doubt the best pilot ever turned out by a Columbus high school. He directed his team in a slow, cool manner and picked the weak spots of the North line to pieces. Harley played for the East team and not for himself. He had innumerable chances to flash for himself, but his whole heart was for a victory. He knew that North's defense was built to break him and he crossed his opponents by sending away one of his smooth-working backfielders on a successful play. Harley was left alone once when his pals missed a signal and he turned the misfortune into a touchdown by picking several holes accurately and outfooting his opponents to the line 20 yards away. That was the only score he made, with the exception of fathering five out of seven chances at goals from touchdown. [Chic passed for two touchdowns and performed all of the kickoffs.]

His open field running was equal to that of almost anything seen on Ohio Field for several years. . . . His forward passing was accurate as could be directed. Harley misfired on quite a few of his throws, but again it was his good aim that resulted in most of East's touchdowns or put the East siders in a position to count. Instead of being an asset to the North offense, the muddy field worked to the detriment of Captain Hohl's eleven. All of East's touchdowns directly or indirectly came as the result of a forward pass. The East offense was a puzzle to the North players. Everyone was primed to watch Harley, but he was not the only ground gainer for Coach Gullum's team. But without Harley to guide them and plan their campaign, the East backfield would have been almost helpless."

The Columbus *Citizen*'s story, headlined "Harley Is a Wonder," called Chic's performance "probably the best quarterback performance ever seen in interscholastic circles in Columbus." It added that the one area where Harley is clearly superior to any of his predecessors is in his "field generalship. Saturday, the youngster was never at a loss to select his next point of attack. There was no hesitation, and he directed his offense with the precision of clockwork."

For the second consecutive season, East had prevailed over North. The fire of football fandom had been stoked like never before in Columbus. The sport was maturing to a new level, fueled by a new generation of speedy, intelligent, multitalented players who captured the imaginations of thousands, and Harley led the way.

Across town at Ohio State University, a rebirth was under way as well with the arrival of John Wilce as football coach and Lynn St. John as athletic director. The year 1913 was the inaugural season for the Buckeyes in the Western Conference, having earlier made the decision to leave the smaller Big Six Conference. Few teams showed any respect for the Buckeye "yearlings," as they were called. At the same time, the large university north of Ohio was grappling with the question of whether its athletic program should return to the Western Conference it had abandoned five years earlier over relatively minor differences involving training facilities. A short article in the *Dispatch* said the University of Michigan would be voting whether to return to the conference.

"A bitter fight is on at Michigan University against the return. The anti-conference crowd last night burned the 'Big Nine' in effigy and paraded around town leading Coach Stagg's goat"—a reference to the University of Chicago's famed mentor whose actions triggered Michigan's decision to leave the conference. Despite the protests, Michigan voted to return and set the stage for one of the greatest rivalries in American sport.

The last three games of the season saw East easily ramble to consecutive shutout victories over Marietta, 16-0; Delaware, 27-0; and Norwood, 52-0. Against Marietta on a very soggy field, Chic at safety intercepted a pass on the five-yard line and ran it back ninety-five yards for one of the game's two touchdowns. This victory gave East the title of the Ohio and West Virginia conference, which Marietta had captured the previous year.

In the drubbing of Delaware, Chic scored three touchdowns, each time displaying superb open field running and use of a deadly stiff-arm he was developing to brush aside would-be tacklers. In the first quarter, he circled around Delaware's left end and ran forty yards for the touchdown, after which he kicked the extra point. In the third frame, he received a punt on the thirty-yard line "and by wonderful side-stepping eluded all tacklers and scored his second touchdown of the game. He again kicked a goal." And with a minute left in the game, Chic received a punt on his own forty-five-yard line and ran the entire distance of the field for the score, promptly followed by the point after touchdown (PAT) field goal. He scampered a total of 125 yards in that contest from the line of scrimmage.

In one of the greatest seasons of any high school football team ever, East outscored all opponents 369 points to 13. The only teams to score on the Orange and Black were West and South, with South's coming on a recovered fumble in the end zone.

As for Chic, he scored at least 109 of the team's points that year. Maintaining complete scoring statistics was not a priority in those years. Just as important, Harley set up most of the squad's other points with his passing and running, preparing the stage for others to take the ball across the goal line.

As in 1912, Chic was named to the three Columbus newspapers' All High School Eleven teams, as were most other starting East players. Gordy Rhodes, North's standout quarterback, was named to the All Eleven as a halfback. Along with many other North players, he would later play with Chic in college and remain his lifelong friend.

Wrote *Dispatch* sports editor Bill McKinnon:

Who would be the All High quarter [on the All Eleven] was a fore-gone conclusion in the minds of every football fan since the beginning of the season. Of course (quit your kidding) it's Harley, and spell it with capital letters, if you please. There may have been quarterbacks 10 to 15 years ago in Columbus high school circles who were better than Harley, but I doubt, and doubt mightily, if there has been a quarterback in Columbus football for a decade of Harley's caliber. He can kick well, bucking the line is mere pastime for him, and open field running is to him what an after dinner cigar is to the man who admires Lady Nicotine—his greatest delight.

"Chic Harley of East is the real find in the history of Columbus football," said the *Journal*. "He is a wonder."

With the end of the 1913 high school football season, the football season at Ohio State also was ending. The Buckeyes played well that year, its first in the Western Conference. Boyd Cherry, the Buckeyes' talented end, had caught the eye of many. Two years later, he earned honorable mention on football expert Walter Camp's All American team. There was little profit in the school's anemic athletic program, however. Total expenditures for the year were $10,077 and receipts $12,820. Football managed a tiny profit. "There is bound to be a deficit at the end of the year because other branches of athletics seldom pay for themselves," lamented the school secretary.

As fabulous a football season as 1913 was for Chic Harley, his senior year, 1914, was even more spectacular. Coach Gullum departed, because of the "press of other duties," and was replaced by Palmer Cordray, who had taught at East in 1913. For several months leading up to the start of the season, rumors spread that Chic would leave East to return to Chicago.

One sportswriter wrote that "if Captain Chic returns to East there remains little doubt about the quality of the Franklin Avenue team for he is a host in himself and will work wonders by his example in spurring on the green men Cordray will have to contend with. Practically the entire East squad was graduated in June. If Harley goes, East's machine will resemble a yacht without sails."

But on September 7, Chic himself told reporters from his parents' home in Chicago that he would return to Columbus. "East's chances of copping the city honors on the gridiron are materially increased by his return," the *Journal* said. A report on September 12 added, "Harley will reach Columbus Sunday night and will start work with the eleven on Monday."

Now safe and sound in Columbus, a guest of the Cordray family, Harley embarked on his senior year at East High School. The season developed into one of the most spectacular of any high school player in Columbus history, if not the nation. Unlike 1913, Harley was not surrounded by a team of almost equally talented players. Nearly everyone from the 1913 team had graduated, leaving Chic with younger, less experienced teammates. Understanding this from the beginning, he never held back in the ferocity of his play. He realized that he had to go all out in every game to ensure that East's team would not lose should it ever show signs of faltering. Like a demon possessed, Harley fired off the year like a shotgun, sparking the season opening win over Doane, 59-0. In this contest, he was instrumental in every score of the day but one, a forward pass intercepted by a teammate, who ran it into the end zone. Chic scored four touchdowns that day and kicked four extra points.

The following week, for some unexplained reason, Chic did not play in East's 21-0 win over Aquinas High School.

One week later, an injury to one of East's halfbacks prompted Coach Cordray to consider moving Harley from quarterback to halfback, meaning his position on the filed would not be directly behind the center, but off to the side. Whoever would be assigned to quarterback would be responsible for calling the plays.

"Chic is being worked at halfback by Coach Cordray," the *Dispatch* wrote in previewing the Saturday, October 10, contest against Delaware. In that battle, East blanked Delaware 34-0. Chic once again was the game's stellar performer, crossing over for four TDs at the halfback slot and kicking four extra points.

At the same time, about 400 miles to the east, the Boston Braves, a traditional doormat in the National League, were facing off with the Philadelphia Athletics in the World Series. A star player for the Braves was its catcher Hank Gowdy, a Columbus native who later became a close friend of Chic's. The Braves lost to the Athletics in four straight games, but Gowdy hit .600 in the series.

Pregame publicity for East's next encounter was at a fever pitch for the Orange and Black's meeting with West High School on Saturday, October 24, at Indianola Park. Most observers believed that punting would play a key role in the contest, with Mulbarger and Chic assigned by Cordray to handle those chores for East. In the stands that day was Ohio State Coach John Wilce, who was interested in checking out some of the game's recruiting prospects. Without a doubt, Wilce's main reason for being there was to scout East's senior sensation he had heard so much about. For this game, Chic was back at quarterback. When the dust had cleared, East had won 42-0. Wilce had to be impressed.

"Harley Sparkles As Usual" read one newspaper's headline, with the article reading, "Of course, the star of the game was Chic Harley, who gave one of the finest exhibitions of open field running that has been seen in Columbus in many a day. He scored a touchdown at the very outset of the game, a second one on a 35-yard run, and a third after taking a punt and rocketing 55 yards through a broken field. He converted every TD into a goal—a total of six PATs."

A week later, East annihilated South High School 55-0. After the first half, Chic and other starters played very little because of the lopsided score. Harley did not score a touchdown in that contest, but kicked five extra points, and Mulbarger, two.

In the season's most lopsided game, East beat Springfield High School 74-0 in a Saturday afternoon game at Indianola Park. All of East's touchdowns except two came in the first half. Substitutes were used wholesale. Harley scored three touchdowns, one on an eighty-yard run from scrimmage, and booted eight extra points. He also completed numerous passes.

Across town at Ohio State, new faces were beginning to shine for the Buckeye football program. Fred Norton was the team's talented quarterback; Swede Sorenson, one of its halfbacks and a strong defensive player; and Bill Havens (Louise's older brother), a senior end who also could play halfback.

The biggest, though not the last, game of the season was set for Saturday, November 11, against archrival North High

School. East supporters and Cordray expressed confidence that they could defeat North for the third straight year.

"They have Harley and why shouldn't they feel a little chesty," a newspaper reported. "Not only have they got the greatest quarter Columbus has ever produced, but they also have 10 other good men who will be in there battling to add another victory over the up-city eleven."

For the entire week leading up to the East-North cross-town clash, both schools held huge rallies. As usual, a down-town Columbus band performed at East's, while North had its own musicians. At one of East's rallies, subscriptions were sold to earn money for musical instruments and other necessities in hopes of starting a band the following year.

In games between the two schools dating back to 1899, North had won 10 and lost 4 with 1 tie. North had scored 174 points to East's 91. For this game, contrary to past practice, East's rooting section was on Ohio Field's east bleachers, and North's was on the west side.

"Enthusiasm and confidence ran riot in the North and East football camps yesterday," read the Ohio State *Journal*. "Today's game should be one of the greatest in the history of high school athletics in this city. North realizes that to win today's contest, Harley must be stopped. Harley has caused every team in Ohio many sleepless nights since he has been at East. At North, the feeling prevails that Coach Swain has developed a defense that will keep Harley within bounds. Coach Cordray is confident of winning, but has warned the East eleven that it is going against the very best team that has been met this season."

On the same day, longtime football rivals Harvard and Princeton were meeting, with Harvard the favorite. It was considered one of the major games in the country that week and would be played at the Yale Bowl with its seating capacity of 70,000.

An estimated 6,000 people attended the East-North game, one of the largest throngs ever for any football contest in Columbus. North Coach John Swain's tactics of shadowing Harley and putting as many as two or three defenders on him at a time paid off that cloudy Saturday afternoon in Columbus, as East fell for the first time in two years, 14-0.

"Harley was stopped," a Columbus newspaper reported. "The great player was played to a frazzle by the game North youngsters. The keen quarterback made several good gains, his longest a 20-yard run. But he was thrown for losses that more than made up these advantages. The losers had plenty of fight, but seemed to be doomed just as quickly as North had put up its 'Stop Harley' into effect so thoroughly."

Mulbarger "apparently lost his head," according to one report, when he was ejected from the game for slugging an opponent. "The blow was directly responsible for North's touchdown in the third quarter."

The sizable gains Chic made running were quickly offset by North players throwing him for losses. On one play, he tossed a twenty-yard pass that was immediately fumbled and recovered by North.

"At times, any number of Maroon forwards would break through and nab Harley or another backfield man before he was fairly started," said the paper. "North was coached to stop him and North did stop him. His generalship was great Saturday. He tackled fiercely and had he been given any kind of interference (blocking) there is no doubt that he would have pulled off many of his spectacular runs."

The defeat was devastating for Chic, as he and many others on the East side of the stadium left the field in tears. While not the final game of his high school football career, the loss proved a foreshadowing of what would happen exactly five years later on the same football field.

The next two contests saw East shut out Aquinas 31-0 and South 55-0. In the last football game of Harley's high school years, East and Bellaire High School tied 6-6 in a fierce battle that featured one of Chic's most spectacular plays of all time. It occurred in the first quarter of a game that siphoned every ounce of strength that players from both squads could muster. On that play, from fifteen yards out, Chic ran the ball around the right end, only to become confused after a wall of defenders blocked his way to the end zone. Rather than ramming ahead for a short gain, he turned around and headed in the opposite direction with twenty-one players—half of them his own teammates—in hot pursuit. Chic was heading in the wrong direction, straight for Bellaire's end zone and six points for the other team, when he came to his senses, shifted gears, and motored his way back in the direction he'd come from. Dodging, darting, and stiff-arming his way around and through an army of desperate tacklers, Harley sprinted into the end zone for six points, ending what turned out to be a 185-yard run. One newspaper story called it "the most spectacular game ever witnessed in this city." A headline screamed, "Harley Saves the Day."

For his miraculous senior season, Chic Harley scored at least 123 points, bringing his three-year grand total to 269 known points in twenty-four games. Columbus had never seen anything like it, not to mention the fact that his superhuman skill as a passer, punter, and safety resulted in dozens more points being scored by East in those three seasons and countless more being saved.

East placed second behind North High School in 1915. Chic Harley, however, had ensured his place in the hearts and minds of football fans throughout Columbus and Ohio. He was not only named to the All Eleven Teams of all three Columbus newspapers, but tapped captain as well.

"There's no doubt that he is the most capable pivot man ever developed in Columbus," the *Dispatch* wrote on November 19, 1914.

Before the end of his senior year, Harley made his mark in athletics overall, displaying his versatility and all around abilities in sports other than football. As the buds of the cottonwoods began to unfurl along the swift-flowing Olentangy, Chic raced to top honors in the first annual outdoor track and field meet of the Columbus Interscholastic Track Association. He ran away with fourteen points the afternoon of Friday, May 8, 1915, easily winning the 100-yard dash, leaving his nearest opponent twenty-five yards behind in the dust. He came within a fifth of a second of the state high school record. He also won the 220-yard dash and the broad jump and was the anchorman on the one-mile relay team. Mulbarger placed second in the shot put, and Vorys, second in the hammer throw. Two weeks later, a headline in the *Dispatch* put a scare into everyone in Columbus: "Chic Harley Off for Michigan U."

According to the story, "Chic Harley, East High's athletic star, left Columbus early Friday morning seeking other worlds to conquer. His destination was Michigan University in Ann Arbor. No, sit down, Clara, he has not deserted East and he will be back in Columbus Monday morning at the latest unless "Hurry Up Yost" happens to hear of him and refuses to allow him to return." Chic traveled to Michigan to compete in the Michigan high school interscholastic track meet. Fielding Yost was Michigan's famed football coach at the time.

In early June, with the school year winding down, Columbus newspapers named their All High Baseball Teams. Harley was named to the first team as its captain, with Mulbarger in right field and Joe Finneran of Aquinas High School at shortstop. Finneran and Chic became close friends, teammates, and room-mates a few years later.

The question of what Chic would do after high school was clear in everyone's mind in Columbus—except Chic's. To local sports fans, his next stop was naturally Ohio State University, where he would continue to compete in athletics on the local stage. Chic, who had little interest in studies, was not so sure where he would wind up and for several months stewed about his future. By this time, several schools were aggressively courting him. Coach Wilce saw all he needed to see early in the 1914 foot-ball season to know he wanted Harley for his football program. Michigan and Notre Dame also pursued Chic with a vengeance.

Unsure, Chic thought about getting a job somewhere. He knew that if he wanted to stay in Columbus, he'd have to find a way to pay for room and board. If not college, then employment. Perhaps a job similar to one he had for a few summer months at the Buckeye Steel Casting Company, where he quietly went about the business of wielding a sledgehammer used in the manufacturing of railroad boxcars. Harley, of course, was no ordinary sledge thrower. As a longtime friend described years later, Chic's ability to use a sledgehammer in the dreary, echo chamber surroundings of an industrial plant was a thing of sheer beauty.

The process required one person to hold a steel rail while his partner, wielding the sledge, hammered the large nails into place. "It was dangerous for the guy holding the item," said his friend Russ Finneran, brother of Joe, who later became Chic's college roommate. "Chic threw it perfectly the first time he had to hit the coal chisel."

On one of Chic's first days on the job, Finneran related, a fellow sledge thrower who considered himself the best in the place heard about the ability of this new kid on the block. Finneran said: "I was told by a fellow worker not to go home for lunch this one day because there would be a big fight at noon between Chic and this big guy, who was six feet, four inches and 245 pounds. He was jealous of the fame Chic had gotten as a sledge thrower. I had to go home for lunch, and I didn't want to see this new guy, Chic, get beat up. I was told that if I went home, I would never see anything like it if I lived to be 300. So when I got back to the plant after lunch, I noticed Chic swinging his sledge so easily and nonchalantly. I said to someone, 'There was no fight, right?' I was told that the big guy was beat up and I should take a look at him. Chic's ability to throw a sledge had spread like wildfire, and this bully had heard about it, so he went up to Chic and threw sand in his face. Chic's only reaction was to tell the bully that he would see him at noon."

Reluctantly, by late July, Chic was forced to decide whether to attend college. He decided to accept the offer—not from Ohio State, but from Michigan.

"Other schools were trying to get Chic," said his friend and college teammate Charlie Seddon. "We were surprised when we heard that he hadn't made up his mind. It was found out that he was literally on the train ready to go to Michigan when Bill

McKinnon, sports editor of the *Dispatch*, and someone else got on the train and took him off. They made him change his mind to go to Ohio State."

But even after enrolling, Chic was unsure that college life was for him.

"Harley May Leave State," reported a Columbus newspaper on September 30, 1915, sending OSU supporters into hysteria. "Harley must work his way through school and if he can find no position by which he can make enough money to pay his expenses it will be necessary for him to leave school. It is likely too that if forced to leave State he will matriculate at the University of Michigan, where he will have no trouble finding means to defray his expenses. Ohio State is his original choice and he would rather go to school here than at any other place."

As Russ Needham reported in a column in 1929, Chic was confused, partly because recruiters from all over the country were pressuring him to enroll in their colleges and partly because no one from his family was in Columbus. Once McKinnon had pulled him off the train and made sure Chic was safely signed up to attend Ohio State, it took another month or so before things settled down. Only a week into college life, Chic confided to his high school senior class advisor, Grace Peters, that he didn't like college and was going to quit.

"Stick it out until they call out the freshman football players," she told Chic. "Just for me, Chic." Wrote Needham, "And Miss Peters being Miss Peters, as all East High School graduates know, Chic promised. After the freshmen were called out and Chic began rambling through the varsity just the same as he had rambled through high school opponents, he began to like it and then began the college football career in which he was stopped only once."

Besides, young Louise Havens was enrolled at Ohio State, too.

East High School coach Frank Gullum adjusts Chic's helmet during game around 1914.

STOP 'CHIC' HARLEY, SLOGAN AT NORTH

Coach Swain Hopes to Rig Up Defense for His Special Benefit.

Annual Championship Game at Ohio Field Should Be Drawing Card.

With the idea of building up a defense that in a measure at least will prove too much for "Chic" Harley to overcome, Coach Swain of North High's football squad will work during the remainder of the week at Indianola park.

A November 4, 1913 Columbus Dispatch headline shows how much Chic attracted the attention of arch-rival North High School in season's biggest game.

Early high school football photo of Chic circa 1912.

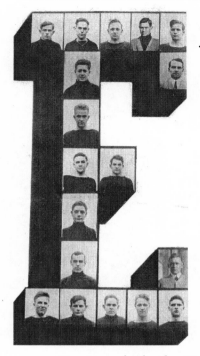

Members of East High School football team form giant "E" with Harley in the center right box.

Mattie and Charles Harley in photo take in late 1920s.

·HARLEY IS A WONDER

Besides the hopeless elimination of North High school as a contender for premier football honors in Columbus, the East's 47 to 0 victory over North Saturday brought out probably the best quarterback performance ever seen in interscholastic circles in Columbus, the work of "Chic" Harley, East's star pivot. The comparison with Barrington, Harley's forerunner at East, is inevitable and in it Harley towers over his predecessor. In only one department of quarterback play, kicking, does Harley fail to show more stuff than the famous "Rink." At running with the ball and starting the forward pass Chic seems far superior.

But where Harley's superiority is most clear is in field generalship. Saturday the youngster was never at a loss to select his next point of attack. There was no hesitation and he directed his offense with the precision of clockwork, this one thing overwhelming the North defense until the maroon and gold's plight became pitiable.

The season of 1913 has surely brought out a new Glen Gray in Columbus.

November 10, 1913 Columbus Citizen headline shows clearly the dominance of Chic on central Ohio football gridirons.

Photo shows 1917 Ohio State offensive squad that includes Chic in backfield at left halfback behind center flanked by Pete Stinchcomb (right) at right halfback and Dick Boesel at fullback (left).

Chic during happy moment around 1916

In his last year at Ohio State Harley played guard on the university basketball team earning his fourth varsity letter.

Chic in track clothing. He set Western Conference record in 50-yard dash running it in 5.35 seconds in one of the few track meets he ever participated in.

During summer months in Columbus, Chic, an excellent swimmer, was employed as a lifeguard at the Franklin Park public pool.

45

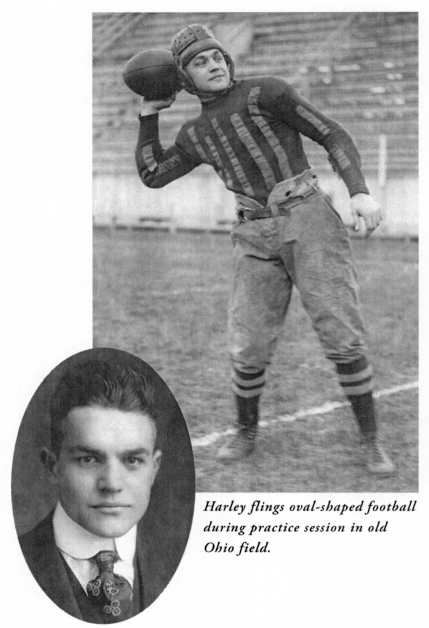

Harley flings oval-shaped football during practice session in old Ohio field.

Harley in photo that may have been taken upon his admission as a member of the Varsity "O" Athletic Association.

CHAPTER 4

The Breakout

As Ohio State's crop of wide-eyed freshmen settled into their new quarters and returning students and faculty renewed acquaintances, a fidgety Chic Harley was chomping at the bit, anxious to get going as a new member of the varsity team. His first opportunity to unshackle his latent skill loomed just around the corner. Both he and Coach John Wilce sensed that great things lay just over the horizon. Yet, they muzzled their enthusiasm. Chic's modesty and quiet demeanor precluded any boastfulness or predictions. Wilce knew that too much talking was bad business and could negatively affect his team. So the two remained reticent as fifty players hoping to make the varsity squad and another ninety seeking placement on the frosh team reported to Ohio Field for the first day of practice, September 20, 1916.

In that era, college football commenced around the same time when classes began in September, unlike today, when preparations and planning rarely let up throughout the year. Wilce and Athletic Director St. John reported for work toward the end of the first week of September. They were the first athletic heads to arrive in Columbus, ready to roll up their sleeves and get to work molding a football team. The rest weren't scheduled to show until the following week. Ohio State's first football game, against

Ohio Wesleyan on October 7, was just a month away, so time was of the essence.

The Buckeyes' prospects looked good for several reasons. Just a year earlier, the varsity team in only its third year in the Western Conference (also known then as the Big Nine) won five of seven contests, losing one and tying one. That was good for third place, highly respectable for the conference newcomers. The team had won its final three games, two by shutouts against Oberlin (25-0 on November 13) and conference rival Northwestern (34-0 on November 20). Two weeks earlier, the Buckeyes edged Indiana 10-9. Another cause for optimism was that a number of gridiron greats who had won fame in high school and performed well as Buckeye freshmen were about to be elevated to varsity ranks. Harley led this group, followed by such notables as Gordy Rhodes, center Ferdinand "Fritz" Holtkamp, guard Irwin Turner, and tackle prospect Jim Flowers. These four players, along with returnees Howard Yerges at quarterback, team captain Frank "Swede" Sorenson, tackle Bob Karch, tiny guard Charlie Seddon, and the speedy "Shifty" Bolen at end, formed the nucleus of a team that had high hopes. It was a team that was small in size, even by standards of the day, but swift of foot and intelligent, which was a reflection of their cerebral coach. Just how far and how high the Buckeyes could go was uncertain. To reach high, Wilce's gridders would have to aim high. The coach knew that even with his team's tremendous skill level, it had to function on all cylinders as a real team that pulled together with all members helping one another. Otherwise, the season would be just another seven-game stretch attracting average crowds of 3,000 to 5,000 and ho-hum interest.

No one knew for sure how Chic, at five feet, eight inches and 150 pounds, would perform in varsity competition, although all predictions were that he would do well. It was one thing to scamper around and through the opposition, as Chic did, when the freshman team was comprised of friends and teammates and the occasion was a scrimmage on the home field with empty bleachers. It was quite another feat to ramble for sizable chunks of real estate in a scheduled contest before thousands of fans and against experienced fleet-footed tackles and guards, some of them weighing more than 220 pounds. A year earlier, Harley, in one of his first offensive plays in the first practice of the year, let it be known that his reputation was well-founded. With the freshman squad serving as guinea pigs for the varsity team in practice, halfback Harley snatched a handoff and zigzagged his way through eleven defenders to score a sixty-yard touchdown. Everyone who witnessed it was in awe. The frosh were jubilant that Chic was able to serve the varsity its lunch in such roaring fashion. Equally amazed were the rival varsity members, embarrassed that this small-sized underclassman could breeze through them as easily as he did.

Chic had commanded great attention as a quarterback and safety during his three years at East High School. In Columbus, as in many towns large and small throughout the country during the first half of the twentieth century, high school football games were the craze. Intercommunity rivalries blossomed, and teenagers became gridiron stars. High school championship games in large towns like Chicago could draw as many as 100,000 fans. Such was the situation, but on a smaller scale, in Ohio's capital city, where the prep competition was fierce, drawing crowds even larger than Ohio State's.

Harley had starred at East High School during his varsity years of 1912-14, as had his new Buckeye teammate Gordy Rhodes at North High School. When these two standouts— both squad captains—and their teams faced each other for the city football championship of 1914, it was Rhodes's school that defeated Harley's 14-0. It was only one of three defeats Harley had tasted in his three years of varsity action at East, and it was a most bitter pill for this shy, sensitive teen to swallow. Two years later, when they were Ohio State teammates, Harley quietly admitted that the championship game of 1914 was the saddest day of his life. Rhodes at the same time said he remembered that contest, which East was heavily favored to win, as one of his happiest. Those two reactions said volumes about their personalities. For Chic, the defeat was heartbreaking. For Rhodes, victory brought joy, but the day was merely "one of the happiest" of his life; it was a football game, not a life-defining event. Later the Buckeyes, led by Harley, would suffer a defeat that proved to be hauntingly reminiscent of that painful day in 1914. It was a loss that not only crushed him, but signaled disturbing events to come.

While Wilce, St. John, Rhodes, Seddon, and others were keenly aware of the skill and talent Harley brought to Ohio State, few could foresee the overall impact he would have in the weeks ahead. On September 22, reporting on the team's second practice, the Columbus *Evening Dispatch* mentioned Harley's name only once (in the sixth column), saying that he and Fred Norton (who died in World War I a few years later) served as halfbacks on the second practice team. Most of the regulars practiced on the first team. Reported as "splendid kickers" were veteran quarterback Yerges and Rhodes, with Yerges picking up where he left off the previous season as the team's number one kicker and Rhodes proclaimed by Wilce as the team's best booter in the last five years.

This story and others before the season opener against Ohio Wesleyan may have been part of a clever strategy by Wilce. As practices progressed, he was well aware he had a very good team and that varsity newcomer Harley was living up to his preseason billing. Within days of the September 22 report, Chic not only wrestled regular punting duties away from Rhodes and Yerges, but was named the team's starting right halfback. It's probable that Wilce had this in mind from the start, but kept his little secret weapon under wraps as long as possible. Still, the die had been cast. Harley's talents, as demonstrated during practices, had promised to elevate the "Babes of the Big Nine" to heights it had never dreamed of. Harley's speed, uncanny ability to accelerate at top stride in just two steps, dodging ability, stiff-arm, sharp instincts, and strength made it easy for Wilce to start him in several key positions, the most notable being halfback. Yerges would fill the team's quarterback slot.

Wilce and others had noticed one other important attribute. While many athletes were naturally aggressive, outgoing, or vain, Harley was none of these. He was unusually quiet and bashful, rarely spoke unless spoken to, and almost always responded in just a few words. He had a magnetic smile and a strong air of sincerity, and when his smile broadened to flash his straight white teeth, people were instantly transfixed. The Buckeye squad knew from the start that Chic was not only an extremely talented football player, but an individual with charisma and charm. He was the kind of guy who let skill, not his mouth, do the talking. Those around him sensed something special, and they wanted to be part of that experience, jockeying for position near this natural born leader whenever the opportunity arose.

Advance ticket sales were brisk. The picture of an up-and-coming football team and an innovative coach with an impressive record from last season was rosy indeed. Early fall in the Midwest is a time of fluctuating weather. On the worst days, daytime temperatures can dip to forty or fifty degrees, setting the stage for winter with its chilling westerly breezes and ominous, swift-moving puffy gray clouds. On Saturday, October 7, there was no sign of winter in central Ohio. It was a fine Indian summer day, and by 2 P.M., the thermometer approached eighty degrees with no wind. For football players, conditions were anything but ideal. The *Dispatch* described the setting as "torrid enough to induce the bleacher fans to remove their coats until the football stands looked like the sun section of a ballpark on a July day."

Wesleyan's Battling Bishops had trekked the seventy miles from Delaware, Ohio, to take on the Buckeyes in the traditional season opener. The non-conference bout had always been a good test for Ohio State. A year earlier in Delaware, the Buckeyes squeaked by Wesleyan 19-6. There was no reason to think that this year's opener wouldn't end the same, especially for the heavily favored Buckeyes. Both sides recognized that the rivalry was such that a rout was not likely. The difference this time, however, was that Ohio State had a speedier, more talented squad than in 1915.

For Chic Harley, it was his first official opportunity to demonstrate that he was more than just a high school wonder. Although typically confident on the football field, he didn't know to what extent Wilce would play him and whether he would deliver when called upon.

Football historians generally gloss over Ohio State's first two games of 1916 because the contests against Wesleyan and Oberlin were non-conference and considered warm-ups to the first Western league battle against powerhouse Illinois on October 21. The importance of these first two games cannot be overlooked, however. For one thing, Chic's playing in the Wesleyan matchup was significant, though brief in time. For another, Wilce's use of the forward pass emerged, an offensive strategy then still in its infancy. Ohio State attempted passes ten times, completing only one. Even with these paltry results, Wilce had already determined that passing and not just plowing through the line would be a major part of his offensive attack. That approach was deliberate because it could utilize not only Harley's running skill, but his passing ability.

Despite playing "only a short time" in the Wesleyan contest, according to *Dispatch* writer Russ Needham in a 1938 feature story about Harley's football career, Chic's performance on the field, along with that of captain "Swede" Sorenson, stood out.

"For Ohio State, Harley, whose offensive and defensive work brings out hopes of a place in stardom, and Captain Sorenson held the posts of honor," wrote the *Dispatch*. "Harley, who too often was hindered by his interference, which was extraordinarily slow, picked his holes well and played nobly as a defensive halfback. Sorenson proved the same old reliable 'Swede' who got the needed yards when called upon." By interference, the newspaper was referring to the blocking for Chic, which on this steamy day was so lethargic and sluggish that he frequently outran his teammates.

Beginning with Ohio State's second set of downs, Harley and Sorenson set the offensive pace and ripped through

Wesleyan's line time and again, picking up three yards here and five yards there.

"Harley stumbled over Wesleyan bodies for seven and then made eight around Wesleyan's right end," continued the *Dispatch*'s account. As 1916 progressed, Harley specialized in runs around right and left ends, utilizing his fancy footwork and uncanny ability to bolt through holes in Wesleyan's defensive line. All the while, the positioning of the offensive players—called formations—created by the innovative Wilce gave Chic the option of passing the ball or running, whichever his instincts told him. In normal situations, Wilce employed the short punt formation, which placed Chic about five yards directly behind the center. This gave him a clear view of what lay ahead as he began to run.

In the third period against Wesleyan, Harley scampered for ten more yards around the end, but the play was called back when a Buckeye was singled out for holding. Finally, with Ohio State ahead 6-0, "Harley and Rhodes carried the ball to the four-yard line, where Yerges, aided by the line, again bucked it over." It was quarterback Howard Yerges's second touchdown run of the day, and it put Ohio State up 12-0, which proved to be the final score.

Defensively, Harley played flawlessly in the backfield against the Bishops. On one occasion, he broke up a fake punt by Wesleyan "and nailed" the kicker for a ten-yard loss. Chic began his varsity career playing defensive back, but became well-known as a sparkling safety in his last two seasons with Ohio State.

Harley's quadruple-threat status hadn't yet emerged in early October 1916. The showcasing of his superb punting skills, handled in so-so fashion by Yerges and Rhodes in the Wesleyan contest, had to wait for a few more games. Also on hold was his ability to toss the football with accuracy and speed from a full sprint, something he quickly became famous for doing.

As tough and hard-fought as Ohio State's bout with the Battling Bishops was, the opposite proved true a week later in one of the most extraordinary games ever played by any college football team. Oberlin College, south of Cleveland, came calling on its longtime rival on the afternoon of Saturday, October 14. Less than a year earlier, in its penultimate game of the season, Ohio State had won 25-0. This time only 3,300 fans, probably expecting nothing more than a scrimmage for the Buckeyes, witnessed the contest on Ohio Field. What unfolded couldn't even be considered a scrimmage. It was a massacre, as Ohio State walloped the Yeomen, 128-0, the most lopsided score in team history. Harley scored twice early and then was taken out to preserve him for bigger games in the weeks ahead. He and fellow halfback Frosty Hurm scored TDs on the Buckeyes' first two offensive plays of the game. Halfback Fred Norton scored five touchdowns, and fullback Dick Boesel, four. Ohio State scored an amazing nineteen touchdowns that day and fourteen conversions in amassing an incredible 1,140 yards. In the first down category, the Buckeyes totaled forty-three to Oberlin's two, and in total punts, OSU kicked only twice, while Oberlin booted sixteen times.

"This score gave Ohio State University the most publicity it ever received," wrote professor Thomas French in the Ohio State *Monthly*. It undoubtedly stoked the simmering fire inside French, who until then had been quietly calling for support to build a new football stadium that could seat at least 25,000 fans. The Oberlin score, Wilce's up-and-coming team, and the solid play and emerging popularity of little Chic Harley had French and others believing more and more in the lofty goal that many thought unattainable.

Discussion of that dream picked up momentum following Ohio State's next game, the first conference encounter of the season, against Illinois. Comparing players in modern times with those who competed fifty, seventy, or ninety years earlier is a tricky business in any era. So is comparing the importance of one game or one season with another. The Buckeyes' 1916 battle against the Fighting Illini is, without question, one of the greatest football games ever played by an Ohio State team. In fact, it may indeed be the greatest. While no one really identified the full significance of the contest at the moment the final whistle sounded, history revealed that without the 7-6 victory, and the way it was snatched in the final seconds by Chic Harley, it's questionable that Ohio State and its storied football program of today would have evolved the way it has.

Heading into the contest on Illinois turf in Champaign, Ohio wasn't given much chance. Illinois had been a perennial power in the Western Conference, winning the league title the year before. In fact, Coach Bob Zuppke, in his third year at Illinois, hadn't lost a conference contest since the 19-9 loss to Minnesota in 1913. His players were big, quick, and talented, with Bart Macomber captain, George Halas at end, and Ed "Dutch" Sternaman at halfback.

A few hours before the 2 P.M. kickoff, Zuppke gave the visiting players a tour of the Illinois trophy room, where awards, balls, and all sorts of hardware were on display. This clever bit of hospitality more likely was a tactic to intimidate the visitors. That day, the weather in Champaign-Urbana and surrounding corn-fields was horrible, with intermittent rain that made the gridiron a sea of mud. Neither team could get on track as 4,388 fans (175 from Columbus) huddled on the bleachers, trying to keep dry and warm. Just moments after play began, a fumble by Ohio State gave Illinois good field position. Two complete passes set up a successful field goal for Macomber from a difficult angle. Two more field goal attempts a few minutes later by Macomber failed, leaving Illinois with a 3-0 lead at the end of the first period. In the second quarter, Harley and Ohio continued to struggle with the wet conditions, picking up a few yards here and there and occasionally thrown for a loss. Finally, on a fake punt play, Harley picked his way through opposing tacklers for a twenty-five-yard gain around the left end. But on the next play, he was thrown for a loss, and a play later, a forward pass from Harley to Shifty Bolen was incomplete. Later in the period, a forty-five-yard field goal attempt by Chic failed. After the Illini gave up the ball on downs, as did the Buckeyes, a punt by Harley was accidentally blocked by one of his teammates, with the referee ruling that the ball belonged to Illinois. Macomber, running and passing, again was called on to make a field goal as the second period ended.

This time it was good from twenty yards.

Buckets of rain continued to fall, forming a sea of small puddles and uprooted turf as the second half of play began. Cleats were like street shoes on ice. Jerseys and padded pants were caked in mud. Players' faces were unrecognizable. Still, the two teams battled up and down the gridiron, with Rhodes and Harley carving out one- and two-yard gains and Macomber booming fifty- and sixty-yard punts following unsuccessful Illini attempts at first downs. A few trick plays netted six or seven yards, not enough to prevent Ohio from punting nine times in the game and Illinois, seven.

In the fourth quarter, with Illinois clinging to a 6-0 lead, play began to open up. Harley, unable to get going for anything longer than his twenty-five-yard scamper in the second period, was called on to handle some of the punting. Macomber went to the air more often for Illinois, and the crafty Sternaman started chalking up four-, five-, and six-yard gains on the ground. Following an eight-yard punt return by Harley to midfield, Ohio State suddenly began gaining sizable chunks of ground. L. A. Friedman replaced Yerges at quarterback, and his hot passing gained eleven yards, then six yards. Their hopes at scoring fizzled when Chic was thrown for a seven-yard loss and a Harley-to-Bolen pass attempt was incomplete. Illinois then came right back, with Sternaman and Macomber leading the way with runs. With just a few minutes remaining, Harley, running for his life after a handoff, "seemed confused," but managed to complete a pass to end Clarence MacDonald for eighteen yards. Two more forward passes put the Buckeyes on the Illini thirteen-yard line as the clock ticked away the final moments. With about two minutes left in the game, the situation was third down and three yards to go for Ohio State. The outcome rested on Wilce's next one or two plays and on the skill and luck of his players, who had to contend with not only an opponent desperate to stop them, but also terrible weather conditions.

"Two minutes of bitter struggle remained," Wilce later wrote of one of his greatest thrills in a three-decade coaching career.

"A long forward pass from Chic Harley to end MacDonald had carried Ohio from its twenty-yard line to midfield, and a succession of short tosses, in which the future aviator Fred Norton figured prominently, made it fourth down with three yards to go on the Illinois thirteen-yard line. Then came a great play."

"The game was nearly over," remembered team center Fritz Holtkamp. "But the Buckeyes were pressing down over a sodden, miserable field. They were inside the fifteen-yard line. A flash of Scarlet and the sophomore halfback Illinois had heard of had raced loose for a touchdown."

As a newspaper described it the next day, "Harley received the ball from quarterback Kelley Van Dyne that started to be a forward pass play. Harley saw the Illinois defense on the right side of the line momentarily sucked in, triggering him to plug the ball under his arm and dart across the field. With his legs carrying him as fast as he could Chic whisked by the outstretched arms of several defenders and dropped the ball across the goal in the far northwest corner."

The roar from the small contingent of Buckeye rooters was deafening, and Harley's teammates went wild, not believing what they had just witnessed. "He faked to pass then ran to the left," recalled Wilce. "Two teammates going to the left as possible pass receivers blocked the defensive end and right halfback. Harley outran the fullback, straight-armed the safety man and dove for a touchdown in the extreme left corner of the field. As teammates jumped up and down, hands and helmets raised, uncontrollable, soaked Ohio fans shrieked in delight, and Illini fans mumbled their disappointment, one more job awaited. Harley was not through thinking. He called time, asked for a clean right shoe to replace the mud-heavy one he had on."

Moments earlier, after scoring the TD in dramatic fashion, Harley punted the ball from his end zone, which in those days was a requirement for a chance at kicking the extra point. Norton, whose catching ability late in the fourth quarter was so important, threw his hands and body around Chic's punt at the twenty-two-yard line, where the ball would have to be placed for the point after touchdown.

"Gimme a shoe," said Harley to team trainer Doc Gurney. The cleat he was handed was not only dry, but a special square-toe design created by team manager Joe Mulbarger, Chic's pal and former high school teammate. In practice, Chic was perfect when he used this shoe; with other shoes he occasionally missed.

"Calmly, as if the battle were just starting, the Ohio sophomore waited while out from the sidelines came the immortal Doc Gurney, the Buckeyes trainer—carrying one clean square-toed shoe that was to be the instrument in deciding a Big Nine championship," wrote Holtkamp.

As Chic laced up his new shoe, Wilce, always the psychologist, briskly and nervously in uncustomary fashion walked up and down the Buckeye bench instructing "all Ohio substitutes to concentrate on just one image—the picture of Harley kicking the winning point after touchdown."

On the field, waiting for Harley, was a calm Van Dyne, who had volunteered to hold the ball for Harley, the first time he had ever been put into that role.

"A scoreboard that showed the score 6-6," wrote Columbus *Citizen* reporter E.H. Penisten, "An almost breathless stillness of suspense broken only by the wind that swept the grey sentinel bleachers on either side of the field. Four thousand spectators who realized that only a simple minute of time remained, whose hearts beat with a mingled feeling of hope for victory and dread of impending defeat. And down on a rain-soaked field a scarlet jerseyed player—a sophomore playing his first big game, lacing his shoes for an attempt at goal that was to mean more than any one play in the two score years of football history of his alma mater."

With mud splattered across his face, jersey, socks, pants, and left shoe, Harley stood nearly ankle deep in muck waiting for the snap to Van Dyne. The hike was perfect, as Chic gauged the distance carefully from the line and sent the ball sailing perfectly between the uprights. For a moment, stone silence. Then pandemonium broke out among State fans. Several people fainted in the bleachers, said reports. With the minute that remained on the clock, Illinois tried desperately to recover, but couldn't. Delirious Buckeye fans—all 175 of them—broke down a fence in front of the bleachers, running up to members of the team to congratulate them, slapping them on the back, hugging, and dancing around like little children. Harley, the hero who had scored all seven points in spectacular fashion, fled in embarrassment for the more comfortable confines of the locker room. As he was running, tackle Bob Karch threw his arms around Chic and carried him all the way into the dressing room, tears streaming down his face.

The final statistics showed that Ohio outplayed Illinois on nearly every level, gaining 221 yards rushing to the Illini's 164. Ohio's passing was superior, as was its punting, and defensively the Buckeyes held when they had to.

Harley hadn't a thing to say after the game. He took it all very quietly and didn't join in the exuberance of his mates. He was one of the first of the squad to climb into his street clothes. There was something more important on Chic's mind at that moment: getting Wilce's permission to leave the team to visit his parents in Chicago for the rest of the weekend. Still celebrating the victory, the coach responded, "Boy, you can go to California if you want to."

Sports columnist Ring Lardner, who was well-known for successfully predicting college football contests during that era, had prophesied that the game would end in a tie. "Whereas it would have been a tie had not Harley of the Buckeyes, as Ohioans are sometimes called, changed his shoes before attempting the goal from touchdown," wrote Lardner, "there is nothing in the rule book legalizing such a sudden change of shoes, and I believe Mr. Zuppke had ground for a protest." League commissioners thought otherwise, as nothing came of Lardner's suggestion.

Following the game, as both squads headed off the field, team rascal Shifty Bolen yelled to the Illinois coach, "Hey, Zup, how would you like to have Harley's shoe for your trophy room?" It was an obvious reference to Zuppke's guided tour a few hours earlier. That comment ignited a small skirmish between the two teams that campus police quickly broke up.

For Ohio State, wrote Penisten, "more was at stake than at any time in Ohio State athletics. The result would mean more than a victory over the famed Illini. It should mean that at last the scarlet and gray had found its place in the sun. It was the first win against a real football leader." That sense of the Buckeyes' finally arriving on the big stage was shared by every follower of the team. The next morning as the squad's special train from Champaign arrived at Union Station in downtown Columbus, "a great throng of students" normally asleep on an early Sunday morning, especially after a long night of celebration, greeted their heroes with cheers, smiling faces, and an air of cautious supremacy.

"It's an old, old story that will live forever in the annals of Ohio State—Chic Harley's first Big Ten game," Holtkamp would write. "Two months later he was Walter Camp's All-American fullback." In his next two years of Ohio State play, Harley would again earn the honor, becoming not only the school's first, first-team All-American, but its first three-time All-American.

Armed with a reinvigorating sense of confidence in their coach, themselves, and especially their new star, the Buckeyes anxiously awaited the remaining four games of the season. Three of those contests would be against conference rivals Wisconsin, Indiana, and Northwestern. The other opponent would be Case Western Reserve, a longtime intrastate rival.

While Ohio State's victory against Illinois on October 21 could arguably be considered the most important game in its football history, the November 4 battle against Wisconsin certainly ranks nearly as high. October 28 was a bye (meaning they were not scheduled to play that week) Saturday for the Buckeyes, allowing them extra time to prepare for the Badgers. Not only would a win keep Ohio State in contention for the conference crown— its first Western League football title—and maintain its unblemished win-loss record, but it would be especially gratifying for Coach Wilce, a Wisconsin alum and former Badger coach.

Chic Harley's thrilling performance in snatching victory from Illinois two weeks earlier had whipped up a frenzy, not only on campus, but throughout Columbus and, to an emerging degree, the state of Ohio. Wisconsin, like the Illini, had been a major power in the Big Nine for years. It was also one of seven charter members of the Western Conference and had already won four league titles before OSU joined the conference in 1913. While Illinois and Zuppke early on recognized the potential of Ohio State's football squad, the Badgers displayed an air of aloofness and overconfidence. Like the Buckeyes, the Badgers had a record of 3-0. In three previous contests, they had outscored opponents 91-10. Badger Coach Paul Withington, so concerned about his team's game against Minnesota in late November, spent that Saturday in Minneapolis scouting the Gophers and then sending his assistant Ed Soucy to Columbus to run the team in his place. It would be Wisconsin's first road game of the season.

The hopes and dreams of Ohio State, fans knew, hinged largely on the shoulders of Chic Harley. Six days before the Wisconsin game and eight days after the thrilling victory over Illinois, the Columbus *Dispatch* published a large drawing of Chic with this tribute:

We can almost hear you say "there they go—spoiling that boy for the rest of the season—turning his head and ruining his chances." But, Mr. Reader, we are sure of our ground. This is no ordinary boy we are dealing with—He is so sane and intelligent, so modest and well-poised, that there is nothing in the way of praise that you or we could say that would harm him—he is a good student and a burner of the midnight oil in his studies, clean, gentlemanly, and a comer nationally in the sport of football. If he fumbles every punt and flubs every game for the rest of the season, his gameness and display of football intelligence out in Illinois will carry him strong with us—he delivered on time at the place and the spot, and we are glad to pay him this tribute.

Columbus's daily newspapers—the *Dispatch, Journal,* and *Citizen*—were becoming quickly and keenly aware of the value of Chic Harley. People wanted to know about not only his extraordinary athletic abilities, but what kind of person he was, his study habits, his origins, his friends, and his appearance. Chic Harley and the Buckeye team as a whole were good business, not only for newspaper circulation, but for promoting the school, city, and state. If Chic and the Ohio State football program succeeded and grew, so would they.

Wilce, well aware of the Badgers' offensive ability, drilled his team relentlessly until dark each evening. Taking a cue from Withington, Wilce also decided to dress his team on game day in uniforms without numbers. This was a ploy often used in those days to confuse the opposition. The excitement that had built up in and around the Columbus campus had transformed Ohio State almost overnight. Tickets to the Wisconsin game were almost impossible to get, largely because rickety Ohio Field could seat only about 12,000. Talk of a bigger, more modern stadium to accommodate larger crowds picked up steady, passionate steam.

Chic Harley's stunning last-second heroics two weeks earlier seemed impossible to duplicate. In that contest, he not only ran with the ball, but punted, passed, and played sterling defense. He almost single-handedly won the contest on the opponents' field in awful playing conditions. Asking him to perform as well against Wisconsin seemed too much to ask.

In the more than 100-year history of college football, there have been many majestic performances by outstanding players. Jim Thorpe, George Gipp, Paddy Driscoll, and Fritz Pollard are just a few of the stellar grid greats who have single-handedly carried their teams throughout their collegiate athletic careers and consistently performed extremely well under difficult circumstances. At the head of that list must go Chic Harley, who in three years with Ohio State set a scoring record that lasted thirty-five years in an era of relatively few points, less passing, and overall conservative play. What made Harley so fabulous as a football player was not just his running ability, but his greatness in every other aspect of the game. He was labeled a multiple offensive threat because he could run with power and grace, pass with pinpoint accuracy, and kick with the best of them. He caught passes as well. But in reality, Harley was much more than just an offensive weapon. As noted previously, he was a terrific safety on defense and considered by many one of the finest and most unselfish blockers around and a deadly tackler.

If ever there was a game that showcased Harley's multiple talents, it was the 1916 thriller against Wisconsin, which Ohio State won 14-13. In this Herculean homecoming battle on Ohio Field, Harley scored all fourteen points for the Buckeyes. In only his second conference game, he literally did everything before an overflow crowd of 12,000 excited fans still slaphappy from the victory over Illinois two weeks earlier. Chic handled the team's punting by kicking seven times, averaging about forty yards per punt. He rushed for 185 yards out of a total team offense of 330 yards. He kicked both PATs, attempted unsuccessfully a forty-yard field goal, returned six punts (one of which was a miraculous scoring effort), attempted four passes, returned kick-offs, and received forward passes. On defense, he played safety, breaking up throws, tackling runners, and constantly being a thorn in the side of Wisconsin. He was as near a perfect football player as one could imagine. As teammate Charlie Seddon said years later, "There was nothing that boy could not do once he made up his mind."

With Ohio State trailing 7-0 in the second quarter, Harley rambled for a twenty-seven-yard touchdown by darting around the right end, barely sneaking past the line of scrimmage to find daylight. Receiving the hike as he stood in punt forma-tion, he veered first left and then right, outrunning Wisconsin's Glenn Taylor. That run was set up by the previous play, which saw Chic rifling a perfect spiral to right end D. V. Peabody. Moments after his TD run, Chic calmly kicked the extra point to tie the score as the first half ended. For the last five minutes of the first half, said the Columbus *Dispatch*, both teams were "pretty well fagged out."

For the next period and a half, the two goliaths of the grid-iron pummeled each other without mercy. The third period turned into a punting match between Harley and Taylor, one of the Badgers' most talented stars and its quarterback, who, unfortunately for Wisconsin, failed on a crucial play late in the game that led to Wisconsin's loss. It wasn't until seven minutes into the fourth period that Harley scored again, this time returning a punt eighty yards on a forty-five-yard punt from Taylor. Chic promptly kicked the extra point, too. His heroics ignited a demonstration of euphoria in the packed Ohio stands as hats, canes, cushions—anything the fans could lay their hands on—were thrown into the air. The punt return was one of Chic's greatest runs. Those few who remember it or have heard of it consider it to be one of the greatest plays in Ohio State history. Without that play, Ohio State would likely have lost the game, missed its first perfect season, and failed to generate the public attention for Harley, his teammates, and the university.

Harley's longtime friend Russ Finneran, Sr. witnessed that eighty-yard punt return in the first football game he ever saw. Nearly sixty years later, Finneran could still describe it in great detail and the lasting impression it had on him:

"All I knew about football was to get the ball over the line. Chic received the ball on the twenty-yard line and ran down the field to cross the goal line about five feet from the sidelines. There were four defending players who attempted to put an end to that run. They came to him at an angle about ten yards apart. He had the ball tucked under his arm. The first man attempted a flying tackle, and I saw his arms around Chic's legs. I said to myself, 'Why doesn't that boy try to evade that man, to dodge or do something? Why does that play have to be over?' I saw the man dive and the hands starting to close, and I was amazed to find that Chic was still running. Now Chic had stepped out of that tackle with that loping action. He had his body under perfect control, perfect rhythm, to step out of that tackle. Chic kept loping down the field. The next man who attempted to tackle him decided to throw his arms around his waist so he wouldn't get away. I saw the hands start to close, and just at the proper moment, Chic twisted his body, and this man rolled harmlessly off of him, and Chic continued loping down the field with that undisturbed even pace. That defense is called 'giving them the hip.' The

third man, another ten yards down the field, decided he would throw his arms around Chic's neck, thinking he won't get away from that. So he threw his arms around Chic's neck, and I saw just at the very proper moment, up went Chic's stiff-arm, where he got under it, under the chin, and the man turned a somersault backwards. None of these attempts resulted in Chic's leaving that straight line five feet in from the sideline, loping down the field. The fourth man, ten or fifteen yards further, came running at him, and what he tried to do, I'll never know. When he got the proper distance, Chic put on that change of speed the same as I do when I put the metal down to the floor to put my car in passing speed. When he did that, this man ran harmlessly out of the way, and Chic ran the last ten yards across the goal line. When I see a play like that again, I'm ready to leave this world."

Finneran, like Harley an Ohio State student, said that eighty-yard punt was an inspiration to him for the rest of his life. "I was just beginning to learn how to sell cooking utensils at the time in the ladies' dorms," explained Finneran. "I thought, *If Chic could do what he did, then I can sell these cooking utensils.* I went out that evening after the football game when everyone else was celebrating and sold enough cooking utensils to make my eighty-five-dollar commission, which was the first time in my life I earned eighty-five dollars in a month." For the next three years, Finneran sold utensils, always remembering that if a man he knows could be so focused, determined, and talented to accomplish what Chic Harley did in November 1916, then he, too, could succeed. "When I graduated, I had $3,000 in the bank, and I bought a new Ford Model T, which I did every eight months," said Finneran. "I give all the credit to Chic Harley, who inspired me. He's been my greatest inspiration, next to my wife."

Following Harley's miraculous run, the fourth quarter crawled toward an end locked at 14-7. With just a few precious seconds remaining on the clock, the Badgers battled their way back by furiously connecting on a combination of passes and runs. A crucial fifteen-yard penalty against Ohio State brought the ball to the Buckeyes' two-yard line, setting the stage for Lou Kreuz's smash across the goal line. Now with the score 14-13 Ohio State, the visitors just needed to tie the game with a successful extra point kick. But it wasn't meant to be. Glenn Taylor, the talented Badger star, somehow dropped the kick out where the ball would be placed for the PAT. When he fumbled, Ohio State took possession, essentially ending the contest.

The loss by Wisconsin was its second 14-13 heartbreaker in two years—in both cases halting its hopes for conference championships. A year earlier, the University of Chicago beat the Badgers 14-13. "We favor the abolition of the numbers 13 and 14 from the category of numbers," wrote the *Wisconsin State Journal.* "Run them out of numberdom, if you will, but give them not to us again. 'Tis too much." It also reported that "the big city of Columbus is wild tonight and if the [presidential] election was tomorrow probably not a thousand voters would cease discussing football long enough to go to the polls. Since its advent into the conference Ohio State has played brave football but never until this year did the Buckeyes really have a team that was championship class. With victories over Illinois and Wisconsin tucked away the Buckeyes promise they will make mince meat of Northwestern's claim to the title."

Harley won high praise from one of the most noted authorities on college football at the time, Walter Eckersall of the Chicago *Tribune*: "Charles (Chic) Harley, who weighs only 153 pounds and who learned to play football on Chicago's prairies, was the all important factor in today's struggle between Wisconsin and Ohio State, which resulted in a 14-13 victory for the Buckeyes and turned Western conference dope upside down." Dope, in the jargon of the time, referred to bettors, or those who predicted the outcomes of games. "Harley scored all the Ohio State points and he is about the best piece of football machinery ever seen in the country this year," added Eckersall. "It was a great game, one which unquestionably has put Ohio State on the football map to such a degree that the Buckeyes must command the respect and admiration of critics in all sections of the country."

With victories over two of their toughest rivals, Harley and his Buckeye teammates still had to get by weak Indiana and Case squads and most likely title contender Northwestern in order to win the championship. Ohio State easily triumphed over the Hoosiers 46-7 on November 11. Harley played only the first nine and a half minutes, scoring on touchdown runs of thirty-three and forty-three yards. Three times he broke away for long runs, chalking up a total of 108 yards rushing. While Chic was easily the star of the game during his play, quarterback Howard Yerges performed sensationally in open field running, scoring two of the team's seven touchdowns. Indiana attempted to pass against Ohio's strong defense an extraordinary twenty times, completing only five for a total of ninety yards. The Buckeyes connected on three of nine passes.

The next Saturday, November 19, Harley and the Buckeyes traveled north to the Cleveland area, where they met old rival Case Western Reserve College. The Buckeyes completely dominated this contest, defeating Case 28-0 on a muddy field. Playing conditions were so bad that Wilce strongly protested, leading some Case fans to worry that the visitors would not go all out. Still, those conditions, which Chic said were worse than in the Illinois game, failed to slow the Buckeyes and especially Harley, "who scooped up punts on any kind of a bad bounce out of the mud and didn't slip once in getting started." Case managed only four first downs the entire contest, while Ohio State amassed twenty-three, accumulating a total offense of 387 yards.

The victory over Case and Harley's superb performance in that game led former Case Coach and Cleveland *Leader* reporter Xen Scott to declare that the Buckeyes may be the best football team in the country: "Today, State has as much right as any other to be classed as the strongest team in the country, and the Columbus team is in direct line for the national championship." Scott reasoned that OSU had achieved records comparable to those of the other squads and had defeated three of the strongest teams in the Midwest: Illinois, Indiana, and Wisconsin." The only teams that rivaled Ohio State at that time, Scott said, were

Brown, Pittsburgh, Nebraska, and Northwestern—the team next on Ohio State's schedule.

Having scored an average of forty-one points per game while allowing some of the best college teams in the nation only twenty-six total for the season, Chic, Wilce, and the Buckeyes had just one more mountain to climb. On November 25 on Ohio Field, they would meet Northwestern, a charter member of the Big Nine led by the talented halfback and kicker John L. "Paddy" Driscoll. Both teams had perfect 6-0 records heading into the clash.

The game was billed as the contest that would decide not only the Western Conference championship and perhaps even the best team in the country, but the better player—Harley or Driscoll. As an interesting sidelight, the battle would feature a team comprised of twelve players who lived in the Chicago area against thirteen players who hailed from Columbus. In some minds, it was a Chicago versus Columbus match to see which was number one.

Chic, of course, said little. He was inwardly excited, not only because the conference championship and a perfect season were at stake, but because his team was playing one of the great teams from Chicago—the town where he was born and where his family lived. The Buckeyes were considered 10-to-8 favorites. Throughout his three years of college football, Chic never took credit. He instead unselfishly heaped praise on his teammates, especially the linemen, whose all important, yet unheralded, role found him daylight. In Chic's mind, they were the heroes, he the byproduct of their hard work. Driscoll, too, was a gentleman whose love for football overrode any pregame criticism of opponents. The fans, especially Northwestern fans, were not hesitant, however, in expressing their belief that Driscoll would outclass Harley once the action began.

"Driscoll, they claim, is as good an offensive player as is Harley, will gain as much ground in hitting the line, in running the ends," declared one Chicago newspaper. "And Driscoll, they also claim, will shine in departments in which Harley will be mediocre—Driscoll will punt with any man on the Ohio team, will handle the ball in the open game with an adeptness excelled by none. . . . Harley and Driscoll have been the sensations of the conference and now they meet in a duel in the last, the most important game of the season, a battle that means the championship of the Big Nine."

In Columbus, confidence in the Buckeyes was at an all-time peak. By this time, Chic was considered a strong candidate for not only All-Western Conference honors, but first team All-American, which—if it happened—would make him the first Buckeye football player to be so honored. Ohio State was a team comprised of many talented, strong-willed players at nearly every position. At the pinnacle was Harley, who had a sixth sense that enabled him to turn sure defeat into amazing success. He always seemed to know the right thing to do on a gridiron at the right instant. When the chips were down, he always came through, regardless of an occasional mistake, such as fumbling the ball or tossing an incomplete pass. But when he had to perform either in the last seconds of play or in a fourth and long situation, Harley never failed. His teammates had supreme confidence in both his playing ability and his demeanor. It was true mutual respect and admiration that lasted until the last day of the last surviving Buckeye of that 1916 squad.

An estimated 15,000 fans jammed into every seat and every corner of Ohio Field on that bright, sunny, cool late November day. The night before, a special train left downtown Chicago for Columbus carrying 150 fans and the Northwestern marching band. The round-trip cost per person was $14.14 coach plus $2 for a lower berth. Arrival time at Union Station in Columbus was 7 A.M.

After Harley opened the game by kicking off to Driscoll, the contest quickly developed into a defensive struggle. Ground gains were small, forcing the teams' two punters, Harley and Driscoll, to engage in a fight for field position. Near the end of the initial period, Ohio State struck first after fullback Swede Sorenson, playing in his final collegiate game, moved the ball to the thirty-yard line. From there, Chic booted a field goal that went squarely through the uprights, giving the Buckeyes a 3-0 lead. Throughout the next two and a half periods, Harley ran, passed, and punted, while Driscoll returned many of those punts, gaining sizable chunks of real estate. But there was no additional scoring. Driscoll tried a dropkick from the forty-yard line for a field goal at the start of the second period, but the ball fell short. Finally, in the fourth quarter, Driscoll connected on another forty-yard field goal, which knotted the score at 3. About halfway through the fourth period, Driscoll, forced to punt, kicked the ball to Chic, who fumbled on his forty-yard line but immediately recovered it.

"On the next play,'" reported the *Tribune*'s Eckersall, "Harley skirted Northwestern's left end for a 63-yard touchdown followed a moment later by booting the extra point." Added the Columbus *Dispatch*, "In the fourth period, Harley gathered momentum, and his run of sixty-three yards around Northwestern's left end, in which he had to cut back into a mass of Purple foemen to elude would-be tacklers, will long be remembered as one of Ohio's greatest athletic incidents."

Ohio State fans were delirious as their team led 10-3 with the clock ticking the seconds away. Northwestern was down, but not out. They came back with a vengeance, abandoning their reliance on the run by passing. They "grew mighty dangerous" as pass after pass connected. That is, until the prowling Harley, now working the safety position and probably overlooked because of his diminutive five-foot, eight-inch frame, intercepted a Purple pass on his own twenty-yard line. After gaining about forty yards on smashing runs by Buckeye left halfback Dick Boesel, Ohio State was forced to punt. Northwestern fumbled the punt on their fifteen-yard line, which set up a sweep around the right end by Harley for another touchdown.

With Ohio State now in command with a 16-3 lead, Chic continued to dominate and to show doubters that he was superior to Driscoll. He ran for another sixteen-yard gain and returned a punt to Northwestern's thirty-yard line. With just a few minutes left in the contest and the wooden Ohio stands rocking, Harley threw a bullet pass twenty-eight yards to end Clarence MacDonald to the three-yard line. From there, Sorenson pushed his way over the goal line and ended his career by booting the extra point. Ohio State had won the game 23-3. The victory sewed up the first-ever conference title for the Buckeyes, put the final touches on a perfect 7-0 season, and propelled them to the top of national football prominence. Chic Harley's stellar performance made it impossible for college football authoritarian Walter Camp of *Collier's* magazine to not choose him as a first team All-American halfback. Strangely, Chic's position on the All-American team was listed as an end. Teammate Bob Karch, a junior tackle, was also chosen All-American.

The moment the final whistle sounded to end Ohio State's win over Northwestern and the season, a tall man wearing a dark overcoat and wide-brimmed hat shot out onto the field and grasped the tired and battered Chic in his arms.

"Walter!" gasped Chic, at the sight of his oldest brother. His look of weariness was instantly replaced with a bright, wide smile. It was the first time Walter had seen Chic play in a college football game. "Chic's my brother. I never saw him play before. I didn't know he could play so well," said Walter, "for Chicago papers have said little about him, and the kid would never send us local clippings or tell us about his games." Also watching that day were Chic's mother, Mattie, and his sister Ruth. Walter said that every time during the game when Chic ran by him, he would duck so his brother would not notice him. "It would have worried Chic if he thought I had come over just to see him play," said Walter.

Newspaper accounts of the game paid glowing tribute to the Buckeyes, most notably the twenty-two-year-old right halfback. "He's one of the greatest players I have ever seen," wrote Walter Eckersall in the *Tribune*.

"As for Harley, he is the easiest dodging back I have ever seen," Gus Axelson of the Chicago *Herald* reported. "Harley's work this season was second to that of no man in American football," added famed columnist Grantland Rice. "It was the brilliant playing of Chic Harley of Ohio State, who not only proved himself to be one of the game's leading stars, but who also accomplished more for his team than any other individual of the year." "November 25, 1916, will go down in athletic history as marking a new epoch in Ohio State football," reported the Columbus *Dispatch*. "Her place in Western Conference circles has been fixed, and it is a credit to have won from such a fine team as Northwestern placed on the field."

Three days later, on November 28, 1916, the subject of quiet discussions among professors, coaches, and administrators at Ohio State now became a loud chant that had found its way into the limelight. "A new stadium for Ohio State is now believed to be assured," proclaimed the Columbus *Journal* in a story headlined "Stadium for State Is Prediction Made."

At a banquet honoring the champions on November 27, Thomas French and Lynn St. John announced that plans for a new 25,000-seat stadium were under way. Coach Wilce warned the team and fans against overconfidence, declaring that winning isn't the most important thing. The *Journal's* coverage of the banquet added that "Chic Harley was another to be greeted with uproarious applause by the big crowd present. Harley's speech was typical. He talked for only a few seconds in which he took occasion to hand bouquets to coaches and his teammates."

Six years later, after Ohio Field had hosted its last regular season football game, the Buckeyes had a new stadium. It resembled a giant concrete horseshoe and accommodated 72,000 fans.

Photo taken in 1917 shows a freezing and tiny Chic (fourth from right) surrounded by teammates. At far left is Athletic Director Lynn Saint John and Coach Jack Wilce.

Chic flashes his famous smile.

CHAPTER 5

Perfection

The clouds of war loomed as early fall 1917 crept closer. For more than two and a half years, President Wilson had managed to keep America out of the war in Europe, but almost everyone knew that U.S. neutrality couldn't last. Entry into the great conflict was no longer a question of *if*, but *when*. Millions of families wondered who among them would respond to their nation's call for help. For Chic Harley, the answer was easy. He long dreamed of a life in the military, especially the Army Air Corps, where he could become an aviator. The sky and all its expansiveness would become his sanctuary. To Chic, the great question was when his enlistment application would be accepted so he could report for duty. Until then, his life at school in Columbus, in athletics, and with his family in Chicago would go on as it had for the previous two years.

Coach John Wilce and his gridders—strikingly similar to the team of a year earlier—would focus on the task of trying to repeat the championship 1916 season. All indications were that at the very least, they could win the Western Conference title again. They exceeded everyone's wildest imagination. Not only did the Buckeyes win another conference championship, but they also were being heralded again as one of the top football teams in the country. Their only equals were Pop Warner's University of

Pittsburgh team and John Heisman's Georgia Tech. By the end of the season, after amassing an incredible 292 points to their opponents' six in an undefeated season, there was universal acceptance that the team of 1917 was the greatest ever put together at Ohio State. And after watching Chic Harley during the 1916 and '17 seasons, many also believed that he was America's best all-around football player. For the second year in a row, he was a consensus All-American.

Scholastically, Chic seemed to have finally found his stride with the beginning of the new semester in January 1917. Unlike his disastrous freshman year of 1915-16, when he nearly flunked everything and was often on academic probation, he now had passing and satisfactory grades. That cemented his eligibility to participate in interscholastic sports, which often had been an iffy proposition. What must have been a source of high anxiety for him eased considerably when his grades improved.

Football, of course, was the sport Harley was most noted for. Newspapers devoted much more space to college football during the autumn months than to any other athletic program at that level. Professional football was considered nothing more than a game of tough opportunists looking to score a quick buck. In spring and summer, professional baseball drew the most attention. But in September, October, and November, high school and college football dominated athletic programs, especially in Columbus.

Ohio was evolving into a football-crazed state where prep and college teams had strong followings. Only a few years earlier, near the bottom of that limited pack in the Columbus area was Ohio State, a small school that had produced mostly mediocre to average teams dating back to 1890. High school football usually overshadowed Ohio State teams. After the turn of the century, the local sports stars were playing in high school, not college.

Thanks to his playing for East High School, Chic Harley was at the top of that list of luminaries. Ever since he was a little boy, Chic had been interested in all kinds of sports. He was especially passionate about baseball, even before football. Both permitted him to unravel a layered personality that was painfully reserved and full of self-doubt. In the outfield, he could run like an antelope after fly balls. At the plate, he could swing the bat, connect with the ball, and tear around the bases. On the gridiron, despite the fans in the stands and his teammates crouched over on the line of scrimmage in front of him, he was free of life's problems—real or imagined—for upwards of sixty minutes.

Other Ohio State coaches coveted Chic's talent for their programs, and one of them was lucky enough to win him. In early February 1917, the Ohio State track team was scheduled to challenge the University of Chicago on the Maroons' campus. Because of his blazing speed, especially his ability to reach full throttle in just two or three steps, it was decided that Harley would run the fifty-yard dash for State at that indoor meet even though he had practiced little with the team. To Chic, a trip with the track squad meant a chance to visit his family in Chicago. His goal was to see Mom and Dad. Running was a means to that end.

"An interesting feature of the meet is the appearance of Chic Harley in the 50-yard dash in his first track effort since his high school days," wrote the Columbus *Citizen* on the day of the race. Back then, the fifty-yard dash determined the fastest runner among the teams going head-to-head. Years later, that specific intercollegiate race was officially discontinued. Thereafter, the winner of the sixty-meter sprint is considered the fastest. But on February 16, 1917, there was no question who was best. In his first ever race for Ohio State, Chic lit up Chicago's Hyde Park neighborhood by running the first heat of the straight fifty-yard indoor course in 5.45 seconds. Minutes later in the final heat, his time was clocked at 5.35 seconds. In his first ever college track competition, Chic won the team's only first place of the meet and set a conference record in the process. It was a record that stood for years and to this day has been exceeded by only a talented few.

With Ohio State coaches fighting for Chic's services that spring, he was forced to split his time among running for the track team, playing on the varsity baseball squad, and maintaining acceptable grades. The track team was going nowhere in the Western Conference. Even with Chic's scorching speed, the team lacked overall talent. In its meet with Chicago, despite Harley's record-setting display, the Buckeyes were shellacked 62-24. Still, Chic made himself available for whatever role whenever asked. On April 21, the track team faced its intrastate rival, Ohio Wesleyan. The Buckeyes were absent many of their first stringers, who temporarily left school to help with family farm work. Nevertheless, State won twelve of its fifteen matches, defeating Wesleyan 94 2/3 to 36 1/3. The headline in the next day's *Dispatch* read: "Chic Harley Without Previous Preparation Steps In and Cops 100- and 220-Yard Dash Events." What had happened was that Coach Frank Castleman had convinced baseball Coach Lynn St. John to free up Harley for the track meet. Chic ran in the 100- and 220-yard dashes, winning both events easily. These two wins, along with his performance in Chicago two months earlier, gave him enough points to earn another varsity letter. His times in the Wesleyan races were 10.3 seconds in the 100-yard sprint and 23.0 seconds in the 220. What was even more amazing is that he won the races without having worked out at all on the Ohio State track that season, and some reports had him wearing baseball spikes.

"The cinder track was slow and soft," reported the *Dispatch*. Chic won the heats "with room to spare. . . . His races were the prettiest of the afternoon. He won the 100-yard dash after being set back two yards." The *Dispatch* added that since he is equally talented in basketball, Harley would undoubtedly become the school's first four-sport letterman. The only basketball Chic had played at Ohio State up to that point was in intramurals, although he did play on the East High School varsity team.

In the first half of 1917, when Chic wasn't running track, he was focused on baseball. For the most part, he roamed right field during his two years on varsity. Just a day before winning the 100 and 220 heats against Wesleyan, Harley was playing for St. John's highly touted varsity squad, and he smashed two hits, scored two runs, and "did about as he pleased on the bases. In the seventh inning he stretched a three-base hit into a home run by a long head-first slide under the catcher's tag who had the ball and was waiting for Chic. In the third inning, he brought the crowd to its feet by scampering home on a short passed ball."

By early May, Ohio State was considered the best baseball team in the Western Conference. If it could hold on and capture the title, it would be the school's second major sports title within a year (the first having been won by the 1916 football team).

"They beat Illinois for the first time ever a week earlier 7 to 3 at Champaign," wrote the Columbus *Citizen* in April 1917. On May 5, the Buckeye baseball squad all but wrapped up the conference crown by blanking Illinois again, 1-0. Playing center field that day for the Illini was George Halas, who batted first in the lineup, went two for four, and stole a base. Chic, batting second for State, also went two for four and was credited with a sacrifice.

"For five years Illinois has held full sway as the premier exponent of the national pastime in Big Nine circles," said the *Dispatch* on May 6. "It appears as though Ohio is about to succeed the Illini as king of the crowd after the second defeat of the champions." Later, a news account read, "Eight members of the 14-member squad were batting above .300. Harley, a threat to always steal, was hitting third best on the team with a .467 average." Following the team's fifteen-game schedule, its record was 14-1—having lost only to Indiana—good for the league crown. The student *Makio* said, "Teammates like to tell how Chic made three bases on an infield hit, how he stole home, made a shoe-string catch, or tore up the dust in a tantalizing fall away slide at third base. Yes, Harley was All American timber in football, but was also all something in baseball."

A switch hitter, and often a left-handed batter because it gave him a head start on his sprint to first base, Chic ended the season with a .437 batting average, second only to Fred Norton, who batted .442 that season. Chic belted twenty-one hits in forty-eight at-bats and scored twenty-two runs.

Meanwhile, American involvement in the war in Europe heightened. On April 6, 1917, Congress voted overwhelmingly to declare war on Germany. The call to arms was like an elixir to young Harley, who was beginning to feel torn between his loyalty to school and friends and the exciting notion of serving in uniform. To Ohio State fans and the school itself, the prospect of Chic heading off to the Army was a scary thought. On April 28, the *Dispatch* reported that his enlistment was probable. A few days earlier, Chic had interviewed with military recruiters in Columbus about signing up and reporting to Fort Benjamin Harrison in Indiana for training. First, though, he wanted to discuss the idea with his parents in Chicago, and the opportunity came when the Buckeye baseball team traveled to play the University of Chicago. The visit in the familiar, happy surroundings of his parents' home resulted in the decision not to pursue military service, at least at that time. It was agreed that he would return to Columbus, finish the school year, and revisit the subject at a later date. To Chic, the help and support of his parents were reassuring and helpful, but not altogether convincing. He was sure he wanted to fly, and the way to do so was to join the Army. *The sooner, the better*, he thought. He would have to wait a little longer.

Coach Wilce's hopes were sky high as Labor Day 1917 neared. He had no doubt that his team was poised for greatness. Most of his players from the championship 1916 squad were returning. It was a given that Howard Yerges would start at quarterback—where he would shout out the plays and help lead the team—for the third straight season. "Shifty" Bolen was again at end. The Courtney brothers would remain the starting tackles, and Kelley Van Dyne would replace Fritz Holtkamp, who had graduated, at center. An addition to the lineup was halfback Gaylord "Pete" Stinchcomb, a talented speedster whom some were hailing as the "second Harley."

In doubt, however, was whether Chic would report to preseason training camp. At the first team lecture of the season, on Saturday, September 8, Harley was nowhere to be found. Two days later, the team held its first field practice without Chic. Five days later, on Friday, September 14, the *Dispatch* had encouraging news for worried Buckeye fans: "Chic Harley isn't in the army. He hasn't appendicitis. No Northern wood bear nipped a couple of his toes. Chic is perfectly healthy and discovered. Harley is on his way to his Chicago home now from a potato farm on the shores of Platte Lake near Beulah, Michigan, where he spent three weeks hunting and fishing as the guest of George Sibert, 259 Nineteenth Ave." It added that Chic would likely be at practice on Saturday, September 15. On September 17, the paper said twenty-one players had reported for practice. Chic was not one of them. Was he again on the verge of enlisting in the Army? The season opener against Case was less than two weeks away.

By September 21, however, under the headline "Ohio Football Stock Soars," the *Citizen* reported that Chic would return to school in a few days and pay his student enrollment fees. Watching practice from the sidelines, Bob Karch predicted another Ohio State championship. On Wednesday, September 26, Harley participated in his first scrimmage of the year. "Chic Harley scrimmaged with State's eleven against the second team for just two minutes Wednesday afternoon and scored just two touchdowns," the *Citizen* wrote. "That was enough to convince the coach that State's All American star had lost none of his cunning and he was dismissed from work for the rest of the afternoon—to take up another kind of work—study for his examination in American History which he will take Saturday morning." Harley passed the exam just a few hours before the opening kickoff against Case.

The first two contests for Ohio State were non-conference bouts against Case on September 29 and Ohio Wesleyan the following Saturday. In the Case game, Harley played little because of a slight injury and his arrival on campus only a few days earlier. Stinchcomb, whose weight was about the same as Harley's, was the offensive star. The sophomore showed for the first time as a member of the varsity that he was a tremendously hard runner who used brute force in his small, lean frame to crash through the line. That style differed from Chic's "wizardry" on the field, which took advantage of his ability to change pace in just a step or two, give opposing tacklers "the hip," and cut back and dodge after sweeping wide right or left. When the dust cleared, Ohio State had annihilated Case 49-0, the worst defeat in the school's history up to that time.

"It is too early to predict what a player will or will not be later in the year, but Stinchcomb showed promise and if he lives up to his reputation as a freshman, he and Harley, with their varied attack, should be a pair of backs that will be hard for any team to head off," said the *Citizen* on October 1.

A week later against Wesleyan, Harley stepped to the fore-front, scoring three touchdowns in a 53-0 Buckeye win. Wesleyan was stopped on a fourth down with four feet to go when a quarterback sneak failed. It was the closest any team came to scoring a touchdown on Ohio State all season long.

For the season's first conference game, on Saturday, October 13, State hosted Northwestern. A year earlier, these two teams had battled in the season finale to determine the conference winner. Harley dominated that game by outplaying and outsmarting Wildcat star Paddy Driscoll and capturing the Buckeyes' first ever Big Nine title. Now, they met again, much earlier in the season in a game that lacked the emotionalism of eleven months earlier. Ohio State buried Northwestern 40-0 in a battle of sheer dominance by the Buckeyes.

Two days before the game, said the Columbus *Citizen* later, most football forecasters predicted Ohio State would win by two or three touchdowns, but not six. "There is only one answer," it continued. "State right now is a much better eleven than at the same time last year. The men are more experienced and their teamwork is wonderful for this time of year."

A former Notre Dame University football player who watched the game from the stands marveled at Harley, describing his contributions as among the best he had ever seen from a running back. His admiration was not for Harley's well-known ability to run with the ball, but for his blocking. "On every play when Stinchcomb carried the ball, Harley had his men out of the way," said the Notre Dame grad. "He showed me he is even better than

I thought him. I always knew he was a wonder at carrying the ball, but I never knew he could block the way he did Saturday." The story continued, "Harley's work in this regard was in a measure responsible for the splendid work of Stinchcomb in carrying the ball, and there is no longer any doubt that these two fellows are the best halves who ever played on an Ohio team at the same time." On October 18, another Columbus newspaper said, "Chic did his through his blocking. Such an exhibition of blocking is seldom seen. It was largely responsible for Stinchcomb's gains. It was a great thing for him because it was the first chance Chic had to show what he could do in this phase of the game and the only department in which he had not already shown superlative ability. Northwestern was outguessed and overwhelmed due to Chic's blocking and Pete's running roles which were reversed in a way."

Following a bye week, Ohio State annihilated Denison University 67-0. It was a long day for the visiting "Big Red," which made the thirty-mile journey to Columbus only to play on a rain-soaked, sloppy field. The two teams had not met the previous five seasons because of strained relations. The drubbing was not enough to keep the two teams from meeting a year later, when Ohio State won 34-0. So in just two contests, the Buckeyes had shut out Denison in scoring 101 total points.

With the warm-up games safely behind, the Buckeyes entered the meat of the 1917 schedule with three conference games against formidable opponents. After those would be games in Alabama and downstate Chillicothe, Ohio, billed as exhibition contests to support the war effort, at Auburn University and Camp Sherman.

On November 3, Ohio State took on conference rival Indiana. The Buckeyes had squeaked out a 10-9 win over the Hoosiers in 1915, followed by a comfortable 46-7 win a year later. This time, the consensus was that Ohio State should win easily. No one, however, told the Hoosiers that. From the outset, the bulky Indiana players believed they were equal to, if not better than, their Buckeye opponents. One thousand Ohio State fans traveled to Bloomington for the game, which attracted a full house of 11,000.

It was a gorgeous fall day in southern Indiana. The sky was blue, and trees in the distance were turning various shades of orange and gold. For a while, there was confusion on the field because Ohio State had packed red "home field" jerseys instead of the visiting "whites." With both teams wearing red, fans and undoubtedly some players were bewildered at first. By the second quarter, things had settled down and the game became a one-man show.

"When Chic noticed that Indiana was obstinate, he assumed the role of morale breaker," the *Citizen* beamed. "The redoubtable Mr. Harley, who seems to aspire to a permanent berth on Camp's All American, decided that it was up to him to stop all the foolishness on the part of Indiana. Enter the morale factor." Six minutes into the second period, Chic scampered on one of his most impressive scoots of the season, running for forty-six yards to the Indiana three-yard line—only to see the play nullified for an offsides penalty. The play counted for nothing on the statistic sheet, but served as a major punch in the stomach of the Hoosiers.

"The score wasn't needed," said the *Citizen*. "The run had served its purpose and the Indiana team watched its hopes sag in the smile of the courageous Chic. With the run went the Indiana spirit although the run was called back and counted for naught in the final reckoning. Indiana crumpled, put up a mediocre resistance, gave a few spasms in the final period and died. All because of a 46-yard trot in which the Ohio star galloped away from the Bloomingtoners."

Chic scored all of Ohio State's points in the 26-3 win. He tallied four touchdowns on runs of forty, eight, eleven, and thirty-three yards. He also kicked two extra points. Indiana's only points—a twenty-seven-yard field goal by Russell Hathaway— came late in the fourth quarter. Those three were the first points scored against the Buckeyes that season.

"Of all the teams in the Western Conference, Ohio State is easily the most feared and most respected," proclaimed the

Citizen a week later. "The 1916 champions are having another wonderful season, though their real test comes within the next two weeks, when they will be called upon to meet Wisconsin and Illinois in succession."

As in 1916, the Badgers and the Illini were expected to be the Buckeyes' biggest challengers in 1917. Both teams were experienced and tough and had exceptional coaches: Jason Richards of Wisconsin and Bob Zuppke at Illinois. Wilce knew all too well that he had his work cut out for him.

Sporting a 5-0 record, Ohio traveled to Madison on Saturday, November 10, to play in brand new Camp Randall Stadium, which had been christened a week earlier when the Badgers upset highly rated Minnesota 10-7. Now, a confident Wisconsin, playing on its home turf, had its sights aimed squarely at the defending conference champs. Avoiding the confusion of the previous week, Wilce dressed his team in gray jerseys with scarlet armbands. Approximately 500 Buckeye fans traveled the 500 miles to join 5,500 Badger loyalists in the bleachers. For those who hadn't made the trip, play-by-play descriptions were telegraphed to Columbus, where men with megaphones screamed out the news to anxious throngs gathered outside the offices of the *Dispatch* on Gay Street and at the Union. "Grid-graf" scoreboards displayed the positions of players, downs, and the score.

Near the end of the first quarter, Eber Simpson of Wisconsin kicked a forty-three-yard field goal that gave the Badgers a 3-0 lead. (It was the only time during the entire season that Ohio State was behind in a game.) Wisconsin's lead was short-lived. In the second period, Harley got down to business. While caged in as a runner by a team that zoned in on him from the start, he turned to his skills as a passer. A forty-five-yard completion to a wide-open Bolen gave Shifty the room he needed to charge into the end zone for a lead the Buckeyes would never relinquish. On that play, Harley faked as if he was going to punt, then tossed a strike.

In the third frame, a long pass from Harley to Howard Courtney drove the ball to the Badgers' one-yard line. On the next play, Yerges ran the ball in for six more points. In the Camp Randall stands that day sat Illinois Coach Zuppke, who was scouting the Buckeyes for the following week's game. Harley's pass to Courtney especially caught Zuppke's attention, and a few days later, he designed a defense that he passed on to his players during practice. But the defense failed because Zuppke thought Harley's pass was to team captain "Hap" Courtney, not his teammate and brother, Howard. Throughout the contest against Wisconsin, Harley's superb punting kept the Badgers bottled up with poor field position. And in the fourth quarter, with Ohio State holding firmly onto a 13-3 lead, Harley sealed the deal by booting a forty-yard field goal, ending the bout at 16-3. Harley's "accurate forward passing and sure toe brought the Buckeyes two touchdowns," said the *Wisconsin State Journal*. "He narrowly missed another field goal try in the second quarter. His punts averaged well over 50 yards."

With Chic at the top of his game in every department, the stage was set for the season's conference finale against Illinois in Columbus on Saturday afternoon, November 17. Both teams were undefeated. The outcome would determine the Western Conference championship. Everyone in Columbus and Champaign was talking about the biggest game of the season. Zuppke and his team had fire in their eyes. The last year they had lost 7-6, thanks to a Harley touchdown in the last few seconds. They wanted revenge so much they could taste it. They were as focused, confident, and talented a crew as the Buckeyes had faced all season long. Their defense was arguably even better than Ohio State's, having not given up a single point all year long. What the Illini feared most was the unpredictable, spellbinding play of Harley and the brainpower of Wilce. In practice, they devoted hours to repeating plays to foil the Buckeye halfback's attempt to take off along right or left ends. Zuppke also believed that his scouting the previous week had helped solve some of the potential forward passing problems he might encounter. Defending against Chic's other offensive weaponry, such as his ability to kick and pass, were harder to prepare for, but not impossible, preached Zuppke to his players.

"The Buckeye backfield calls for all the resources that Coach Zuppke can command," warned the Champaign *Gazette*. What opened the eyes of Illini players and coaches was not just the outstanding play of Harley, but the "perfect team play from whistle to whistle" of the entire Ohio State squad. "Coach Wilce has one of the best teams that ever played the game," said the *Gazette*. "The men from Illinois realize what they are up against and entered the week's practice with a never say die spirit." They were two great teams with first-rate defenses and offenses.

Though the day was a "trifle warm for the players, no power of nature could have supplied a better day," the Ohio *Journal* reported. "A dull November sun shone from the sky; there was a slight twang of autumn in the air. And the gridiron, with its light brown turf, offered a perfect footing for the players." The clock struck 2 P.M. No bleacher seat was empty. Nearby trees and buildings were occupied with people trying to catch a glimpse. "Ohio Field was surrounded by 15,000 human beings. It was an artistic crowd. Almost all the ladies wore great bobbing yellow or white chrysanthemums. Many men were decorated in similar fashion. Everything was color."

In this contest, as in nearly all of Ohio State's matches the previous two years, Harley's superhuman skills unfurled. Ohio State defeated Illinois 13-0 in a game that saw Chic work loose from defenders on just a few occasions. The prolific yard gainers for the Buckeyes that day were Dick Boesel and Fred Willaman, not Harley. But as a testament to Chic's overall contributions to the team, when his halfback offerings were stymied, for whatever reason, he had more than enough fuel in his arsenal to ignite. "Harley, As Usual, Is Star in Great Game Which Nets His Team a Second Championship," announced the Chicago *Examiner* sports section the next day. The short ground gaining of Boesel and Willaman and the superb quarterbacking of Yerges set the scene for Harley to kick twenty-nine- and fourteen-yard field goals. The twenty-nine-yarder came in the first period. The score remained 3-0 until the final frame, when Harley kicked his second field goal and flipped a twenty-yard pass to Howard Courtney for a touchdown. Moments later, Chic booted the extra point. A big break for Ohio State came at the end of the second period, when Illini fullback Dutch Sternaman fumbled the ball on Ohio's forty-five-yard line, ending a threatening offensive drive. In the third period, a pass intended for Illinois end George Halas was intercepted by Yerges on the thirty-yard line.

"In its deciding game here today, Ohio State, led by the indomitable Chic Harley, defeated Illinois 13-0 in one of the hardest fought games in conference history," one newspaper stated. "Chic Harley was the outstanding star of a collection of brilliant players. He carried the ball most of the time, and twice during the contest sent the ball between the uprights for field goals. He scored his first field goal in the opening period, and after only a few minutes of play. From that score until the final period the two teams battled away savagely using every known modern means to advance the ball, but without success."

Harley's brilliance as the nation's best football player was unquestionable at this moment in his three-year collegiate career as regular season play came to an end. In the three November conference games, Harley scored all the Buckeye points except for the one touchdown notched against Illinois. But on that play, he passed the ball to the player who scored the six points. In the early season league game against Northwestern, Harley's blocking for running mate Pete Stinchcomb was recognized as one of the main reasons that Ohio State blitzed the Purple 40-0. A second year on Walter Camp's All-American first team was assured. Columbus and the state of Ohio were ablaze with confidence in their college team, their community, and themselves.

Two postseason games remained for the Buckeyes following the victory over Illinois, both benefits for servicemen. The first was on Saturday, November 24, against Auburn, and the second was five days later, on Thanksgiving Day, against a team from Camp Sherman. The Camp Sherman contest was for the benefit of the servicemen with the 37th Division of the Ohio National

Guard. The Auburn game produced the only real blemish on an otherwise flawless season for Ohio State, with the two teams fighting to a 0-0 tie. Several State players, including Van Dyne, Seddon, and Yerges, were out of the lineup due to injuries. Rarely hurt, Chic suffered an excruciating wound to his right hand when a player with long cleats stepped on it. Many thought his hand was broken when it swelled to nearly twice its normal size and turned a horrible blue. The inability of Ohio State's key players to perform that day robbed the team of any offensive punch.

Harley's hand was not broken, and the team was intact when Ohio State swamped Camp Sherman 28-0 a few days later. Known as the Sammies from Chillicothe, the team consisted of five former All-Americans, one All-Western, and two All-Ohio stars. They had taken on all comers during their fall season and had never lost. This time they never knew what hit them.

"The champions performed like real champions, making no such blunders, and were quick to take advantage of every error made by the khaki-clad performers," wrote the Cincinnati *Enquirer* on November 30, 1917. "The collegians came back with a wide-open, twelve cylinder attack and the varied movements of the back field at times completely bewildered the all star lineup." Said the Chicago *Tribune*, "Chic Harley outplayed a team of former All American stars today and Ohio State, Western Conference champions, won easily from the Camp Sherman football team, 28-0. Harley broke away from the army team several times for long gains. Stinchcomb also got away for good runs." Chic passed to team captain Courtney for one touchdown and ran through the entire Camp Sherman team for another six points. "Harley was the center of attack in every touchdown. When he was not ramming his noble bean through the line he circled the flanks or pulled the forward pass."

With the exception of the meaningless exhibition contest against Auburn, the 1917 Ohio State football team showed it was invincible. It was a team that relied on speed and intelligence at a time when football had just emerged from the dark days of brute force and frequent serious injury. The halfback duo of Harley and Stinchcomb was the best in the country. Ohio's offensive and defensive lines averaged only 180 pounds, yet they unselfishly and skillfully paved the way for their jackrabbit halfbacks and held opposing teams to just two field goals the entire nine-game season.

"But when all is said and done, the great eleven of 1917, the second Buckeye team to win the mythical Western Conference championship, is still the first choice of many who have seen it," wrote James E. Pollard, Ohio State's publicity director, in 1926. "Harley, in his second varsity season, was close to perfection. There seemingly wasn't a thing he couldn't do instinctively and well on offense or defense. His offensive prowess has been stressed so often that many have lost sight of the Harley who fitted into the team play with a nicety and who never hesitated to sacrifice himself for his teammates."

"Harley stands out in a class by himself among the half-backs," concluded the Columbus *Citizen* on December 1, one day after the season ended. "Though not showing the running form of last year because every team he met was laying for him, he was consistently the main factor in his team's success through his kicking, passing and blocking. He was the best punter in the conference."

Football fever was sweeping Columbus, with Harley clearly leading the way.

This drawing shows that the football heroics Harley had displayed for Ohio State propelled him in the nation's limelight ahead of such greats as Jim Thorpe and Walter Eckersall.

*Harley, with goggles, flyer's headgear, and leather jacket
striking a happy pose.*

CHAPTER 6

Crash Landing

The air was crisp, and the sky, remarkably clear the evening of January 17, 1918, just north of downtown Columbus. With a stretch of the neck and the head tilted backward one could see white stars twinkling in the heavens above the cold, fast-flowing Olentangy River and the small Ohio State campus.

Members of the Western championship Buckeyes had had a near-perfect season, and tonight they were gathered for a celebration banquet on campus. Postseason dining in a semiformal setting with white linen tablecloths and sparkling silverware had become a ritual. The entrée was steak, served with potatoes. Liquor was conspicuously absent. Just water, milk, and a few soft drinks had been put in place. Congregated on metal folding chairs at long wooden tables that stretched across the room, the team joined Coach Wilce, Doc Gurney, and team trainers to reminisce about the season that had ended less than two months earlier. That night the players also would select a captain for the 1918 team.

Not in attendance were teammates who had been yanked away by military service. Just ten months earlier, America had entered the war that had been raging across the Atlantic since 1914. Many young men from Ohio had reported for duty to Army, Navy, and Marine bases all around the country. Others were clinging to their young lives in the muddy, rat-infested, disease-plagued trenches of

93

Belgium alongside hardened British and French troops. Death was everywhere. Stretching in front of them for a hundred yards—the length of a football field—was "no man's land." Lying in wait beyond that were Germans armed with machine guns and bayonets. Football on old Ohio Field, encircled by those rickety wooden bleachers and adoring fans, seemed so far away.

Just days after Ohio State had pummeled the Camp Sherman team in the 1917 football season finale, Chic Harley had withdrawn from school to enlist and by now had received the news he longed for: acceptance into flight training. Despite several rejections for Army officers training, the new year brought him to the brink of his dream of becoming an aviator. He couldn't wait to get started. His friend Eddie Rickenbacker was already flying. Even though Rickenbacker was four years older than Chic, they'd known each other growing up in the same East Side neighborhood of Columbus. By May 1917, Rickenbacker had gone from racecar driving to the Army. A month earlier, when America entered World War I, he was recruited to become part of a secret troop movement to France as an Army staff car driver. Eleven months later, Eddie became a genuine flying ace by shooting down five German planes in just two days. By war's end, he had destroyed twenty-five enemy aircraft and become the United States' most celebrated military hero. Maybe the same fortune awaited Chic.

The choice of a football captain for the 1918 Buckeyes was a foregone conclusion as the twenty teammates sat down for dinner. Even though Chic was no longer enrolled at Ohio State, the reason was his military enlistment two months earlier, not disinterest in school. Student ranks at universities across the country were quickly becoming depleted because of the war. That night Harley was at his parents' home in Chicago awaiting his first official orders. And while those dining in Columbus knew that Chic would likely not be available to play football next season, everyone knew who the choice of captain would and should be.

"New honor was heaped on Charles W. 'Chic' Harley, Ohio State's famous halfback, at the annual football banquet held in

January for the 1917 Western Conference championship squad," the *Ohio State University Monthly* magazine reported a few weeks later. "The letter men of 1917 unanimously elected 'Chic' captain for 1918." Election of a new captain, said the article, usually didn't occur until it was known who would be eligible to play next year. "But when Harley's teammates gathered on January 17 they decided without hesitation that 'Chic' merited the honor of being chosen captain whether or not he could compete that fall."

Four days after the banquet, Chic returned triumphantly to Columbus, not as a student, but as a candidate for Army aviator. Orders had reached him in Chicago to report for duty to the School of Military Aeronautics at Ohio State on February 1. The Columbus *Dispatch*'s magazine section (September 23, 1917) called the institution "the Best Ground School in America." Major George E. Stratemeyer, who later became World War II chief of Air Staff, headed the Signal Aviation School at OSU. Chic's early arrival in Columbus would give him time to visit with friends, teammates, and coaches before military training started. Together they watched Ohio State's varsity basketball team beat Michigan at the Armory on January 21.

The loss of Harley to the Army was not the only blow to the Buckeye football team of 1918. It was the most notable, however. Running backs Pete Stinchcomb and Frank Willaman "will do their gridiron work this year at Great Lakes where they are seamen," said one newspaper account. Nearly all team regulars from 1917 were gone. Only six "scrubs" from that year were planning to return, with one news account adding that "Ohio State loses more veteran men than any other school in the Big Ten for it must be remembered that Ohio last year was composed of virtually all seasoned players." One of the few major college football programs not strongly affected by the war was John Heisman's Georgia Tech University team, one of the nation's best in the years leading up to the war.

For eight weeks beginning February 1, Harley spent much of his time in the classroom consumed with learning the basics of aviation. When not studying, he and others in the program of would-be aviators drilled endlessly on the grounds of Ohio State, marching in formation for what seemed like thousands of miles back and forth. After satisfactorily completing the initial coursework, Harley was shipped out to Souther Field near Americus, Georgia, to get more training. Built by the army in 1918, Souther served as a primary Army flight training facility. By May, the base was teeming with activity as twenty-five cadets at a time regularly arrived for their two months of extensive work and practice. By the middle of the year, 1,500 service personnel were stationed there, and 147 planes—mostly the JN-4 "Jenny"—were available for training. Overall, the air corps was bursting at the seams as thousands of young Americans enlisted and the Army was starting to comprehend the military ferocity of the new flying machine. After the war, in 1923, a young Charles Lindbergh visited Souther to buy a surplus Jenny for $500. Four years later, he became the first person to make a nonstop transatlantic flight, considered one of the great achievements of mankind.

For the next ten months, Chic and the other cadets trained from sunup to sunset learning about everything from ailerons to lift. When not training or drilling, he watched the war in Europe rage and subsequently subside that year. The continuous drilling of the young flyers was something Chic hated with a passion. Fortunately, for escape, Souther had a football team comprised of former stars from throughout the country who had found themselves and each other on the military compound's dusty gridiron. In the fall, as in college, the Souther squad played teams from other military bases and put on shows for their fellow aviators and curious locals.

"Still At It," screamed the headline of the Columbus *Citizen* on November 29, 1918. "The most famous player ever developed at Ohio State is up to his old tricks." The story told a community starving for news about Harley that in a football contest against Camp Johnson on Thanksgiving Day, he had starred by running through the opposition over and over again. Harley by that time was practicing and playing for the Carlstrom Field team, based in Arcadia, Florida, another training spot for aviators. He had been shifted from Souther, which closed as a military training ground in November 1918, to Carlstrom, where he was the team's top player and captain. Chic's bunch defeated Camp Johnson 21-0 in that game, the only one he played in that year.

By the beginning of 1919, with the war over for a month and a half and Chic still a cadet yearning for flight time, he was transferred yet again to another new air facility, Kelly Field, near hot and dusty San Antonio, Texas. Almost from the beginning, Chic knew that Kelly Field was not the place he wanted to be.

"There are far more desirable fields than Kelly," wrote Chic to OSU Athletic Director Lynn St. John in a rare letter fashioned neatly in his distinctive penmanship on February 23, 1919. "It's one of the jumping-off places of America." Chic had arrived at Kelly from Carlstrom about a month earlier, and by now his attitude about flying and life in the military was clearly changing. Besides apologizing to "Saint" for not writing to him earlier, Chic complained about the lack of flying time he and other cadets were given. His "crabbing," he said, has gotten him nowhere.

"Since leaving Arcadia, Florida," he wrote, "I've got less than five hours flying. There are plenty of ships here to get time in, but the men learning are far too numerous. There being 500 cadets—more than ever before—many keewees [*sic*] taking flying instruction and student officers taking advanced work. Now what chance has a poor kaydet [*sic*]. Anyhow, with good weather I expect to get thru soon." Those who aspired to fly in the military but were confined to ground service were called kiwis during the early part of the twentieth century.

Even with expressing a glimmer of hope, self-doubt flows throughout Chic's three-page letter concerning his future in the military and whether to return to Ohio State. On one hand, he vigorously asserts that he's "made such a mess out of college work . . . it's hard to see what I can get out of it, other than the pleasure of playing football." A few lines later, he writes that perhaps he'll "play football or fly for a while though I admit there's not much of a future in flying." He was likely referring to his personal future of finding work in flying, not what lay ahead for the field of aviation. Later Chic writes that perhaps he will return to Columbus to either enroll in summer school or get a job.

"So, please let me know just how I stand," he asks Saint, referring to his standing at Ohio State and their willingness to have him return. He also says he is looking forward to the day when he will be a commissioned officer.

At this point in his letter, Chic tells Saint that he's been "downhearted thinking my affair was public scandal and wanted to drift away from everything. I didn't write anyone. But I've since learned that little c.w. [Chic himself] was lost in the excitement, hence I don't worry anymore.

"I haven't any hours, no decorations, etc., but have learned many lessons which will stick and best of all (am forever gloating over it) I've the honor of being the oldest cadet in America—how's that (not in years, but length of service)?" Chic was twenty-five, while these aviator hopefuls who were all around him were around twenty to twenty-three.

In a postscript, he adds, "Don't let any of those news-hounds put anything in the paper about me going to school. I think it best for me to keep out of the papers—don't you?"

Exactly what "affair" Harley was referring to is uncertain, although most likely it concerned his inability to become a commissioned officer after more than a year in the service. Military documents written just a few months later, after he had become consumed in trouble with one of his superiors, indicate that something happened after he finished his preliminary flying work and awaited assignment. Perhaps it was his frustration at not being able to advance or maybe the continuous seemingly unproductive drilling in the dust of Kelly Field that led Chic to the threshold of trouble. Whatever it was, he had embarked on a road headed toward disaster.

"At that time he was disciplined for some breech of conduct, dismissed from the service, reinstated in a short time and made to repeat the training," said military records. Rumors surfaced that Chic had commandeered a military airplane without authorization and flew to an undisclosed location in Texas to meet up with a young woman. Nothing exists to verify that rumor. No evidence exists that Harley ever had a sexual affair with any female at any time in his life. To the contrary, he was extremely introverted except among his closest friends and family. His only girl was the pretty and personable Louise Havens, whom he had known and befriended since their days at East High School. In 1919, Louise was in Columbus, having earned a degree from Ohio State in 1918.

Everything appeared in place for Chic in early May 1919 as he was wrapping up his second round of military training, having paid the price meted out months earlier. Chic paid little mind to an ugly encounter he experienced just a few days earlier with commanding officer Lieut. Art Wortman over his sleeping past the permissible time of 7:30 A.M. On May 1, Chic was preparing to receive his commission and return to Columbus. Suddenly, however, everything changed. When Wortman discovered Harley in his bunk, he confined him to his barracks. On May 2, as Chic was preparing to receive his commission and then be discharged, Lieutenant Wortman met up with Harley while walking on the base and asked why he was not in the barracks as ordered a day earlier. Harley responded that the cadet sergeant had given him permission to leave the barracks for a short time to turn in his clothing. Wortman said that he could order Chic back to the barracks if he wanted. Chic asked Wortman if he thought the offense deserved such punishment. That's when all heck broke loose.

"Wortman then went into a rage and had Chic confined to the guard house and wrote him up on charges of disrespect to a superior officer, breaking arrest and other minor charges," wrote fellow cadet Morgan Moore to a now anxious and worried St. John on June 15. Wortman ordered Harley in confinement for three weeks, after which a special court-martial was scheduled to hear and rule on the charges. On May 24, the court-martial, comprised of ranking officers, was convened at Kelly Field. The first count against Chic charged that he displayed disrespect to a superior officer, Lieutenant Wortman, on or about May 1, "by smiling in a sneering manner while being reprimanded and by contemptuously saying to him, 'Can you do it?' or words to that effect." The second charge was that Harley broke away after Wortman ordered him arrested. That was quickly proved untrue. The third charge was that he was found "lying asleep on his cot in the barracks after 7:30 A.M." and appeared in the orderly room with his shirt unbuttoned.

Two days later, on May 26, after the tribunal heard testimony, much of which pitted the higher-ranking Wortman's word against Chic's, Harley was found guilty of most of the infractions and sentenced to three months of hard labor in the Kelly Field jail—an unbelievably harsh punishment for such minor infractions against a man who was literally hours away from receiving his commission.

"The whole affair is a damned outrage," Morgan wrote to Saint, "and it is a seemingly well-founded rumor that the court went to trial with the intention of giving him a long sentence."

"The boy does not deserve this punishment he is getting and his companions in the guard house are most of them ignorant and dirty coming from the lower strata of society and a number of them have every conceivable venereal disease," Mrs. W. F. Cunningham wrote in a personal letter to Saint. The OSU athletic director had mistakenly been told that Mrs. Cunningham was involved with the War Camp Community Service, an organization that looked after young men in the military who are away from home for the first time in their lives or need some form of help. Mrs. Cunningham was not with the War Camp, but was the mother of a U.S. serviceman in France. She had taken a liking to Chic and wanted to help him in any way she could. She later wrote to St. John that Chic "was a general favorite in the field, but it was the lieutenant that got him wrong as he did every cadet he could. I think he was jealous of the boys and wanted to show his authority." She closed saying, "Thanking for your interest for I was doing for him what I would my own son."

When word finally reached St. John and the Ohio State community that Harley would probably not be enrolling in summer school by the June 23 deadline, panic set in. For if he was unable to return to Columbus by late June because of his violation of army rules, no matter how minor or trumped up, the threat loomed that he might not be back by the time football practice opened just after Labor Day. By being found guilty, Chic was ordered to perform hard labor at Kelly Field until his scheduled release from jail on August 26. Where he would go from there was in question. Would he remain at Kelly Field or take a train east to Ohio? By then, it was clear that Chic wanted out of the army at any cost.

"Some men from rival institutions have done their best to make it difficult for Harley," wrote St. John to army authorities. "He has been twitted with, 'Being an All-American halfback won't help you here.' We have been told that an effort is being made to keep Harley away from the university this fall. If he is back here he will surely be a factor in football and most dangerous to the opposing teams."

St. John not only was charging that football rivals were directly involved in Harley's unfair imprisonment, but stated the obvious: that Chic had enormous financial value to Ohio State because his ability to win football games attracted lots of fans who would pay handsomely to see the Buckeyes play. "Considering his popularity here and his ability," continued St. John, "he is a most important factor in the success of the university from the standpoint of success in winning games and from the point of receipts."

About three weeks after his sentencing, Harley was calling himself "thickheaded" and "of course, in trouble again," in a second letter to St. John. But, he added, "for once, Saint, I am not to blame." He writes that the charges filed against him are trumped up, "full of lies," and "petty."

"Everybody tells me it's a frame up, but don't seem to help," wrote Chic. "The charges were made up by the lieutenant and therefore, are his side of the affair. After all that's happened, I haven't the heart to tell any people. I started to write you many times—had even finished a couple of letters but tore them up being ashamed to heap any more woes upon you or afraid that I might get in bad as all mail is censored in the G.H. [guardhouse]. Everyone home is writing and wondering what's happened. They wouldn't understand. Mother, especially, would worry thinking it was just like being a regular criminal. Had everything gone right I would have been in Columbus early in May." He added, "And I fear I'm getting in bad condition as I'm smoking like a demon. It's that or go cookoo from worry." In despair, Chic pleads, "Now, old daddy friend of mine, get busy, please. You can do it all. God, I hate to ask you to come down here. Everything and everybody is so suspicious. One can't trust anybody the way I've been ganged on." He signed the letter, "Heap down-hearted." Chic was desperate to get out.

Saint had already gone into action. Desperate for news about his prize star, he asked a friend in San Antonio, V.R. "Bill" Billingsley, to look into the situation. "You know how much this is likely to mean to the athletic association and to the supporters of Ohio State University," wrote Saint to Billingsley. The letter he had received from Chic two months earlier, he said, "was one of the few he has ever written to anyone. I want the straight dope on Chic. I can get something started as high up as necessary but want to do the best thing and the right thing." He assured Billingsley that, contrary to Chic's feeling that he was a disgrace to Ohio State, "such is not the case, and he can come back here with apologies to no one."

To another acquaintance from San Antonio, David Rause, St. John wrote asking for "the names and addresses of the officers in command of the Field at present. If you can find out who the men in authority are—I mean where they came from, whether they are college men or not, where there is any avenue of approach to them or not would be a real help if there is anything to be done in helping Chic along.

"Of course, the real point is to get him back here in college this fall where he is sure to be a big factor in the football champion-ship possibilities. Being in some haste about the matter I wish you would wire me collect as soon as you receive this letter, acknowl-edging this letter and giving Chic's address if you have been able to find it at once."

Saint even considered contacting U.S. Secretary of War Newton D. Baker for help.

"Harley is a member of Phi Gamma Delta fraternity. Secretary of War Baker is a Phi Gamma Delta and a strong one," Saint wrote to a friend. "On the facts of the case and with the proper personal appeal, it would seem to me that Secretary Baker might act in this case—commission him and discharge him." To Mrs. Cunningham, he wrote, "Baker is a Cleveland man and we can reach him through a number of influential political and financial men. He [Chic] is probably being made a horrible example for the benefit of others but surely they have done enough to him by this time. Although the boy has served a lot of extra time in order to get his commission, I suppose he would be glad to get out regardless of the commission. I sincerely hope you may be able to get some prompt action in this case."

St. John's determination to help Chic—and the future well-being of the university—shifted into the highest of gears. Letters asking for help in gaining Harley's release went out from numerous top administrators at Ohio State, including its president, William O. Thompson; Eugene F. McCampbell, dean of the College of Medicine; and Thomas French, head of the Engineering Department.

St. John's letter-writing campaign, along with his numerous inquiries for help, paid off in spades. Within two days, the mood of cadet Chic Harley went from discouragement and misery to hope and delight. In a telegram to Saint on June 19, Chic was at his wit's end: "Have been in guard house since May second. Will not get out until August 26. Charges petty including disrespect to an officer." Two days later, his telegram to St. John required only a few words: "Everything lovely. Expect to start north in a week."

Chic, Lynn St. John, Ohio State University, and the city of Columbus could now breathe a sigh of relief. Harley would return. Football practice was two months away.

One of Chic's great ambitions was to become an aviator. He served as an Army Air Corps cadet in 1918-1919 earning his commission after being court martialed on trumped up charges.

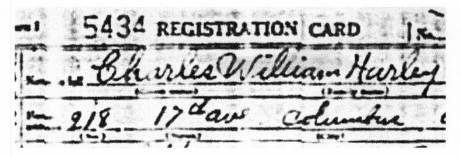

Military registration card that Chic Harley filled out on June 13, 1917, lists his full name as Charles William Harley. He served in the Army Air Corps until the middle of 1919 when he returned to Ohio State.

Chic was often asked and agreed to help worthy causes in Columbus and elsewhere by selling newspapers on street corners with proceeds given to local charities. This is what he was doing in this photo taken around 1919.

Newspapers back in the early part of the 20th century often published caricatures and cartoons like this one that appeared in the Dispatch just six days before Chic's last game as a Buckeye.

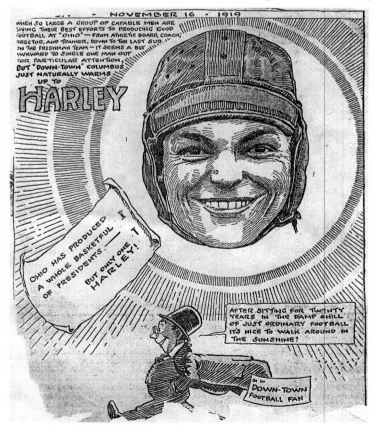

105

In this photo, Harley is preparing to run around and through four Michigan defenders in October 25, 1919 games in Ann Arbor which was the first time the Buckeyes ever beat the Wolverines. This run is considered one of the greatest Chic ever made and ignited what many consider the greatest rivalry in American football.

Photo of helmetless Chic taken around 1917 during perfect Ohio State football season.

CHAPTER 7

Showdown With Michigan

By summer 1919, football fever was like wildfire in central Ohio encircling and engulfing everything and everybody in its path. Months of rumors of Chic Harley's return finally became reality in early July when Gov. James Cox was informed by the army that the country's top running back soon would be discharged. That day would come none too soon for the beaten, but not broken, Chic. For football fans across America and especially Ohio, the news was almost too good to believe. Chic's homecoming meant that he would re-enroll in school and, of course, play football. Once again acclaimed as one of the country's best football teams, with the war over and their star player back for his final season, Ohio State and Chic, many felt, were destined for heights never before imagined. Nothing could prevent the Buckeyes from reaching another perfect season, as in 1916 and '17. Chic, back home, would see his best season ever. He was going to go out in a blaze of perfect glory. Columbus and the nation's heartland had never seen anything like it. Opening day couldn't come fast enough.

Just a year earlier, the 1918 season was dreadful for every college athletic program. With the world still at war and the nation gripped in a devastating outbreak of influenza that killed tens of thousands, nearly every collegiate sport had dwindled to just a shell of what it had been. To most, the 1918 season really didn't count. It was more a year of exhibition games than a period that showcased the finest talent schools could muster. That was fine with Ohio State fans, having witnessed a 3-3 record that year without the benefit of watching the great Harley. For 1919, with the suspense building, expectations were at an all-time high. The world was finally at peace. Soldiers and sailors were coming home. Chic was not the only one returning. Team standouts Pete Stinchcomb, Jim Flowers, Jack Farcasin, Iola Huffman, and many other Buckeyes had also spent the previous year in uniform. Some dared to think that 1919 could actually be better than the unbeaten Buckeye seasons of 1916 and 1917. With Chic and Pete back in the fold, nothing could stand in the way of another undefeated season capped by the retirement of Harley after the final contest against Illinois. Ohio State as a school and with its heralded football program was now firmly on the map as one of the best in the country.

Having been granted an honorable discharge from the air corps and his virtue as a cadet and a person restored, Chic faced a bright future. His fame had spread well beyond the borders of Ohio into major cities like Chicago, where he was born, and across rural farm communities, where he was regarded as a hero. His mystique lay in his sensational ability to snatch victory from defeat as he had done on countless occasions. Where many in all walks of life would reluctantly accept defeat, Chic never accepted losing. His small size gave hope to people of all shapes, sizes, and backgrounds that being bigger, stronger, or better looking does not necessarily make someone a better athlete or a better person. In fact, he was one of the first in modern day football to disprove that stereotype. The period just before and after World War I was a time of rebirth for football where talent mattered most.

And then there was Harley's famed smile, which no one could miss, and his complete lack of self-absorption. His squinting eyes and dimpled chin were irresistible. In an era before electronic media, the primary forms of communication were newspapers and the spoken word. People read and talked constantly not only about Harley's astonishing skills on the gridiron, track, and baseball diamond, but about his shyness and strong connection to friends and family. He was most at ease standing in the background when allowed to do so. He bedazzled not by talking, but by performing and then minimizing the heroics he had just performed by simply saying, "It was nothing." His unabashed modesty was so contagious, people couldn't help but be drawn to him.

"Chic Harley looks like football king of 1919," bellowed the September 24 Chicago *Post* above three photos of Chic running, passing, and kicking. The first game of the new season was just two weeks away. Coverage was intensifying, and all eyes were transfixed on the local boy, who was entering his last year of football eligibility.

Two weeks earlier, the *Post* kicked off a series titled "Lessons in Football" that featured Chic's pointers on how to pass, kick, and "learn to be cool." Said one lesson: "A star punter must be one who won't wilt under fire. The ball should be received from the center with arms straight out. The punter then sizes up the situation and drops the ball. His toe will strike it almost as it leaves his hands. The bulk of the ball should fit into the curve of the foot as in the picture. Keep everlastingly at it. Practice, practice, practice!" There were few punters in the country better than Harley, who in '16 and '17 averaged 42 yards per kick—a stellar accomplishment in any era.

Two days before State's October 4 season opener against ancient rival Ohio Wesleyan, Harley was officially elected captain of the team by unanimous vote of fellow players. He had been appointed to the top honor on a temporary basis by the school's athletic board a few weeks earlier. But following the return to campus of all football team lettermen after summer break, the crowning became official.

Regular team workouts, which began on September 17, were light due to hot weather in and around Columbus. Practices were excellent, featuring a lot of pep and concentration on tackling the many equipment dummies that had been pulled out of storage. Two days earlier, Coach Wilce had gathered about thirty of his players for a "mental exercise" by reviewing the rules during a session in the athletic house.

Looking on from the stands during an early practice, Howard Yerges, the Buckeye quarterback in 1916 and 1917, beamed with delight at what he witnessed. "Spirit among the students this year is greater than ever before judging from the crowds that gathered out [at] the field Wednesday and took a peek at the practice between the iron pickets," said Yerges. A few days later, all OSU freshmen were invited to watch practice from the bleachers. More than 2,000 showed up, an astonishingly high number.

As for an anxious and reinvigorated Chic, his presence at practice was felt immediately. He delighted in being back home in Columbus, away from the hell he experienced in the army. Everyone felt that with Chic back, another conference title and a perfect season were assured.

"Harley lost none of his speed while in the service, easily outstripping any man on the squad," said one newspaper report. "Stinchcomb is in excellent trim already. Yerges is assisting in the coaching of the backfield. Much interest is being shown in the Michigan game, to be played at Ann Arbor on Oct. 25, not only by the students but also by the alumni."

As in past seasons, the first three games of the year were considered tune-ups for conference play. Wilce, Harley, and the others realized from the start that there was no time for easing into the main part of the schedule. The game with Michigan, the first conference game and maybe the year's most important, was shaping up to be the best chance the Buckeyes had ever had to beat their rival to the north. In twenty-two years of competition, Ohio had never beaten the Wolverines—in fact, Ohio had been outscored 369 points to 21. If ever there was a time when the stars were lined up for a Buckeye win over Michigan, this was the year. Already arrangements were being made to transport 500 Buckeye rooters to the game in Ann Arbor.

But first was the season opener against the Wesleyan Methodists of Delaware, Ohio, on a hot and humid Saturday, October 4, in Columbus. The weather made for sluggish play, with the Buckeyes fumbling numerous times—twice as they were about to score touchdowns. Wesleyan entered the game with confidence. Regarded by some as fielding their best football team in years, they could give Ohio State a run for their money. But twelve and a half minutes into the game, the outcome was not in doubt, with the Buckeyes romping to a 21-0 lead. Chic's end-around sweeps from his famous punt formation position set up line plunges by Fred Willaman that resulted in the three touchdowns. After the first quarter, play slowed, and both teams made wholesale substitutions. After sixty minutes, the referee mercifully signaled an end to the game, with Ohio State the 38-0 victors.

A week later in Columbus, the University of Cincinnati came knocking, hoping to at least play a respectable game. The field was described as made "slimy" by a "miserable, drizzling rain." Cincinnati players were chatterboxes intent on disrupting the Buckeye machine, which had trouble at the outset due to the wet conditions. The only score of the first period was a Harley field goal. After that, the sea opened for the Buckeyes as Stinchcomb, Harley, Willaman, Davies, and Farcasin went on a running and kicking rampage. After realizing that his backs were going to have trouble with their footing, Wilce used a remarkable strategy. He ordered quarterback Stinchcomb to punt on first, second, and third down situations, rather than waiting for the normal fourth down. This not only surprised Cincinnati players and coaches, but resulted in numerous fumbles by the receiving team. Perched to recover the fumbles were the speedy Ohio Staters. The only threat Cincinnati mounted came in the first quarter, when they tried some razzle-dazzle plays, such as double and triple passing and on one occasion a "submarine" forward pass in which the pigskin was tossed underhanded. After that, the Buckeyes, much improved from the first week of play, demolished Cincinnati 46-0. The visitors managed to gain only eleven yards the entire game. They even failed to get a first down. Wrote *Dispatch* reporter Karl Finn, "Scarlet and Gray slow in getting started, but after Chic Harley dropkicks goal in first quarter, team slides over for six touchdowns."

Despite being a "marked man," Harley scored two of the touchdowns and kicked three extra points and two field goals, making him three for three in that category after two contests.

In the third game of the season, Kentucky State University arrived in Columbus hoping to give their hosts stiff competition. In the week of practice prior to this game, Wilce continued to work his players hard, trying to perfect tackling and blocking techniques. Occasionally, freshmen players were brought in to practice against the varsity. When one of the flashier freshmen got loose and headed downfield, Chic displayed his talent as a defensive player, frequently being the first tackler on the scene.

"The freshmen stand in awe of Captain Chic Harley," read an account in the October 17 *Citizen*. According to the story, during a practice in which a frustrated freshman Coach Red Trautman ordered his players to "get in some way and break up" runs by Harley and Stinchcomb, a freshman who had gained a reputation of being able to quickly spot runners on offense and then complete the play with a skillful tackle spotted Stinchcomb rumbling through the middle.

"He almost had Stinch when Harley stepped up, grabbed the fresh by the collar and held him until Pete got around the end. Instead of getting up and sputtering rage against Chic, the tackle meekly turned to Harley and said, 'That's holding, isn't it, Captain Harley?' 'Naw, get back over there,' Harley growled. 'Awright,' replied the first year man. 'But I thought sure that it was.' Chic turned away to hide a broad grin and the freshman vanished."

Despite Kentucky's best efforts, the Buckeyes ripped their way to a 49-0 win. The Ohio State *Monthly* magazine graciously described the Wildcats as a "scrappy team." Ohio State scored seven touchdowns and seven extra points. On the first play of the game, Harry Bliss scored on a sixty-yard touchdown romp. Harley later made two runs of forty yards each. Stinchcomb returned one kickoff for seventy yards. Kentucky made two first downs the entire game, with those coming in the fourth quarter after Buckeye substitutes entered to play. After three games, Ohio State had given up only three first downs while making sixty-four of their own.

The stage was now set for Ohio State's biggest football game in its history. To say the Buckeyes were out for revenge is an understatement. For twenty-two years dating back to 1897, the humiliation fans had experienced was so aggravating that at one point before the arrival of Harley, serious thought had been given to dropping out of the Western Conference. Of the fifteen games played by the two teams over that time, Michigan had won thirteen (eleven of which were shutouts), and two ended in ties. The Wolverines had tallied a total of 369 points to Ohio's twenty-one. In 1902, Michigan handed the Buckeyes their worst defeat in history, an 86-0 shellacking. In those fifteen games, Ohio State had led only twice. For a few minutes in 1904, the Buckeyes led Michigan 6-5. But when OSU quarterback "Runt" Jackson broke his nose, any hope of victory vanished. Four years later, Ohio led Michigan after halfback Millard Gibson ran for a seventy-five-yard touchdown. The lead didn't last long. Michigan won 10-6. But the fame Gibson gained with that single run led some people to say that he should be named to Walter Camp's All-America team—the first time such a suggestion had ever been made about an Ohio State football player.

Football fans throughout the country were transfixed on Ann Arbor on Saturday, October 25. Old-timers, who had endured two decades of disappointment, felt that the day of redemption had arrived.

"With such a record of defeats and shattered hopes, it is little wonder that the Ohio State old guard looks forward to what they believe is the best chance they have ever had of seeing Michigan defeated," said the Columbus *Citizen*. "Probably most of them would rather see this happen than to see State win the Western Conference championship if they had to choose. They base most of their hopes on Chic Harley and point to the fact that State has never lost a game with him in the lineup."

To the Ohio State alumni, this game was the biggest of them all. "There will indeed be a broken-hearted bunch of old-timers in Ann Arbor next Saturday night if Ohio State does not come through with a victory," added the *Citizen*. "Never in the history of the university have students and alumni rallied to the support of the team in such a glorious manner."

In the days leading up to the showdown in Ann Arbor, Coach Wilce put all his skill and strength into motivating his team. "Nine Practice Games Before Michigan," exclaimed the sign on the varsity bulletin board in the locker room. It had been in place even before the season opened, and the number was reduced after every game and practice game as the season wore on. Players were constantly reminded of the October 25 clash with the Wolverines. They couldn't help but see the sign every day before practice and after daily drills. There was no chance to forget about Michigan.

By late Tuesday before the big game, Buckeye rooters had reserved more than 1,600 seats at Michigan's Ferry Field. All spots sold for $1. Students with their university fee card could get in for 50 cents.

On Friday night in University Gymnasium, 3,000 students and supporters went wild with the greatest ovation ever given a Buckeye football team. Cheering lasted for five minutes after captain Harley and the rest of the football team walked on stage and seated themselves. When Harley was introduced by committee Chairman Huntley Dupre, secretary of the local YMCA, more wild cheering erupted. "In his usual quiet manner of understatement, Chic stated the team expected to go into the game with a fighting spirit and do its best to put across a Buckeye victory." Coach Wilce congratulated everyone for their "splendid enthusiasm. It is performance and action that counts. Michigan's string of victories doesn't mean anything now. It's action, the staying power and ability to do the little things right that count in the coming game." Wilce also said, "Michigan has had far greater experience than we have, and they believe Ohio State is still growing and hasn't caught up to itself. This kind of talk is all rot, for the team that will win will be the one that can perform properly regardless of past actions."

The only solemn moment during the raucous rally came when all heads bowed in memory of Fred Norton, a star halfback in 1916 who had died in the war while serving with the Canadian Royal Flying Corps.

The Michigan campus was equally excited about the game. A "Monster Pep Rally" at Hill Auditorium packed in 5,000 students in what was billed as one of the most anticipated football contests in years. "Everything has been done that could possibly be done to put the eleven in the best of shape. There can be no alibi," said one newspaper. Another report described Ann Arbor as "cuckoo."

"Stop Harley" is the Wolverine slogan, declared the *Citizen*. Michigan Coach Fielding Yost concluded early on that the only hope his team had was to stop Ohio's top star. "Michigan's defense will be principally against Harley," said Yost. "Every Michigan man will be out for the honors of stopping the fast halfback."

Chicago *Tribune* college football writer Walter Eckersall echoed Yost:

If the Buckeye captain is permitted to put up his usual capers, the Wolverines will be out of the running for the title. With all things pointing to a bitterly fought battle in which neither can be said to have an edge on the ground gaining ability, the situation reverts to Captain Harley. When all other means to score have failed, the captain will be brought into commission to attempt field goals. His punting will aid materially in placing the oval in Michigan territory for he should out-kick the Michigan booters. No one knows better than the crafty Wolverine mentor that Harley must be stopped and that he must be hurried on kicks. If the Buckeye leader is hurried on his place kicks he can change to drop-kicking which will enable another player to block. Harley is equally good at place- or drop-kicking and the style he will employ will depend largely upon how fast Michigan hurries his kicks.

Not only were the Wolverines extremely worried about Chic's running and kicking abilities, but they also feared his passing. As later proved, they also should have worried about his defensive skills as a safety. Said Eckersall, considered one of the premier football writers of his day:

There is no better forward passer in the conference than Harley. He is one of the few players seen so far this year who tucks the ball under his arm, takes a few steps to either side as if to run, which pulls the defense in, and then shoots the ball on a short or long forward pass. He can hurl the oval with the accuracy of a baseball and he possesses that football instinct of knowing when to run with the ball and when to throw it. All angles considered, this should be a great contest, one of the hardest fought of the season. If Ohio State is the victor it undoubtedly will win the conference championship.

Promptly at 6 A.M. Saturday, a Hocking Valley Railroad train packed with fans slowly pulled out of Columbus's Union Station for the five-hour trip to Ann Arbor. Fans had paid $11.36 for round-trip tickets. The return trip would get under way by 6 P.M., win, lose, or draw. The Boost Ohio Committee had set up headquarters at the Hotel Allenel. Going along for the train ride was a motion picture operator who would record details of the game to show to people back in Columbus who were unable to attend. A few days earlier, the committee, with the help of campus fraternities, had launched a last-minute campaign to raise $300 to send thirty members of the football team who could not suit up.

The team train had arrived at 5:30 Friday night in Ann Arbor, where the "Stop Harley" slogan was on the lips of all Michigan loyalists. Signs hung from railings and dorm balconies. Wilce took his squad to Ferry Field to look over the potential playing conditions and to limber up. Chic, Pete, and other punters kicked while others passed and drilled. The next day, a newspaper noted that "Harley himself seemed more concerned over the curious gazes directed at him by the Michiganders than over the game." Another report added, "Probably no match in history has aroused as much interest here." Shortly before game time, Chic received a telegram from Columbus Mayor George J.

Karb praising the team and hoping for victory: "Columbus and all of Ohio today are behind you and your wonderful football team in its game with Michigan. We feel certain here in good old Columbus town that you, who have done so much for football in Ohio, can lead your team to a victory today. As Mayor of Columbus, I can safely say that every citizen is behind you. I send you the best wishes of the city in this most important struggle and feel confident that you and your team can bring home the bacon."

Despite threatening weather earlier in the day, by 2 P.M., kickoff time, specks of blue sky and sunshine lit up the gridiron. The field was still slippery, forcing players to lace up long-cleated shoes. The wet grass would significantly increase the chances of fumbling. The two school bands had performed their traditional pregame show and got everyone in the right mood by marching up and down the field and playing their school songs.

Back in Columbus, Buckeye fans were gathered in two locations where they could get nearly instantaneous news via the telephone (radio was still in its infancy). Edward Drake, manager of the Ohio Union, had arranged for a big electric scoreboard to display each play as it occurred. Drake himself would serve as a spotter from Ferry Field and relay the plays by phone. Each play also would be called in to Hennick's Confectionary store, a popular student hangout, and announced to those in attendance via megaphone. Everything was in place. The stage was set.

Harley led the Buckeyes out of the locker room at 1:45 P.M., running onto the gridiron to a deafening chorus of cheers from State fans. Ten minutes later, Michigan came out, and the bleachers exploded with excitement. The Michigan band played "Yellow and Blue," and the Ohio State band played "Carmen Ohio." During both songs, the crowd stood, heads bared. At midfield, captains Harley and Goetz met, with Michigan winning the coin toss. They elected to punt to Ohio. Coach Yost ran up to Chic to shake his hand and wish the Buckeyes good luck.

One Ohio State student described Ferry Field at that moment as a picture of unequaled beauty:

The hills of Ann Arbor rolling up on all sides of the huge stadium made a glorious sketch. Like dots on the landscape, the two teams with the brilliant contrast of flashing colors rambled on the green blot. Airplanes circled overhead performing stunts and dips and dives and gave a fairy-like touch to the scene. Michigan's band in uniforms of maize and blue, with capes thrown back, like the costumes of a Red Cross nurse, took the co-eds' eyes.

A minute after Yost's sterling sign of sportsmanship, there was the thump of the shoe slamming into the football and the crescendo of 25,000 delirious fans screaming all at once. The game was on.

On the opening kickoff, Stinchcomb received the ball and immediately fumbled. Michigan recovered, but in the scramble for the loose ball, Wolverine Harold Rye suffered a broken leg and had to be carried off the field. Michigan was unable to move the ball and had to punt. For more than half the period, neither team could move with any consistency. "Both lines were fighting like wild men," read one account. Finally, Harley, "slippery as an eel," broke away for a twenty-five-yard gain, followed by three more yards and then two yards. A penalty against Michigan placed the ball on the Wolverine fifteen, prompting a field goal attempt by Harley. It failed, going wide of the uprights, giving the ball back to Michigan. Still unsuccessful on offense, Michigan was again forced to punt, but this time, Ohio saw an opening and took advantage. Wolverine Cliff Sparks's punt was blocked with four Buckeyes in hot pursuit. Flowers recovered the ball in the end zone, giving State a 6-0 lead. Chic upped it to 7-0 by kicking the extra point.

For the remainder of the first half, the two teams continued to engage in a contest of punts, with Harley performing all the kicking for Ohio. State came close to scoring in the second quarter when Harley's pass to Flowers was completed on the Michigan two-yard line. But Flowers immediately fumbled the ball, with Michigan recovering, eventually leading to a three-point field goal. Their backs against the wall, the Wolverines now had hope as the referee blew the whistle signaling the end of the first half. During the halftime intermission, rooters from both sides managed to regain their composure. A collection for the Roosevelt Memorial Fund was taken up, with fans jammed in the bleachers and on the sidelines, flipping silver coins into two huge stretched-out American flags. Concession sales were as brisk as ever, and the talk was whether Michigan could overcome its 7-3 deficit, or whether the Buckeyes and Harley could put the game out of reach.

As the third period began and the outcome of the clash was uncertain, both teams burst out of their locker rooms playing equally well. All of that changed a few minutes later. With the ball on Michigan's forty-two-yard line, Chic took the hike from the center. In the absence of chalked field hash marks in those days, the ball was always placed where the play ended. In this case, on the far right side of the gridiron. It was obvious to everyone that if Wilce or quarterback Stinchcomb called for a run, it would be to the left, leaving the defense with a decided advantage. Still, with Chic on the field, anything could happen. Hunched over in punt formation, once Chic had his hands on the ball, he had the option of running or passing. Acting on instinct and split-second timing, he chose to run in what many regard as his greatest ever rush from scrimmage. He elected to scurry right, not left, heading toward the sidelines and what would surely be a short gain.

"With two men shifting to the strong side, the Buckeye leader broke through the secondary offense with his inimitable change of pace and sidestepping he evaded Sparks and made a touchdown to one side of the field," said one writer. The next day, the Cleveland *Plain Dealer* described Chic's run: "Just after the start of the third quarter Chic was in punt formation at about the fifty. Dashing around the end, he sidestepped one player, stiff-armed Vick, and slipped out of the grasp of Sparks, all of who made flying tackles."

Several years later, Yost called Chic's run that day the greatest thing he'd ever seen as far as getting out of a hole and away from many defenders focused on tackling him.

Harley started off on his run with four men after him. Peach, an end, was the first man to miss him. Vick, who played full-back that day and later made All-American, a deadly tackler, also missed him. "Beak" Weston, a halfback, was the third, and Cliff Sparks, the quarterback, was the fourth. When he slipped by Peach, he was within ten yards of the sidelines. It was a shin tackle play (below the knees). He sneaked outside without any interference at all. Peach had a clean shot at him but missed, and so did Vick, Weston, and Sparks. All four were unusually good tacklers. These men came at him fast and furiously. It was like dancing on a red-hot stove. How did he do it? It was a thin shade of a pause, a side step, and little bursts of speed. He slowed up to get his opponents to come after him. Then he did his dirty and wonderful work.

In later years, Harley's famous run was regarded as one of the greatest offensive achievements in college football. The game itself is ranked as one of the greatest in Big Ten football history.

Harley missed kicking the extra point. Now with the score 13-3, Yost was forced to change his strategy. In the fourth quarter, he ordered more passing in hopes of quickly gaining large chunks of real estate. So hard and aggressive was the playing that there were wholesale substitutions. As Michigan opened its offense, the speedy Harley and his good friend and backfield mate Stinchcomb lay back, waiting for the right moments. A long pass by Weston was intercepted by Harley on Michigan's twenty-five-yard line. Several more passing attempts fell harmlessly away or were intercepted by Harley. At game's end, a desperate and dismayed Michigan had lost 13-3 before 25,000 stunned fans crammed into Ferry Field. Harley had scored State's only touch-down from scrimmage, having been set up by Stinchcomb's seventeen-yard run. He performed all the punting and kicking, and had intercepted four passes—a record that still stands. The *Dispatch* reported:

> *Chic Harley, the premier football player certainly of the Western Conference, if not the entire country, became a captain of achievement*

*here today, rather than nominal leadership, when 25,000 football fans
gathered from the plains and valleys of two states watched this superman
of the moleskin lead an attack with all the dash of an old time cavalry
chieftain that resulted in a 13 to 3 victory for the Scarlet and Gray.
When it was all ended and the October sun was sinking in its setting of
gold, the crowd went its way slowly, but on the lips of thousands there
was praise for Harley.*

"Head and shoulders above all other men in the game was
Chic Harley," reported the Chicago *Post*. "It was Chic who carried
the ball two-thirds of the time."

Pandemonium reigned in the Ohio State locker room as
Buckeye teammates embraced one another and Coach Wilce's
teeth flashed a wide smile from ear to ear. But the hoopla was
silenced when, to everyone's astonishment, Coach Yost appeared
in the doorway, a look of disappointment on his face. It was well-
known that Yost rarely visited an opponent's locker room after
a game, but the game he had just witnessed nullified that policy.
Humbly, he asked to speak to the team for a few moments. He
first congratulated Wilce and Buckeye Athletic Director St. John
on their victory. Then he turned to the group of about two dozen
half-dressed, exhilarated football players standing before him.

"You deserve your victory. You fought brilliantly. You boys
gave a grand exhibition of football strategy, and while I am sorry,
dreadfully sorry, that we lost, I want to congratulate you. And
you, Mr. Harley, I believe, are one of the finest little machines I
have ever seen. Again, I want to congratulate Ohio State." Yost
then disappeared from the locker room, leaving in his wake a
team and coaching staff bursting with pride. Chic only smiled
as fellow Buckeyes patted him on the back, the only way they
knew to show their respect, appreciation, and affection for their
star teammate.

In the final stats, Ohio State had gained 176 yards, and
Michigan had gained only 85. Ohio State managed six first
downs, Michigan only two. Ohio completed four of eleven
passes; Michigan completed no passes in seventeen attempts.

Chic personally intercepted four of those passes setting a school record. Harley punted eleven times for an average of forty-two yards. One of his kicks traveled sixty-five yards.

Immediately after the game, the exodus from Ann Arbor to the Ohio state line began. Autos filled the highways, and the special trains belched their smoke promptly at 6 P.M. A worried northern Ohio farm lady, confused at the long stream of cars heading south, asked one carload of fans if a dam had broken or whether Lake Erie was overflowing. Men from Columbus who filled the special train, joyous at the victory, were bemoaning the fact that they had been unable to convince any Michigan fan to cover their $10,000 pot. Buckeye fans in Toledo filled the streets, flinging streamers and singing "Across the Field" and "Carmen Ohio." There was even a snake dance during the wild celebration.

Back home in Columbus, 6,000 frenzied fans, beside themselves with joy, awaited the team. Even though the train was an hour late arriving, no one minded as midnight approached. As they waited, students, parents, and ordinary residents of Ohio's capital city sang "Across the Field." More than 1,000 automobiles were parked along High Street and adjoining avenues. A special contingent of police had been sent in to preserve order on the streets, but good-naturedly gave up. So excited was everyone that they even cheered the mention of the Hocking Valley Railroad. Finally, the train arrived, triggering a chorus of "Hail, Hail, the Gang's All Here." A "wild delirium of joy" never before witnessed in Ohio sprang up. According to one description, "Ohio State's great football eleven came back home from Ann Arbor early this morning to find—it seemed to them—a city suddenly gone wild. A shrieking, howling mass of humanity packed the big station. There never was such a celebration here." Even Pat Moran's Cincinnati Reds, who had won the World Series just a few weeks earlier, didn't get this kind of welcome.

Mayor George Karb expressed his pride in the returning heroes, then suddenly and without warning planted a big kiss on Chic's forehead, prompting a roar of approval from the throng.

On Monday, when Chic showed up for his regular classes, he refused to verify Mayor Karb's show of affection and blushed a deep shade of red when the kiss was mentioned. "Starting a habit of kissing Chic after football games might meet with popularity among the girls and be dangerous," said one newspaper report.

With the mayor holding onto his arm, Harley led the procession of victorious players upstairs to the front of the station and a tremendous ovation. From all sides, Ohio State rooters jammed in toward Harley to greet him, express their joy, or touch his sleeve. Also alongside Chic were Wilce and Pete.

One account: "Several machine loads of students with fireworks, a cannon and noisy torpedoes blazed the way and announced to downtown sleepers that Harley and Company were back in town. Massed from curb to curb, State rooters, among whom were hundreds of girls and women, marched back of the team shouting and singing. Everyone [paid no attention that it] was Sunday morning. When the Buckeye team finally reached the Statehouse a few blocks away, cheerleader Johnny Jones led the crowd in a 'Yea, Chic.' Urged on by everyone around him, Harley reluctantly rose to speak."

"I'm glad to get back to Columbus and glad we don't have a game today," said Chic in his soft voice. "But the rest of the fellows did their share in winning the game. They cut the path. Call on them." Following several minutes of applause for Chic, Coach Wilce stood up and said, "The boys gave the university, Columbus, and the state all they had today, and we have a right to be proud of them. The team won by exceptional ability and teamwork. It beat Michigan nicely, fairly, cleanly, and decisively."

After one last singing of the school's anthem, the celebrants disbanded. It was 1:30 in the morning. Chic Harley was at the top of his game.

Louise Havens, one of Chic's closest friends, who he pinned in 1919. Harley family members maintain that the couple was planning to wed before Chic became ill in 1922.

CHAPTER 8

Not Meant to Be

After Michigan's loss, the only unbeaten teams in the conference were Ohio State, Chicago, and Wisconsin. If the Buckeyes could defeat Chicago and Wisconsin, the path would be cleared for another championship. The final game of the season, against Illinois on November 22, was not considered a threat—a risky assumption, as it later turned out—because the Illini already had one loss. Ohio State would also face Purdue, a team many considered much improved.

Taking advantage of a bye week for Ohio State, Chic decided to visit the folks back home in Chicago the weekend of November 1. Arriving by train Saturday morning, and after saying his hellos, he quickly took off for the University of Chicago on the city's South Side, where the Maroons were hosting Illinois in what was predicted to be a fierce inter-league clash. Chic was anxious not only to enjoy the cool fall air in a setting he loved, but to see for himself just how good Illinois was and to report his findings to Coach Wilce. Crammed into the wooden bleachers about twenty rows above the field, Chic quickly grew concerned. Illinois, he realized, was no slouch of a team. It had running backs who weren't afraid to tear into the defensive line low and hard. He knew the win over Michigan was not the best test for Ohio. By the time the referee blew the final whistle, there was no doubt

125

in Chic's mind that danger lay ahead. Illinois had just blanked a good Chicago team 10-0. Its offense had power, its defense was solid, and its best weapon was the brainy Coach Robert Carl Zuppke.

"Our team has not been put to the test," Chic told the *Tribune*'s Walter Eckersall in a rare, unusually candid moment when he was not at a loss for words. He continued:

The Michigan game cannot be taken too seriously. The Wolverines were not a strong team and we could have beaten them by a larger score if we had turned loose our complete attack. We had instructions from the coach to win and not try to run up the score. Of course the team looked good because the opposition was weak. Wisconsin and Illinois are much stronger teams than Michigan, in my estimation. We have won all our games and most plays have gained. Just what we will do when we meet a team which has just as strong a line and an evenly balanced backfield remains to be seen. It is my opinion that Illinois hit its stride in the Chicago game. Coach Zuppke has been shifting his men all season, but at last has decided upon a combination which will be used for the remainder of the year. The eleven has a lot of power and the backs drive hard and low. If they beat Minnesota they will give us a hard battle.

Chic's extreme concern about Wisconsin and Illinois was undeniable. Eckersall agreed: "If Illinois defeats Minnesota November 8, the Buckeyes will have something to worry about."

First, though, the Boilermakers had to be dealt with. Conditions at old Ohio Field were slippery at early morning. By noon, overcast skies had been replaced with a beautiful layer of dark blue sky. Nearby maple trees were nearly stripped of their leaves, leaving behind dark, bare branches. It was the first encounter between the two teams, and Purdue, the solid underdog, was determined to make a good showing. Practices leading up to the game were intense; one of them three days earlier in West Lafayette lasted five hours. During those workouts, freshmen Purdue players were used as guinea pigs for the varsity, running known Buckeye plays in an effort to shore up their defense. One frosh was given the name Harley, and every time he was handed the ball, he ran for his life with beefy first stringers in hot pursuit, screaming, "Stop Harley!"

An overconfident article in the Columbus *Citizen,* "State Ready for Hard Going Ahead," said, "The Buckeyes are now the only Big Ten team that has a clean record and a fighting chance for the title. All possibilities of a tie have been sidetracked and the scarlet and gray gridders can start on the last lap of the race with a clear field ahead." A week earlier, Purdue defeated Michigan State 13-7. A few weeks before that, Michigan drubbed Purdue 26-0.

Ohio State had little trouble with Purdue, winning 20-0. The key moment of the game came in the second quarter, not long after Chic, in his number 10 jersey, appeared on the field for the first time. After an exchange of punts, Chic rambled around the right end for a thirty-yard touchdown. Without the benefit of any blocking ahead of him, he eluded five sure tackles while skimming along the sidelines into the end zone. The Indianapolis *Star* called the run "brilliant." Later in the game, Chic's all-around talents once again bloomed in full when he passed to end Bill Slyker for a thirteen-yard TD.

But despite the lopsided score and the Harley heroics that every Buckeye fan had come to expect, there were worrisome signs. The physical condition of many Buckeye players was below par. Many suffered nagging injuries; several key members had to deal with "poisoning" when dye from their crimson stockings infected their skin. In addition, throughout the year, Ohio had been called for an atypically large number of penalties, including two for holding during the Purdue game just when Chic was crossing the goal line. The two TDs were called back.

What if that happened against Wisconsin or Illinois? Columbus football writer Charles S. Nelson said that OSU fans were far from satisfied with the team's performance in general play despite its undefeated record: "A large amount of it was undoubtedly due to overconfidence. The Buckeyes entered the game against Purdue feeling superbly confident of an easy victory. But the contest served to take the Ohio team off its high horse and did more to open their eyes than a volume of speeches by Coach Wilce." Chic, on the field and during play, was far ahead of most others when it came to concern about the Buckeye team. Just a few days before the Purdue battle, a newspaper article quoted him as calling Illinois a "great team." He added, "Illinois has a wonderful team and is to be feared more than Michigan and possibly more than any other eleven we have to face."

With two games left on the schedule, Chic was well aware that the biggest tests for a perfect season and a perfect college career hung in the balance. Wisconsin, at 4 and 1, was next, in Madison. The Ohio State-Wisconsin game three years earlier in Columbus was still fresh in everyone's mind. It was one of the first battles where Harley's tremendous overall abilities first unfolded on the college gridiron in which he scored all of the Buckeye points in a thrilling 14-13 win. There was no doubt that Wisconsin deeply wanted not only to avenge Harley's winning performance in 1916, but to show Ohio Coach Wilce that his alma mater still had a crackerjack football team.

Northwestern University graduate and football great Paddy Driscoll, writing for a Chicago newspaper, described Ohio State as a team packed with veterans while Wisconsin was a "green" team with one, perhaps two star players. The Badgers, he added, were full of confidence, having beaten Minnesota a week earlier in a dramatic, come-from-behind victory.

The Buckeyes' sendoff from Columbus on Thursday, November 13, was the noisiest ever for an Ohio State team as tens of thousands of fans smelled a third conference championship in four years. Student demonstrations began in the early evening on campus, moving to a monster pep rally at University Gym. Streets were jammed half a mile in every direction, and when Chic was introduced, the cheers roared through the cavernous building. From there, throngs of fans walked the several blocks to Union Station, where "several thousand loyal supporters had yelled themselves hoarse and were fit subjects for padded cells. Like they had done just three weeks earlier, students walked to the station behind the playing of the Buckeye band, yelling and singing. Streetcars, filled to capacity, with some students even sitting on the roofs, slowed to a crawl to avoid hitting any of the revelers. Autos were not allowed to motor down High Street unless they were filled. At the train station, the frenzied crowd forced its way through the gates to the track platform, waiting impatiently for the team to arrive. Then just a few minutes before 10:30 P.M., the scheduled time for the train's departure, the team showed up to a deafening roar of fan approval. As the players stepped onto the platform ready to board the train, there were insistent calls for Chic, who moments later appeared seemingly out of nowhere. The thousands who jammed in suddenly and in an eerie display of reverence quieted to a hush. Then cheerleader Johnny Creps, seemingly on cue, called for a "Yea, Chic!" The response was more than just a yell. It was a rocking, crashing, roaring thunder of sound never before heard or witnessed in Ohio's capital city.

Somehow, fifteen enterprising Buckeye fans managed to stow away on board the team train without being detected. Hiding under berths and in other nooks and crannies, they weren't discovered until the train chugged out of the station. "Football was at a fever heat in Columbus," exclaimed a local paper.

As the squad filed its way toward the train, the crowd broke through the ropes, forming a narrow lane through which the eighty-one players and trainers and three coaches walked while eager hands reached out for encouraging pats on the back. In the middle of the single file was Chic, grinning from ear to ear. Dozens of school faithful patted him on the back. Many grabbed to touch his hands. All around were yells of support, such as, "It's up to you, Chic." At the rear of the line was Coach Wilce, the second most popular man in Ohio at that moment. Traveling with the team were school cheerleaders, who normally didn't make the trip because of the high expense. But two Columbus companies offered to handle the bill. The Columbus Athletic Club had no problem filling two extra train cars comprised of their members, and the Elk Club Antler rooters arranged for another car of their own. Long after the players had piled into their berths and turned out the lights, the roaring kept up, echoing and re-echoing through the smoke-stained train shed. Then the train pulled out.

Unable to sleep during the ride to Madison, some of the older alumni played poker. The only sound from the healthy young players was snoring. The only gleam of light in the otherwise darkened train car came from Coach Wilce's berth, where he sat, propped up by a couple of pillows, studying game charts. Early the next morning, about two-thirds of the way to Madison, the team had to change trains in Chicago. They were greeted by a small group of Ohio State graduates and curiosity seekers wanting just one thing: a glimpse of Chic. When a newspaper columnist on board pointed out Chic as he dashed for the connecting train, the reaction of some was disbelief. They had imagined a much bigger man, not one who measured only five feet, eight inches and weighed 158 pounds.

Finally, four hours later, the Buckeye train arrived in Wisconsin's cold and snowy capital city. Piles of straw that had been carefully strewn over the Camp Randall gridiron to protect it from the harsh elements had been removed and piled along the sidelines. Despite the best of efforts, the field remained frozen, hard as concrete. Ten thousand fans, 1,000 from Ohio, jammed the stadium bleachers. Ohio State elected to defend the south goal, which provided the advantage of having the frigid wind at their backs. Other than an unsuccessful thirty-five-yard field goal attempt by Harley in the first quarter, there were no formidable scoring drives by either team. In the fourth quarter, with the score still at 0-0, a pass by Chic was intercepted. The Badgers, however, could muster no offense for another punt. For the Buckeyes, Chic had handled all the kicking, to that point punting eight times. In the fourth frame, Ohio State got on track, with Chic completing a series of passes to bring the team to the Wisconsin twelve-yard line. A successful pass from Harley to Stinchcomb over the goal line was not allowed because it was ruled that Chic had violated the rule that prohibited throwing passes within five yards behind the line of scrimmage. After that, Ohio's only chance to score was to try a field goal from a difficult angle. Chic carefully measured the forty-three-yard distance and after the snap, looking straight down at the ball, rammed it through the uprights, not raising his head until he heard the groans and roar of the crowd.

Throughout the game, Wilce used Harley as a battering ram to try to push Wisconsin players off their feet. On the five end-run plays he attempted, Chic rambled for forty-two yards. Whenever the Badgers looked as if they were going to mount a solid offensive attack, the quick-footed Ohio State safeties, Harley and Stinchcomb, saved the day with strong tackles, preventing sizable gains. His running, passing, field goal drop-kicking, and defensive talents aside, Chic's punting was considered the deciding factor in the game. In this category, he netted his team seventy-two yards of field position advantage. On straight football, which takes into account total team running and passing, Wisconsin performed better than the Buckeyes. But it was Harley's punting, which averaged 39.5 yards per kick, that consistently drove Wisconsin into a hole they could never dig themselves out of. Wilce's strategy was to rely not totally on Chic's running and passing, but more on his kicking. When his opportunity came in the fourth quarter to put three points on the board, he didn't fail. That field goal had been set up only a few minutes earlier by Chic, who had coolly booted a seventy-yard rolling punt.

The 3-0 victory, while not a picture of perfection, was nevertheless a win for the Buckeyes, who now had to win only one more time for a Western Conference title and a perfect college career for their hero and leader Chic.

The scene at Union Station in Columbus early Sunday morning was tumultuous. The school band, which couldn't afford to make the trip, belted out "Across the Field" over and over as the team train inched its way to a complete stop. Early morning editions of the *Dispatch* ran a full-page drawing of a grinning Chic, captioned, "Ohio has produced a whole basketful of presidents—but only one Harley!" In a corner of the cartoon, a tiny man in a derby hat said, "After sitting for twenty years in the damp chill of just ordinary football, it's nice to walk around in the sunshine." As the players and coaches exited the train, Chic momentarily appeared small and out of place as he tried to hide behind two bulky linemen. His maneuver proved fruitless, as two giggling coeds spotted him immediately. They grabbed his arms and shoulders and planted kisses on his cheeks. The shy superstar blushed to a bright, fiery scarlet and, after being buffeted from one group of frenzied fanatics to another, ran for cover and out of the limelight. The unrelenting school band led the entourage of snake-dancing celebrants south on High Street. It was a full fifteen hours since the Buckeyes had beaten Wisconsin, and there was no letup in the revelry. "Goofy?" asked one writer years later. "Perhaps. But somehow football was a lot more fun in those days."

Harley's overall performance in the 3-0 victory over Wisconsin was enough for many to conclude that he should be named an All-American for the third time. Said the Chicago *American*: "With apparently no effort he will elude the most properly timed tackle ever attempted. He does it much in the same way as a boxer clipping a punch. Chic seems to know just where the tackler's effort will spend itself and instead of jumping vigorously to this side or that, he merely crooks his knees inward and the frantic grasp of his opponent is wasted on thin air." *Tribune* writer and former player Eckersall said Harley is "the original knee bender and twister in the football game." Another observer said he had never seen anyone perfect the art of conserving energy better than Harley. "Most players are keyed up to the highest pitch throughout a football game. But not so with Harley. The uniniti- ated would think him to be a lazy player between formations. But once a play is started Chic is all power and force and nerve. This is one reason why he is never fatigued at the end of a game regardless of the character of the competition."

A Wisconsin newspaper described the Ohio State win as "one of those rip-snorting, slam-bang battles devoid of thrills in which the contenders were so evenly balanced on the whole that a tieless score would have done both justice." With Illinois next—and last—on the Buckeye schedule, Harley "may do better a week from today, and if he doesn't Ohio State will find that Illinois is a foe not to be trifled with."

As Thanksgiving drew near in the cooling fall of 1919, there was a buzz never before seen or felt around the Ohio State campus. No longer was the focus simply on winning games and a conference championship. Less than a month earlier, the unimaginable had occurred: Michigan had been beaten for the first time. And the 3-0 victory over Wisconsin on November 15 had positioned the Buckeyes for another perfect season if they could just beat Illinois on November 22. In many respects, the season of 1919 was already the greatest ever for Ohio State football. Only one more accomplishment was needed to make it the most perfect season of all.

Everyone knew that Ohio State's game against Illinois on Saturday, November 22, was the last time the great Chic Harley would ever play in interscholastic football. For 17,000 lucky fans packed into the rickety bleachers at Ohio Field and standing around the gridiron, and the hundreds more perched on rooftops and in leafless trees that day, it would be the last time they would see Chic play for the Buckeyes. It truly would be a historic occasion. In his three seasons on varsity, Chic up to that point had played in twenty-three games, scored 194 points, and performed nearly all of the team's place kicking, drop kicking, and kickoff chores. He was considered the best punter in the league and one of the best in the country. He was the squad's most accurate and prolific passer and runner. Perhaps more important than all of that was his ability to quietly lead and inspire his team to unprecedented greatness.

"To me, Harley was the perfect football player, if there is such a thing," said teammate Jack "Farky" Farcasin years later while reminiscing about his former team captain. Added Charlie Seddon: "He would kick over the goal line on kickoffs. He did all the passing, running, drop kicking. He ran back punts for touchdowns and kickoffs for touchdowns. There isn't anything the man couldn't do. He's got to be one of the greatest, if not the greatest. He was a great leader. We all got a lift. There was something about the guy. I don't know. Tremendous. He had tremendous speed, and he was a tremendous defensive player. He was a great inspiration. How many players can you say laid the foundation for a dynasty? We were nobody in football until he came into the picture. He built the tremendous hysteria you see today. He got everybody riled up to where they raised the money to build a new stadium in just one year."

But with all the adulation and success, on the eve of what could become his final glory, Chic Harley was a man who suddenly and mysteriously became gripped by self-doubt. The fact that he had suffered a rare, nagging injury to his right ankle during the Wisconsin game did not help matters. Whether he could perform at top speed was in question. But Chic had had injuries before and played through them. Squarely on his mind was the fact that Illinois would be no pushover. His scouting of the Illini a few weeks earlier in Chicago taught him that Zuppke's team had come a long way since an early season loss to Chicago. Chic was well aware that Zuppke hadn't forgotten his team's loss to Ohio State in 1916, when Chic scored a touchdown and kicked the extra point in the final seconds of a 7-6 victory. Zuppke, the veteran and well-respected coach, predicted that no one in the Western Conference would go undefeated. Besides being Chic's final game as a collegiate, their upcoming match was also the final college football game of Illinois's talented running back, Dutch Sternaman. Chic, Wilce, and most newspaper writers were mindful that the win over Wisconsin was anything but convincing. Ohio State, while undefeated, had also chalked up an extraordinarily high number of penalties against all of its conference opponents, and its overall performance for the season was not considered stellar.

What haunted Chic the most was his performance five years earlier on the same football field under nearly the same circumstances. East High School, a powerhouse in Columbus for the three years Chic had played for the team, 1912-14, had faced archrival North High School for the coveted city football championship. In his three seasons on varsity, Harley had tasted defeat only three times in twenty-three games. The prep champion-ship game would show not only whether East would win the city title, but whether Harley could end his career in near perfect fashion. In that game, he and his teammates were shut out in a 14-0 licking, in which Chic could not produce as he had in nearly every game before. Now, in the fall of 1919, nearly five years to the date of that major high school loss, Chic came face to face with the prospect of the same fate.

"Losing that big game in high school preyed upon him," said Farcasin. "He walked the campus all night. He was worried. He couldn't shake it." His good friend, Joe Finneran, stayed with Chic throughout the evening, walking the campus, giving him comfort, and urging him to try to keep his injured right ankle loose.

For the students and fans of Ohio State, Saturday's game against Illinois was not so much a battle for the Western Conference title as it was a final, fitting tribute to the most admirable man they knew and Ohio State had ever seen. More than anyone, Chic Harley was commonly credited with almost single-handedly generating the excitement and attention that propelled not only Ohio State athletics, but the entire school, with all its areas of study, to a place of national prominence.

A long line of people snaked its way to Ohio Field's entrance along the great iron gate that ran the length of the gridiron. Smoke billowed from the many campfires that had been lit since late Friday night. Men and women, snuggled in army jackets and hats, huddled around the fires to keep warm.

"Throughout the night they [students] stood about the entrances hoping to be among the first to get a chance at the standing room tickets which are to be placed for sale just before the game," reported the *Citizen*. "These loyal fans kept up their spirits with Ohio yells and songs."

At the traditional Friday night rally in a packed University Gym, Chic broke down after being introduced, realizing that he was about to play his last game as an Ohio State football player. "The wonderful reception that was given him was more than the sturdy little lad could stand," said one observer.

A newspaper cartoon showed the Ohio State team at a Thanksgiving dinner table: "Chic and his bunch of ravenous bloodthirsty pigskin hounds." Being served was a huge turkey labeled "Western Championship," with Illinois as the dessert.

The Chicago *Post* predicted that if Illinois could stop Harley, it could win the game, although every team Ohio had faced that year had tried just that and failed. "Who can stop Harley? Well, any team can stop him if all eleven of the men will tackle him at once. And generally no matter how hard they hit him, he generally comes up smiling, brushing the dirt from his face and rearranging his headgear. He has remarkable stamina." A former famous college football player, who had watched Harley play for three years, called him one of the greatest players of all time. In particular, he admired Harley's baffling change of pace, wonderful straight-arm, and a side step that made nervous wrecks of opposing players meeting him in open field. "And the greatest of all his offensive tactics is a little twist of his own that enables him to shift with the tackler. He does this in such a way that every so often there is no collision at all when tackler and runner meet. That tackler just slides off."

Chic's father and his five brothers and sisters arrived in Columbus by train on November 21. Mattie, Chic's mother and his biggest fan, stayed in Chicago. That evening, Chic entertained his father at the Phi Gamma Delta fraternity house. A few days earlier, Charles Harley had told a reporter that after attending the OSU-Wisconsin game in Madison, he declared that if his son didn't show improvement, he would "take him out to the woodshed."

At noon that day, the Illinois team arrived from Champaign-Urbana. Coach Zuppke had little to say when he disembarked the train. His only comments were about how Wisconsin gave the Buckeyes a fight for their money a week earlier and that Ohio will "find us a much tougher proposition." Also noticeable when exiting the train was Ralph Fletcher, considered to be Illinois's best player and a deadly place kicker. Walking with a slight limp,

Fletcher said he was okay and the recent pains in his bad leg were rapidly disappearing under careful treatment. His younger brother, Bobby, also a member of the Illinois team, attracted little attention.

Football fans throughout Ohio were referring to Saturday's contest as the greatest ever to be played in Columbus, at least up to that time. Lynn St. John was a nervous wreck trying to accommodate everyone who wanted tickets, even though every seat had been sold two weeks earlier. He was nevertheless besieged by people willing to pay record prices. Scalpers were charging as much as $80 for a reserved seat. Standing-room-only tickets, which normally sold for $15, were being sold for $50 each for this game. Nearly all wagers placed on the game were even odds. The Champaign Elks Club arrived with $5,000 and placed the entire sum on Illinois. Columbus's Elks did the same for their home team.

In the Chicago *American*, Paul "Shorty" Des Jardien, former All-American center for the Chicago Maroons and now captain of the Hammond, Indiana, professional football team, predicted Illinois would win, adding that "with the exit of Harley from the ranks of intercollegiate football following this game, other schools in the Big 10 fold will heave copious sighs of relief. Four battles of major importance he won almost single-handedly and in the other games he has been Wilce's biggest ace."

"It will be a game desperately contested to the finish, too, without doubt, and probably won't be decided until the whistle blows," wrote *Dispatch* writer E.H. Penisten. He added that someone he knew who had witnessed the Ohio State-Wisconsin game immediately placed a $5,000 bet on Illinois. "Everything points to the fact that Illinois will go on the field next Saturday right at the height of its power," said Penisten.

For weeks leading up to the November 22 contest, Ohio papers played up the approach of Chic's final game and wondered whether he could end his career on a perfect note.

"Will Today See History Repeat Itself?" asked the Columbus *Journal*. Photos of Chic covered all the local newspapers. Some of the pictures showed him in football uniform, others in his civies, and a few in his army uniform. A few weeks earlier, the Buckeye football program carried a full-length picture of Chic not with his famous broad smile, but with an unusual look of concern.

"In four games, Harley has scored all points made by Ohio State," said a report on game day, "and he has rolled up 191 (there is some question whether it was 191 or 194 points) of the 719 points (nearly one-fourth) made by the Buckeyes in three seasons. His presence on the team has been even a greater asset to the Scarlet and Gray." The article summed things up by recalling Chic's presence on the same football field in 1914. "It has been pointed out that one of the main factors leading to the defeat of East in 1914 was due to the fact that when things began to go wrong, Chic alone was capable of bearing up under the strain. In the event that things begin to go wrong in today's game, Captain Chic will be supported by 10 of the best football players ever grouped together in one team."

Two hours before game time, the area around Ohio Field was an ocean of humanity. People carrying OSU pennants and wearing scarlet and gray armbands pushed and crowded around the gates. Scattered about were Illinois supporters, many clad in orange and blue attire. Fans holding bleacher and general admission tickets rushed the gates as soon as they opened. The crush was terrific. Reserved seats and boxes filled more slowly. Autos lined the streets on all sides of the university, and the extra cars on the Rail-Light were jammed with fans. Volunteers and a cordon of special police walked posts around the field to guard against attempts to rush the fence. Housetops, porches, and trees outside the field on High Street and Woodruff Avenue were occupied almost as fully as Ohio Field itself.

Thirty minutes before the start of the contest, an airplane circled the field and performed stunts. The crowd was in a festive spirit, cheering everything that moved. Chic Harley Aquila, the three-year-old son of groundskeeper Tony Aquila, who was named after Chic, got a huge hand when he trotted across the field in football clothes. He waved his hands and shouted, "We're

138

going to beat 'em," prompting a huge roar. Balloons bumped above the heads of the bleacherites, and streamers were thrown in every direction. One startling illustration of the interest in the game came from a plot involving eighteen ingenious students who were determined to gain entry to the stadium. Led by a senior in the university's Mining Engineering School and an expert in tunneling, they had hatched a plan to dig a tunnel to a location under the bleachers. Each had pledged secrecy. For three nights, they tunneled and made great progress, only to be foiled by a tipoff to the authorities, who made them replace all the dirt.

"Old Chris Columbus would be amazed if he could see the city named after him today," wrote columnist Malcolm MacLean in the *Citizen*. Reviewing Chic's record, MacLean said in his three years, Chic had scored 191 points, for an average of slightly more than 9½ points per game (many of which he played for only a period or two). He scored twenty-two touchdowns, kicked thirty-five extra points, kicked four field goals from placement and four drop kicks. He failed to score in only two games: his first game in 1916 and a 1916 game against Indiana, in which he ran numerous times for long gains.

Weather conditions at game time were ideal. Unusually mild breezes throughout the day left the field in good shape. The student newspaper, the *Lantern*, was preparing to publish a story immediately after the contest about plans to build a new football stadium. Editors were also readying type that would allow publication of an "Extra" edition moments after the end of the game that would shout the news of a Buckeye win to fans leaving Ohio Field. Hundreds of people, the *Lantern* said, had traveled to Columbus for the Illinois game, only to be turned away because no seats or space was available. Instead, they had to walk to the student Union to see play-by-play accounts of the game being posted. All 15,000 seats were occupied with another 4,000 or so people standing along the sidelines and end zones and literally hanging from trees just outside the gates. Later, St. John proclaimed that 60,000 tickets could have been sold. The story pointed out that the school's present football facilities provided inadequate practice space and permitted anyone, including spies, to enter the field to see new plays being developed. Although she had gradated six months earlier, Louise Havens was one of the lucky alums to have secured a bleacher seat inside the stadium. She, like everyone else, was bundled up in a long winter coat and hat that day, consumed with anticipation, excitement, and concern about the man she loved. To Louise, it was unthinkable for her not to attend Chic's last football contest, to be with him to celebrate his last victory—or in the case of defeat—to provide him comfort. For most of their high school years and throughout college, the couple had grown so close, having spent their summers at the Franklin Park public pool, where Chic lifeguarded and Louise swam and perfected her diving. Louise, like Chic, rarely let her emotions get the better of her. She was always in control, soft-spoken, kind, compassionate, and well-liked. "She never raised her voice," said her only daughter, Connie, years later. Louise's affections for Chic were undeniable, although in Connie's estimation, not necessarily sexual. "She took him under her wing," guessed Connie in explaining that Louise saw in Chic a person who longed for the nurturing of a close friend. But, as Connie conceded, "who knows?" leaving open the possibility that there was more to their relationship than anyone other than the couple knew. The fact that Chic had "pinned" Louise at some unknown time during their college years lends credence to the belief that marriage was planned. The Varsity "O" pin Chic presented to Louise contained a sparkling blue stone. Etched on the backside are the initials "CWH" and "VOA," the latter which stands for Varsity "O" Association. "She was thought of as a very sweet person," described Connie of her mother. "She majored in English literature and after school did a lot of volunteer work. Mother especially liked to watch Edward G. Robinson movies because she thought the actor looked like Chic."

Promptly at 2 P.M., after the Buckeye band had marched up and down the field playing the ever-popular "Across the Field" fight song, Illinois won the coin toss and elected to receive the ball at the south end. A fumble by Dutch Sternaman on the Illinois twenty-nine-yard line was followed by three short runs by Harley, who then was called on to kick a thirty-four-yard field goal. The ball fell low and short, allowing Illinois to go on the offensive. Their efforts proved unimpressive, with OSU eventually regaining possession. The first of several unusual miscues by Harley occurred when he threw a pass that Illinois intercepted on its forty-three-yard line but failed to score on. But as the period neared an end, following a well-placed punt by Harley that was caught by Bobby Fletcher, Sternaman brought the crowd to a stunned hush. Handed the ball, Sternaman stumbled and nearly fell after maneuvering outside. Thanks to perfect blocking, he raced fifty yards for a touchdown. It was the first and only touchdown scored against the Buckeyes all season.

The second period saw both teams battle it out, with numerous punts exchanged in a battle over territory. Harley's punting was exemplary, as he kicked for sizable yardage. His passes, however, were off the mark, and throughout the first half, he was unable to break loose on runs. In the third period, it was obvious that Ohio's strategy was to ram holes through the center of the Illinois line, as Harley time after time slammed forward, gaining three and four yards at a crack. Chic also started connecting on passes, even though on one, Sternaman stepped in front of Clarence MacDonald to intercept Harley for the second time. Finally, as the seconds ticked off at the end of the third frame, Chic hit MacDonald on a fourth and nine with a forward pass at the two-yard line. On that play, Chic, in punt formation, carried the ball to the far right side of the field. Looking to the left, he found MacDonald waving frantically in the far left corner of the field. MacDonald made a spectacular play, catching the ball just in front of the goal line. Next, Coach Wilce called on his 210-pound fullback, Dick Boesel, to push the ball into the end zone. But after three attempts, the ball was now on the three-yard line.

"Let me have it," demanded Chic. On the next play, Harley, running from five yards behind the center, snatched the handoff and hit the defensive line with such ferocity that one Illinois guard bounced back left and a tackle bounced back right. Chic found himself six yards into the end zone for the score. The touchdown triggered such a display that many thought the old wooden grandstand would fall under the strain. A second later, Chic barely made the extra point after it hit the inside of the upright. No matter, Ohio State was ahead in the game for the first time, 7-6.

If Ohio State could keep Illinois from scoring for the next fifteen minutes, a Western Conference championship would be theirs and Chic's perfect record would be intact. At first, things went well for the Buckeyes, as their defense held Illinois to short gains. But the situation grew dark following another interception of a Harley heave, leaving Illinois with a slim possibility of kicking a field goal. Fortunately, the attempt was blocked, and the ball went back to the Buckeyes. For the next several minutes, the gritty OSU squad gave everything it had to gain two, three, and four yards at a time the hard way, on the ground. Stinchcomb, Willaman, and Harley did the running, grinding out precious real estate. With the ball beyond the forty following a run by Chic of twenty-five yards, the team captain decided to call on Butch Pixley to attempt a field goal for the Buckeyes. Chic believed that the distance was too great, though Pixley and his 230-pound frame had a chance to make it. The attempt was blocked. On the next set of downs, Illinois failed to move the ball, giving it up to Ohio State. But the Buckeyes couldn't move. With just a few minutes left, Ohio was forced to give up the ball, and once again Chic was called on to punt and hope to put the Illini in a deep hole. As he had done so many times, Chic came through, miraculously kicking the ball forty-seven yards into the Illinois end zone and forcing a touchback. With only about two minutes to go, an anguished Coach Zuppke ordered quarterback Larry Wahlquist to throw on every down. Three Illinois starters, unable to play due to injuries suffered in the game, lay spread out on the sidelines.

"It was growing dark and all seemed lost," reported the Chicago *Tribune*. "One beauty pass by Sternaman put the ball in midfield after Chic Harley himself had touched but failed to hold the ball. It flew out of his arms into the anxious hands of an Illini. After this, three more passes were tried and all failed. A fourth attempt by Illinois was somehow miraculously completed. It was on Ohio's 35-yard line." Now, with less than a minute left, Illinois, desperate as could be, attempted three more passes. All failed to hit their target, but a fourth try succeeded, putting the ball on Ohio State's twenty-two-yard line. Zuppke, half-crazed himself and surrounded by pandemonium, managed to keep his head and ordered a substitution, which bought him a few seconds of precious time. His best player, Ralph Fletcher, the man he would normally call on to kick a field goal, had been crippled earlier in the game, aggravating his already hobbled leg. Brother Bobby, who attracted little notice when the team arrived in Columbus a day earlier, had played brilliantly throughout the game at quarterback. Zuppke told him to get out there and kick a field goal—something the younger Fletcher had never done. Now, with time running out and autumn's long shadows enveloping the entire field, Fletcher, at the thirty-two-yard line, moved forward as soon as he saw Sternaman snare the ball from the center and place the rounded end on the grass. The only visible lights flickered in the press box and in distant windows.

The ball sailed low over the scrimmage line, as if some tall rival had leaped up just far enough to tag it and start it spinning end over end. But the ball went tumbling on and finally carried over the crossbar. Eight seconds remained on the clock.

Illinois players and substitutes went mad. The groans from the Ohio rooters drowned out Illinois's screams. Chic Harley crumpled to the earth beneath the goal posts and cried. Only eight seconds remained in the game. Chic knew the end had arrived. He was called on to make one more play from scrimmage for the Buckeyes. With tears streaming down his cheeks, he threw a forward pass, which fell harmlessly to the ground. Crying as though his heart would break, the little halfback made his last effort as an Ohio State football man. The field judge approached the referee and told him of the game's end. The flood of tears coursing down Chic's cheeks became a torrent just as it had five years earlier. He was not alone. Most likely weeping with him was Louise, as were many others. "But it was the sight of Harley, Ohio State's wonder boy, weeping in his first defeat and in his last game that opened the lachrymal glands of hardened rooters and soft-eyed maidens," said one postgame report. Besides most of Chic's family, others who witnessed the heartbreak included former OSU guard Charlie Seddon; baseball great Joe Tinker; former OSU Coach Jack Ryder, who guided the Buckeyes two decades earlier; top high school football players from throughout Ohio; prospective OSU freshmen; and Harry Saxbee, captain of the 1897 Buckeye football squad.

Many players from both sides were physically spent at game's end. Stinchcomb collapsed after the last play, utterly exhausted and in dire need of assistance. He was carried to the athletic house, where he responded quickly to treatment. At one point in the game, Illinois players were nursing so many injuries that the team was assessed a two-yard penalty for delay of game.

As Chic slowly walked off the field, tears streaming down, teammates surrounded him, offering words of consolation and soft pats on the back and head. Many spectators turned their faces away, for they were little better themselves at maintaining their composure. The school band struck up "Carmen Ohio," to which thousands of disappointed fans bared their heads, stood erect, and sang the words of the school anthem. Copies of the *Lantern* telling of an Ohio victory and ready for distribution immediately after the homecoming game had to be scrapped.

"Harley left Ohio Field weeping as though his heart would break," read a local newspaper. "History has a queer manner of repeating its odd pranks." Among those emptying the stands were Charles Harley and Chic's five siblings. The elder Harley had little to say when reporters asked for his reaction, except to express his regret that Ohio State did not win. He decided to stay overnight to spend the evening with his son. The others left for Chicago.

In the locker room, a distraught Chic cried for hours, despite words of encouragement from his teammates and coaches. He blamed himself for the loss, which everyone knew was utterly untrue. "It's all my fault," he said repeatedly, continuing a chant begun even before the final whistle blew.

"We couldn't get him out of the dressing room until after midnight," said Farky Farcasin, who believes that game unveiled the beginnings of what only a few short years later would prove to be Chic's total mental collapse. Added Farky, "Chic was tough as steel." In later years, Louise expressed her belief that something mysteriously wrong had overcome Chic during the final moments of the final game against Illinois. "It was like he couldn't move, like he was in a trance," said Connie Havens recalling the story her mother told her. "He just couldn't catch a pass." Louise, more than anyone, knew of the enormous stress that had been placed on Chic by thousands of Ohio State fans, by the community of Columbus, by many people throughout Ohio and the country, and by Chic himself. For nearly the last seven years, he was continually called upon to be the best, to snatch victory from defeat when those occasions arose, as they often did, and to live up to the superhuman expectations of his coach and teammates. He always came through—that is, until his very last game, leaving him in a state of tortuous mental anguish that not even Louise could bring him out of.

Finally, late Saturday evening, after nearly everyone had left and Ohio Field was nothing more than a ghost of its earlier self, Chic emerged from the locker room. A few reporters had hung around to record what Chic had to say. "I will remain in school until I graduate and preserve my amateur standing until I am through at Ohio State. If I can be used in other sports, I will be here and ready to do what I can. I may play professionally next fall but not until then."

"Ohio State had a great team on the field and it played me hard," said a relieved Illinois Coach Zuppke following the game. "Illinois in my opinion was just a little bit better, though, because of its success with the forward pass. I really felt sorry for Harley and that his record of no defeats had to be broken. He has been a wonderful player and I certainly am glad he is through annoying us."

At the homecoming dinner that Sunday night, despite the

previous day's tragic loss, the mood was upbeat, and for good reason. Ohio State's football program had just completed a run of twenty-six wins and two losses dating from 1915, not including the war year of 1918. It was an amazing record that would become even more magnificent a year later, when the team went undefeated once again. Announced at the homecoming dinner was the hope of school officials that a new 70,000-seat stadium would be ready by the 1921 season. They were a year off. Ohio Stadium opened in 1922. Already $600,000 had been raised for the project. With Chic and Wilce at the head table, President William O. Thompson predicted that in just a few years, OSU's student enrollment would reach 10,000, and OSU would be regarded as the leading university of the Midwest. He declared it imperative that the state of Ohio realize what a wonderful institution it has and give it adequate financial support. To the riotous cheers of the full house, Thompson added that colleges in the East, such as Yale and Princeton, should visit Columbus to see a real game of football.

Eleven years after he played his last game for Ohio State, local newspapers were referring to him as the greatest player ever produced in the Western Conference.

Harley Stars in the Victory of Staleys

DECATUR, Ill., Oct. 10. — Six thousand former service men and visitors attending the American Legion convention saw the Staleys football team defeat the Rock Island Independents, 14 to 10, today. Both teams relied on the open style game and the fans were treated to some beautiful forward passing from Harley to Hueine, and Conselman. In the third quarter a fizzled punt by Woenig gave the Staleys the ball on the Islander 18-yard line, from where Harley passed to Halas, who was downed on the five-yard ark. On the next two plays Huffine went over. George Trafton intercepted Conselman's pass on the Rock Island 20-yard line soon after the opening of the fourth quarter and a pass, Harley to Halas, gave the locals another marker.

Ohio State Journal carries story in October 11, 1921 issue that tells of Chic's early success as a pro player.

Near the end of the 1921 season when the Decatur/ Chicago Staleys won the professional football title, The Chicago Tribune carried a story declaring the popularity of pro football. During Chic's single season of professional ball, the Staleys attracted large crowds nearly filling Cubs Park on several occasions.

PRO FOOTBALL MAKES BIG HIT IN CHICAGO

BY HARRY NEILY.

Professional football is here to stay. That fact has been demonstrated in Chicago during the last few weeks, when really worth-while attractions were presented for the entertainment of the common and ordinary variety of fanatic.

A few years back when some daring promoters leased the Cubs' park and hired ex-collegiate stars, the recognized authorities of football let loose the loud hoot. Motions were passed by the Big Ten conference that officials who judged plays in unauthorized games (the conference being the only "authorized" brand that the conference recognized) could not do business with the conference. Also a resolution was adopted that former college stars who played the pro brand must return their letters, earned honestly in competition for their alma mater.

Just how a man could value a letter ahead of $250 or $300 a week was not apparent, but the faculty commit-

CHAPTER 9

Halas, Dutch, and the Staleys

The agony Chic felt in late November slowly faded as the months drifted by. Outwardly, he seemed to rebound. Inwardly, there was an emptiness. The tears that cascaded down his face in the closing seconds of his last game of 1919 flowed not just because his team had lost for the first time in three years. To Chic, it was a bitter end to one of the most important times of his life, his college playing career. True to his nature, he blamed himself for the loss to Illinois—a preposterous notion, of course, but one he nevertheless believed and expressed.

What lay ahead for him was uncertain. A professional career in football or baseball? A sales job? Maybe working with his father as a Linotype operator? Chic had little taste for playing sports for money, especially football, as did many athletic giants of that period. His aversion came not only from personal principles, but from loyalty to his mentor, Coach Wilce. With that in mind, Chic decided to stay in school, get his degree, and, if given the opportunity, stay connected with the football program as an assistant coach under Wilce. That way he would be close to the things that were dearest to him. He remained enrolled in the College of Commerce and Journalism, where he took mainly business-related courses. His expenses for that school year totaled $595,

149

which included $288 for board at $8 a week for thirty-six weeks. His room rate was $15 per month.

In his three and a half years at Ohio State, Chic always struggled to keep up his grades. After the disastrous school year of 1915-16, when he failed nearly everything, he made mostly passing grades. He earned a "good" grade in economics, his final course at Ohio State. In all, Chic earned a total of forty-eight credit hours—not nearly enough to graduate.

Ohio State's 1920 football season was as grand as ever, even without Chic in the lineup. He remained connected, however, as an assistant coach. As in 1916 and '17, the team went undefeated and won the Western Conference title with a perfect 7 and 0 record, the culmination of one of the greatest periods of football for any major college ever. In six short years, Ohio State football had emerged from near total obscurity to become one of the nation's true powerhouse programs. By winning its last three games of 1915 and going undefeated in 1916 (7 and 0) and 1917 (8 and 0), the Buckeyes won eighteen and lost none. Add to that the seasons of 1919 (6 and 1) and 1920 (7 and 0)—leaving out the war year of 1918—and the Buckeyes' amazing record through 1920 was 31 and 1, with 1 tie, the 0-0 exhibition game against Auburn.

In the fall of 1920, with Chic now on the sidelines, his former backfield running mate and good friend Pete Stinchcomb was the star of the squad, earning All-American honors. For the first time ever, the Buckeyes were invited to play in the Rose Bowl on January 1, 1921. Chic would accompany the team on its journey by steam train from Columbus to Pasadena where they would meet the University of California.

In the weeks leading up to the trip, Harley stayed busy with his studies the best he could. In sports, he began focusing more on basketball, a game he enjoyed and competed in during high school and in intramurals at Ohio State. "Chic's debut on the basketball floor was hailed with delight, although he had but little tested experience at the court game. He soon proved his athletic versatility by winning a regular berth on the five," reported the

Makio in late 1920. "Harley proved himself a whiz at running guard and did much to work the ball into enemy territory at opportune moments."

Harley's skill as a running guard and leader that season earned him his fourth varsity letter in sports. He had already lettered in football, baseball, and track, making him the first four-letter-man in school history, a distinction only a few attain.

Whenever an invitation arrived to play in a local sporting event, Chic could not resist. He even agreed to participate in a play to help raise money for Ohio State's Scarlet Mask Society, which was staging *Oh My! Omar*, on the evening of Saturday, February 5, 1921, in Memorial Hall. Scarlet Mask was a popular student organization that staged campus theatrical productions. Chic and Pete were the headliners of a cast that included sixty-eight men. Their specific roles are unknown, and it is not certain that they even performed. His and Pete's names generated enough interest from Ohio State faithful to pack the hall. Ticket prices ranged from 75 cents to $1.50.

As the westbound special train slowly chugged out of Union Station toward Pasadena promptly at 9 A.M. on December 18, 1920, the send-off was thunderous. The school band played "Across the Field" over and over again. Thousands of exuberant well-wishers, mostly students, crowded onto the platforms next to the dark brown Pullmans. Impossible to ignore was the occasional sound of steam hissing from the underbellies of the long cars. Just a few days earlier, Gov. James Cox had predicted, "It's going to be the biggest going away party in the history of Ohio State. Be there!"

Word had circulated that the Rose Bowl-bound team would be traveling through sleepy towns and a few major cities that stretched across Indiana, Illinois, Kansas, and other prairie states. Harley and other big names, such as *Tribune* columnist Eckersall, would be on the train. While fans along the 2,500-mile route were curious to see the team, they were specially interested in catching a glimpse of the greatest name in football, Chic Harley. Bundled up from head to toe against the harsh winter, people waited all

151

along the way, straining their necks to see Chic and the Buckeyes as they passed by and sometimes stopped to stretch their legs as the train took on new passengers.

Less than a week earlier, Chic's continued interest in competing in the sport he loved took him to Neil Park in Columbus to play in a charity football game against the tough Columbus Panhandles pro team. Chic had been named captain of a squad comprised of collegiate football stars. The professional Panhandles consisted of hard-nosed area all-stars coached by Lee Snoot. Chic prepared for the game by scrimmaging with Red Trautman's Ohio State basketball team, and before that, against the Buckeye football team.

The next day, the *Dispatch*'s popular "Sports Mirror" column, whose byline was "Ham," reported that thousands had gathered primarily to see Chic play and to recall the "delightful championship days." Ham wrote:

We never realized just how great a hero this chap is with the Columbus public until Saturday afternoon. Everyone was there to cheer him. If by chance a Panhandle tackler handled Chic a bit rough, a roar of protest went up from the spectators. Then, just to make the picture complete, after the victory had been earned and Harley was walking off the field with a dirt-streaked face, covering somewhat the old smile, it was in a living setting of at least 100 kiddies who gathered about him. They were admiring their hero. These kiddies, for the most part, had crept through the chinks in the fence, too, to get in and were urchins of the shop district. But they knew Harley, and they were around him because he was their hero. Yes, we know what Harley means to Ohio State and Columbus football. The larger meaning came when we saw him at Neil Park Saturday afternoon under odd circumstances. No college cheers. No acrobatic cheerleaders. No waving of college banners. But just folks and more folks who were for him because he was Harley.

The Harley-led collegiate stars beat the Panhandles 9-0. Chic kicked a field goal, and Howard Yerges, Chic's old high school rival and college teammate, scored the lone touchdown.

Leading up to the Rose Bowl game, Chic helped the Buckeyes prepare by playing the role of the California halfback/quarterback to help Wilce plot defensive strategies. Despite everyone's best efforts, California was too strong and blasted Ohio State, 28-0. The defeat was disappointing but not devastating. The trip to Southern California, with its warm, Pacific breezes and swaying palm trees, was a break from the frigid temperatures of central Ohio. The team did its best. Victory wasn't meant to be that day.

Less than two weeks later at the annual Columbus Press Smoker, a banquet for local notables to gather and chat about local affairs, especially sports, the main topic of discussion was the Rose Bowl loss. Every seat at every table was taken. Attending as honored guests were Harley, Wilce, and most of the Buckeye team, and at one point Chic was introduced, to great ovation.

"Mr. Harley," asked Ohio Lt. Gov. Clarence Brown, "what is your alibi for that defeat of Ohio State New Year's Day?" Chic, embarrassed, didn't quite know what to say. The question was repeated. Then he rose to his feet. "Well, if you really want to know," declared Harley, speaking out for what seemed to some like the first time in his life, "I'll tell you. I think it was because California wouldn't let me play." The surprised crowd roared and yelled its approval. Not only had Chic spoken, but his words expressed an unexpected confidence in himself—something few people had ever heard him do.

Chic's modesty was well-known. In "His Niche Is Secure; Vale Harley" in *Makio*, Fritz Holtkamp wrote: "It is only fair to say that Harley gave Ohio State her place in the sun. Chic Harley, Ohio State's and probably the nation's greatest football player, was as wonderful in defeat as he has been after his many victories. The only difference was that in defeat, he took all the blame for the loss while in victory, all his praise was for the other man. There's Chic Harley's measure."

Holtkamp went on to express the debt of gratitude the Ohio State University owes to this clean, modest, unassuming athlete, who has done more to put the university to the front in the college world than any one individual whose name appears on its records. With the good of his alma mater at heart, this sterling warrior of the gridiron, diamond, and track has never wavered in supporting clean athletics and good sportsmanship. He has always been wonderful in defeat, as in victory. Big as he may be as an athlete, still bigger he is as a true supporter of the Scarlet and Gray and that for which it stands, and when the last name is carved in Ohio State's hall of fame, near the top will be found the name of Chic Harley.

Early in 1921, a report surfaced that Pete Stinchcomb would be playing in a game with the Logan Square football team—the Logan Square Fairies—in late January. Logan Square, a bustling neighborhood on Chicago's northwest side, was the home of the Harley family (and earlier the Rockne clan—it was where Knute learned to play football before moving to South Bend, Indiana, and the University of Notre Dame), and the man who recruited Stinchcomb for that contest was Chic's brother Bill. When a newspaper reporter pressed Stinchcomb about playing, Pete said he had decided not to pursue the matter. There was no mention of whether Chic had been invited to play or had had a role in trying to involve Pete. The article, however, was a foreshadowing of things to come.

Bill Harley, age thirty-three, was an aggressive, outgoing sports promoter and a good baseball player, but not nearly as skilled an athlete as his younger brother. Bill was good at the business side of athletics and organized and managed various enterprises, including the semipro Logan Square team. In later years, he managed Mills Stadium in the Logan Square neighborhood. Bill's interest in recruiting Pete to play at least one game points to his strong business sense; attracting a star for a game would trigger interest and boost gate receipts. The biggest prize, however, was not Pete, but Chic. If Pete agreed to play, could Chic be persuaded too?

It was no secret that Chic was no fan of professional football. Despite his coolness on the gridiron and baseball diamond, away from athletics Chic was a worrier. When the subject of turning pro came up, which it undoubtedly did on several occasions, he agonized over how it would affect his reputation and what other people would think, especially Wilce. Going pro might also jeopardize his membership in Phi Gamma Delta fraternity, something he dearly prized.

In those days, professional football was thought to attract money mongers interested first and foremost in the buck. Bill Harley was a businessman who wanted to make money. Chic's interest in money was minimal. Among the strongest critics of professional football were Wilce, Amos Alonzo Stagg of the University of Chicago, Rockne of Notre Dame, and Fielding Yost of Michigan. In 1921, when 100 of the nation's top coaches formed the American Football Coaches Association, one of the first matters they took up was the emergence of professional football, which they denounced as "detrimental to the best interests of American football and American youth." A motion to adopt that stance was approved unanimously. But by then, pro football had taken root, and there was no stopping its growing popularity.

Even Decatur, in downstate Illinois, had a pro football team, a club established by the A. E. Staley Manufacturing Company. In early 1920, the company was looking for a new and unique way to promote its cornstarch products. The nation's economy was robust. The company was making money. It already had a base-ball team. *Why not add a football team comprised of some of the most talented ex-college stars?* thought Staley's general manager, George Chamberlain. It could make some money for the firm and attract a strong following throughout the Midwest. The open land next to the plant in Decatur would be the practice and playing field. Company owner Augustus Staley agreed with Chamberlain and gave him the green light.

To manage the team, the company hired George Halas, who later recruited his University of Illinois teammate Dutch Sternaman. Earlier, Halas had been playing for the minor league baseball club in St. Paul, Minnesota, which won the American Association championship in 1919. *Why not continue playing into the 1920 season?* thought Halas. He was still single and twenty-five years old. His needs were minimal. Here was a chance to play with a championship team even if it wasn't in the majors.

As he was preparing to report to baseball training camp in 1920, Halas received a letter from Chamberlain asking to meet at the La Salle Hotel in downtown Chicago. Chamberlain had heard of Halas's athletic abilities, organizational skills, and college degree in civil engineering. Would Halas join the Staley Company to learn the business and play baseball for the company team? A few years earlier, Chamberlain had signed Joe McGinnity, a future Hall of Fame pitcher with the New York Giants, to manage the team. To the ambitious Halas, it sounded like a good opportunity. That summer he played baseball and learned the cornstarch business in Decatur. He was elected team captain and, because he had played Illinois varsity football for three years, was soon asked to manage the football squad that Chamberlain wanted to develop.

With the company's urging and approval, Halas and Ralph Lanum, another ex-Illini player, visited a number of Western Conference universities, recruiting standout football players who were willing to work in the Staley plant during the mornings and early afternoons and practice and compete for the Staley football team in late afternoons and Sundays. What they put together was a very good football squad of college stars, including Sternaman. In 1920, the Staleys chalked up a record of 9 and 2. Could 1921 be even better? Could the Staleys win the league championship? Could money be made? A top-notch player or two might put them over the top.

With Halas and now also Sternaman as managers, they would take the team north to play most of the games in Chicago, which had a potentially huge fan base and opportunity to make money. The decision to move north was part of a deal the Staley company was implementing that would lead them out of the football business due to tough economic times. To accommodate all the fans Halas and Sternaman hoped to attract once the move was made, they became involved with William Veeck, president of the Chicago Cubs baseball team, to let the Staleys use Cubs Park starting around mid-October. In exchange for use of the park, Veeck and the Cubs would be paid a percentage of the gate receipts. At that time, Cubs Park could seat 14,000.

Halas and Sternaman knew they also needed a big drawing card if they were to succeed at professional football. Someone like Chic Harley, who by early summer 1921 was no longer in college. No one, not even Chic, knew whether he would ever return to Ohio State as either student, coach, or just plain resident. The timing was perfect for Halas and Sternaman to strike, and they found a willing partner in Bill Harley, who was eager to be involved in the running of a professional football team. All he had to do was convince his brother—the era's most famous and gifted football player—to go along.

Safely back in Chicago and away from the pressures of making grades and playing high-stakes sports, a more laid-back, unstructured, and uncertain way of life seemed to lie before Chic. He enjoyed being at home with his family. He relished the idea of playing baseball in Logan Square. Like football, baseball and Chic were inseparable. Mills Stadium was an oasis for him, and his favorite pasture in that serene, green setting was right field. There, Chic could find momentary peace, do as he pleased, and settle in a place where his tremendous speed, strength, and coordination could blossom to its fullest.

The semiprofessional Logan Square baseball team consisted of Chicago athletes that included Bill Harley and, in earlier years, George Halas. For a while, Chic, Bill, and George were outfielders, with a genuine liking for each other. The Harleys had known the lanky, square-jawed Halas since 1914, and they respected his athleticism in baseball, football, and basketball. In 1918, he was good enough to attract the attention of scouts from the New York Yankees. He was even on the parent club's roster for about half a season that year. He was a good fielder, ran well, and possessed good baseball sense. He just couldn't hit major league pitching, especially sharp-breaking curve balls. An injury during that 1918 season sent Halas shuffling off to the minor leagues. He liked to tell a story about being replaced in the outfield by Babe Ruth. But Ruth didn't join the Yankees until after the 1919 season when his contract to play was sold by the Boston Red Sox.

Chic regularly performed very well for Logan Square. His blazing speed enabled him to steal bases with ease and to lope around the outfield chasing down line drives with little trouble. Offers from professional baseball clubs, such as the Chicago White Sox, Chicago Cubs, and St. Louis Browns, landed in Chic's lap. Some scouts thought so highly of his abilities that they concluded he needed no seasoning in the minor leagues. He was good enough to play in the "bigs." Self-conscious and with a huge inferiority complex, Chic never pursued a professional baseball career. He was comfortable playing for Logan Square with his family nearby. Big-league life, away from home and most of his friends, seemed too complicated and stressful.

One evening in the spring of 1921, the telephone rang at Bill Harley's home at 2448 N. Sawyer Avenue. It was George Halas. "I have a proposition for you, Bill," said Halas, and he asked if he could come over to talk. Within an hour, Halas, sitting on the edge of a chair in Bill Harley's parlor, explained that he recently had leased Cubs Park for the 1921 football season of the Decatur Staleys, the team he played end for and managed. He wanted Bill and Chic to join them. The idea was to play the season's first two games in Decatur and then move the team north to Chicago. "How about it?" asked Halas.

Chicago, compared with Decatur and most other towns where professional football was staged in those years, was the big time. It offered opportunity to draw large crowds willing to pay good money to see some of the best football players in the country. Decatur, stuck in a vast stretch of cornfields some 150 miles south of Chicago, was too small. There simply weren't enough fans to support a profitable professional football operation, especially one led by the ambitious Halas. He knew that Chicago and Cubs Park were major components of success.

An intrigued and curious Bill Harley thought for a few seconds and then responded, "I'll talk it over with Chic."

Halas and Sternaman were well aware of the Harley magic and remembered vividly the 1916 Illinois-Ohio game, which Chic single-handedly won in the last seconds. Presumably, his legendary skills on the football field had not diminished. He was strong and physically in the prime of his life. People loved his quiet, modest personality and good looks. He was a clean competitor, and even his fiercest opponents on the football field had strong regard for him. Chic and his family lived in Chicago only about two miles from Cubs Park, where the Staleys would practice and play. The Staleys needed a star to attract fans and help lead the team. Chic Harley would be perfect. While there were great names around who had drawing power, like Jim Thorpe and Pudge Heffelfinger, they were either too old or committed to other teams. To get Chic, Halas and Sternaman knew they had to go through Bill. They were willing to pay Chic a huge salary (rumors say anywhere from $300 to $1,000 per game), and to give Chic and Bill a combined one-half share in the team's profits.

Bill was excited about Halas's offer. The proposition was a golden opportunity to work in sports, be part of a new professional football league, and even make some money. Convincing Chic, Bill knew, would not be easy. It wasn't that Chic had soured on playing competitive football again. He loved the game, the roar of the crowds, the thrill of running, scoring, and passing, and the sense of accomplishment it gave him. The problem was that with the formation of this new league, participants competed not out of loyalty for a school, but mainly for money. Something's not right with that, Chic felt.

Bill knew that Halas and Sternaman first and foremost needed Chic to make their dreams come true. If Chic agreed to play for the Staleys, where would Bill fit in? If his powers of persuasion were strong enough to convince his brother to go professional, might there be others he could recruit and bring to the table, strengthening his relationship with Sternaman and Halas? Chic's college teammates Pete Stinchcomb and John "Tarzan" Taylor might be available. If Bill could convince all three to join the Staleys, he could single-handedly deliver to Halas and Sternaman the nucleus of what could become the finest team in the league. But to get Pete and Tarzan, convincing Chic was an absolute necessity.

While it took some doing, Chic agreed to meet in Decatur with Bill, George, and Dutch to discuss Chic's turning pro.

July 18, 1921, was a hot, humid day. Downstate Illinois in July and August can get extremely uncomfortable; the heat is stifling, and days seem endless. That sultry afternoon, Halas, Sternaman, Bill Harley, and an insecure, unsure Chic sat down in Halas's room at the Blackwood Hotel, which served as Staley team headquarters during the playing season. Once the four got settled, the conversation quickly turned to the upcoming 1921 season and whether or not Chic would play.

"Chic was undecided if he wanted to play pro football," said Bill Harley three years later in recounting that day. "Sternaman and George both went after him pretty strong." Chic worried whether turning professional would hurt his standing in his fraternity and even his ability to get a job in future years. Halas and Sternaman, taking turns, pressed Chic harder and harder. The Illini grads explained that they played for paychecks the previous season. "We had no problem with it, and neither would you," they asserted. "Nothing wrong with earning a living playing sports," they reasoned. Halas and Dutch were not the only aggressors in trying to convince Chic to sign. Brother Bill pressed him, too.

Four different drafts of the agreement were written before everyone signed, including an exhausted and worried Chic.

"Finally, a worn-out and unsure Chic agreed to sign the contract with the understanding by everyone involved that once they arrived in Chicago, a new, more formal contract would be drawn up," Bill later explained. "It was drawn up hastily, and we got Chic to sign it before Chic had a chance to change his mind." Halas and Sternaman had their star player and, they believed, their ticket to financial and competitive salvation. They also had two more equal partners. Bill had his entrance onto the stage of big-time professional sports. Chic wasn't sure what he had done other than to sign his name to a piece of paper that committed him to playing professional football, a very risky proposition at best.

The written agreement Chic, Bill, Halas, and Sternaman signed stated that the four of them would be partners in running the Staley football team and would share in the profits and losses. Chamberlain and Augustus Staley had determined earlier that, because of an economic downslide that began in early 1921, the company could no longer finance and field a professional football team. It couldn't afford to keep nineteen men on the payroll who didn't produce full time in the cornstarch business. Their dream of a football team traveling throughout the Midwest and perhaps someday the country, promoting the company, was nearing an end. For 1921, they agreed, Halas would run the program as if it was his own, collecting any profits. They would also give Halas $5,000 for the season, much of which was for players' salaries. In exchange, the team would retain the name Staleys for that season so the company could benefit from publicity.

With Chic on board, Stinchcomb and Taylor followed a few weeks later. Bill Harley became the first professional football agent by negotiating contracts on behalf of the three players. The Staleys now had what could become the best professional football team around by signing for the 1921 season two of the country's best halfbacks to go with Dutch at fullback. At right halfback, Chic would be used to not only run, but also pass when the opportunity arose. He also would handle much of the punting and kicking duties. When Stinchcomb was called upon, Chic, an expert blocker, would be put in that role, and vice versa. Taylor would serve as an anchor of the offensive line.

A few weeks later in the lobby of the Planters Hotel in Chicago, an impromptu press conference was held to publicize the signing of Chic, Pete, and Tarzan. The Decatur *Review* reported on August 16, 1921, that Chic had turned down a number of $5,000 offers to coach that coming fall:

Chic is the idol of the Buckeye state and will prove to be one of the greatest drawing cards in the pro game this season. While the locals had a wonderful eleven last year, close followers of the game saw a great weakness in the fact they did not have a man who could combine the

*passing and kicking. Coach Halas was forced to bring back a different
man for the passing and the same for the kicking which was a great
disadvantage to the locals. [It was an era when players played the full 60
minutes of a game.] With Harley, it will be eliminated this season.*

At age 27, Chic clearly was having more and more difficulty
making important decisions. Although he had attended Ohio
State for more than five years, excluding his year in the military,
he had not been able to graduate. In the summer of 1921, it was
obvious that he would never return to Columbus as a student or
a coach. He had little interest in a job, despite numerous attractive offers. He declined the coaching job at Kansas, citing his
need to study for an exam. He did not act on similar offers from
the University of Tennessee and DePauw University or sign a
contract to play professional baseball. He failed to pursue an offer
from Mooseheart Vocational School in the far western suburbs
of Chicago to coach football, basketball, baseball, and track for
the hefty annual salary of $4,000. Making decisions was, for Chic,
becoming increasingly difficult. No matter what he did, he would
disappoint someone, and he couldn't bear that. Only the hard sell
of Sternaman and Halas coupled with the presence of his older
brother finally broke Chic to reluctantly agree to play pro football.
Left alone, he never would have taken the plunge.

With Chic Harley in the fold, Halas, Sternaman, and Bill
Harley went to work to stir up interest and gate receipts. Bill's job
was primarily to handle most of the administrative duties of the
club, such as accounting and writing promotion for Decatur and
Chicago newspapers. In those days, few newspapers assigned
reporters to cover pro football because the spectacle was
regarded as unlikely to succeed in the long run. Bill, George, and
Dutch had to whip up excitement by not only signing players,
but begging newspapers to publish their articles about the team
and upcoming games. There were no sports radio broadcasts.
Television broadcasts were decades away.

By the time of the season's first game, in Decatur on
Sunday, October 2, all the pieces were in place. The partners

had designed posters and plastered them around town. The Staley newsletter heralded the recruitment of Chic as "the landing of the biggest fish in football." A crowd of 8,000 was expected for the game against the Waukegan American Legion team, thanks to a huge Legion convention in Decatur that weekend. The Staleys won 35-0. Chic was the hero, leading the team with his "brilliant forward passing attack" to the team's right end, Halas, and All-American left end Guy Chamberlin. Chic and Ken Huffine did much of the running, and Sternaman, the place kicking. Chic threw two touchdown passes, kicked an extra point, and ran for another TD.

The next game, against the Rock Island Independents, would be the last contest the team would ever play in Decatur. "Harley Stars in the Victory of Staleys," shouted the Chicago *Tribune*. Harley treated the 6,000 fans to beautiful passing, including a TD toss to Halas after Notre Dame graduate George Trafton intercepted a Rock Island pass, for a 14-10 win.

The Staleys played in Chicago for the first time on October 16 in a game against the Rochester (New York) Jeffersons. By now, the Starchmakers (so nicknamed) were becoming known throughout the country. Winning the Western professional football title the previous year and the addition of Harley, Stinchcomb, and Taylor attracted much acclaim. One newspaper syndicate in October distributed a lengthy story about the team to its 450 clients in every corner of the country. Not only were Chicago, Decatur, and other mostly Midwestern towns being introduced to a new and exciting brand of football on Sunday afternoons, but so was the rest of America. The signing of Chic Harley was proving to be a gold mine not only for the Staley partners, but also for the new business of professional football.

A total of 7,239 fans paid to watch the Staleys take on the Jeffersons at Cubs Park, later named Wrigley Field. In a thrilling game, the two teams battled to the bitter end, with the Staleys rallying to win 16-13. The Staleys started the game poorly, fumbling numerous times. Listed as the starting right halfback,

Chic did much of the team's punting, but one newspaper account said he did not play up to standard. Nowhere is he credited with contributing to the scoring. Ken Huffine played a strong role at fullback and throwing the ball, while Sternaman did most of the place kicking.

A week later, on October 23, the Dayton Triangles came to Chicago. Pregame publicity, most likely written by either Halas or Bill Harley, declared that the two Buckeyes, Harley at right half and Stinchcomb at quarterback, would probably make the difference in the battle. Chic ran well, "clicking off several good gains around the ends while carrying the ball in a position to pass." The Staleys won 7-0, with the one touchdown coming when Sternaman passed to Halas. The next day, the Columbus *Citizen* said Harley repeatedly engaged in "clever passing" and that on one play he ran for forty yards to the Triangle ten-yard line.

The Staleys' fifth game, against the Detroit Tigers on November 6 in Chicago, proved to be a pivotal event in Chic's life. In it he suffered the worst injury of his football career, one that later may have contributed to other major medical problems. Rarely injured, Chic might hurt a finger but say little or nothing about it; in the 1917 exhibition game against Auburn, an opposing player wearing cleats had stepped on his hand and smashed it. He accepted pain and played in such a controlled way that he never wasted energy or exhibited signs of exhaustion. To some, he appeared lazy until the moment he was handed the ball. Then, all hell broke loose.

But on that Sunday in Cubs Park, a jolt from one or more Tiger tacklers late in the game resulted in three broken ribs, sending Chic to the sidelines in pain and eventually to bed. More significantly, it was what family members later identified as the beginning of Chic's mental decline. That day more than 100 Buckeye fans had decided to stay over from the previous day's game against the University of Chicago. Approximately 6,500 fans huddled in Cubs Park that Sunday, the same day it was announced that Chic, Taylor, and Stinchcomb would play in a charity game on November 26 in Columbus. It would be the last time Ohio Field would host a football contest because a new stadium would be ready for the 1922 season.

In the game against the Tigers, the Staleys won easily 20-9. Exactly what led to Chic's injury is unclear. Years later, when Chic was suffering terribly and family members were at their wit's end, doctors were told that Chic's injuries that day were not accidental. Bill, in particular, was vocal in asserting that Chic suffered many injuries that year, but the injuries in the Tigers game were caused by jealous teammates who deliberately failed to block for his brother, resulting in his frequently being gang-tackled behind the line of scrimmage. At the root of the jealousy, Bill believed, was the tremendous publicity Chic attracted and his high salary. The salary was none of Chic's doing, but rather the work of the other three Staleys managers, who had hammered away at him to sign in Decatur.

Chic's injury left him bedridden for nearly three weeks. The Staleys continued their regular schedule of games, barely eking out a win over Rock Island, 3-0, on November 13 in Chicago, and then defeating Jim Thorpe's Cleveland Tigers 22-7 on November 20. The weather was described as "unfavorable" with the field snow-covered.

The famed and aging Thorpe was not in the lineup because of injuries. A pregame newspaper headline read: "Thorpe Injuns After Scalp of Staleys." Ten thousand fans, anxious to see the great Olympian athlete in action, packed into Cubs Park. Stinchcomb starred for the Staleys, galloping for eighty-five- and thirty-yard touchdowns. Harley did not play. Three days later, an analysis concluded that pro football in Chicago was a "big hit." Many college coaches and players, however, were still opposed and said pro players who had earned school letters should be forced to return them—an excruciating thought to the immensely sensitive Chic.

"The spectators were rewarded with a sharp, snappy, interesting contest," wrote *Tribune* sports reporter Harry Neily. Having observed University of Illinois grads filing into Cubs Park, most of who were men between the ages of eighteen and twenty-six, Neily wrote:

There is a reason for all of this. Football has an urge, but it's almost impossible for the common folks to obtain tickets for the big college games. The ducats are issued first to the alumni and the undergraduates and the public gets the leavings. Hence, the ordinary fan is left out in the cold. If he has read the newspapers and has accumulated a thirst for football he can quench the same only on the professional field. The professionals, by the way, play a wonderful brand of football. They are the pick of the universities.

Despite the gut-wrenching pain, Chic joined Pete, Tarzan, and a group of about twenty-five of the greatest players in American football on Saturday, November 26, in a game to benefit the Family Service Society of Columbus. The two teams were named the Starbucks, a squad comprised of past Ohio State greats, with Chic as captain, and the Rainbows, great former players from other colleges throughout the country. In uniform for the Rainbows were Thorpe, halfback Eddie Casey of Harvard, Bobby Fletcher of Illinois, and Pudge Heffelfinger, the fifty-three-year-old former star for Yale. Thorpe, in the twilight of his career, could not play due to injuries. He nevertheless thrilled the crowd of 5,000 with an exhibition of his punting skills, with one traveling seventy-five yards. Weather conditions were miserable, with rain and a soaked field. Heffelfinger had a great time, playing the entire contest. He wouldn't wear one of the leather helmets, saying players didn't wear head protection when he competed thirty years earlier, so he didn't feel he needed to start now.

Chic wore jersey number 29 as well as protection for his sensitive ribs, probably a steel plate. With him were former teammates and close friends Iolas Huffman, Pete, Tarzan, Shifty Bolen, Howard Courtney, Clarence MacDonald, and others.

"There is no apparent change in Harley's appearance; in fact, he stands in the backfield with his hands on his hips, unexcitable-like as in Western Conference days," said one newspaper account. The story referred to the cracked ribs that had kept him from playing football for the last two weeks. Bobby Fletcher was asked whether he still had the shoe he used in the November 22, 1919, game to kick the field goal that beat the Buckeyes. He replied that he still has it and had received offers of $1,000 to buy it. "It would take more than money to buy it," he said cheerfully.

Chic played fairly well, although it was obvious he was still hurting and could not go all out. He punted five times, averaging thirty-eight yards per kick. He completed one pass and rushed several times, including one dash for twelve yards. The Rainbows won 16-0. At a banquet after the game, Chic was asked to stand up and speak, with chairman John Vorys, later elected to Congress, joking that Harley had ninety minutes to talk. "Boys, I'm glad to be here, and I'll be back next year," was all Chic could muster.

"That was the long-winded speech of the man who put Ohio State on the map. Chic is still as bashful as he was when drilling in the Army," a newspaper reported the next day.

Two days before the Rainbows-Starbucks charity game, the Staleys lost its first contest of the season, against the Buffalo All Americans, 7-6. The Thanksgiving Day defeat resulted when Sternaman failed to click on an extra point. A few days later, on Sunday, November 27, the Staleys rebounded, defeating Curley Lambeau and the Green Bay Packers 20-0 in Chicago. Pete and Dutch started at the two halfback slots. Chic played for a few minutes, substituting for Stinchcomb. A pregame article said, "All of Green Bay is excited about the affair, and a big band will accompany 3,000 enthusiasts."

With an 8 and 1 record, the next battle on the Staleys schedule was being hailed as the game that would determine the professional football championship. It was a return match with Buffalo, again at Cubs Park. The Roaring '20s were just beginning to roar, with one of the hot spots of Chicago being the swanky LaSalle, where room rates ranged form $3.50 per night to $10. A classy Stevens-Duryea automobile could be purchased for $6,800, and silent screen star Fatty Arbuckle was making headlines being accused of attacking a woman who later died. At the same time, more and more people were becoming interested in sports, and this new brand of football for pay was gaining increased attention. Pro football fans were turning up the noise for an intracity showdown between the Staleys and the Chicago Cardinals, whose big star was Northwestern grad Paddy Driscoll, whom Chic left in the dust five years earlier. But the first order of business was to avenge the one-point loss to Buffalo. A win for the Staleys would mean the title. On Sunday, December 4, the air was cold, and the skies, overcast. Winds from Lake Michigan only five blocks away sliced through the wool jackets of spectators. While each team had lost only once so far, Buffalo had tied twice. Chic, his ribs still raw, suited up. His orange and blue uniform included a steel plate snuggly in place under his jersey. Cubs Park was nearly filled to capacity with 12,000 fans. The Staleys won 10-7. The star was Guy Chamberlin, who intercepted a Buffalo pass early in the game and raced ninety yards for a touchdown. Sternaman added a field goal.

The game marked a turning point in Chic's life, not only as a football player, but also as a person. Still hurting from the physical beating he had taken several weeks earlier, his contribution for most of the contest was as a substitute. As later learned, Bill Harley believed that teammates on the Staleys' offensive line, with not only the blessing, but the direction of Halas and Sternaman, had given way to opposing tacklers to allow Harley to be dumped, demoralized, and injured. At the time, Bill said nothing. Even if Chic was suspicious, it would have been totally against his nature to say anything. The final humiliation in both Bill's and Chic's minds came when Chic was directed to enter the game as a substitute. As recounted a year later and in subsequent family interviews, during the season's biggest game and with a near capacity crowd looking on, Chic was sent in to relieve a player. He was in the game only a short time when he was sent to the sidelines. A few minutes later, Chic was told to return to the team, then on the field in a huddle. This time, the player he was sent in to relieve refused to leave the field. No one else in the lineup sided with Chic. He was forced to return to the bench enormously embarrassed. The name of the Staley who refused to leave the huddle is not known.

Family members later recalled that following the humiliating episode, Chic questioned why his teammates had treated him that way. Why had he been shamed in such a manner? A week later, speaking to Bill on a street corner in downtown Chicago, Chic asked what he had done to the other players for them to embarrass him the way they had. He felt as if the Staleys were against him. The matter would not leave his mind. It haunted him, and he could not get over it. "From that time on, Chic was never himself. He seemed to crawl into a shell," said family members in later years. No hard evidence exists that some Staley players conspired to abuse Chic physically and mentally. All that remain are opinions expressed to physicians years later. Perhaps, as they said, Staley players were jealous of Chic's popularity and high salary, just as some in the army had resented him in 1919. Or perhaps Halas and Sternaman saw the team becoming so popular that they didn't want to share future profits with Bill and Chic Harley.

Within a month of the Buffalo game, Chic was so distraught that he was admitted to a sanitarium in Columbus for treatment and diagnosis. Amazingly, between the Buffalo contest and his admission to the sanitarium, he continued to play for the Staleys. The regular season finale pitted the Starchmakers against the Canton Bulldogs at Cubs Park. In spite of cold rain and a muddy field, coaches for both teams decided to play the contest rather than disappoint the large crowd of 10,000. Chic, substituting for Stinchcomb at quarterback, tossed a forty-yard touchdown strike to Guy Chamberlin. Both Pete and Chic performed the punting chores well. Chic even did some of the running in the 10-0 win over Canton.

With the regular season now over, one final long-awaited contest was agreed upon. The Staleys and Cardinals would clash in a bragging rights game at Cubs Park on Sunday, December 18. Four days earlier, an indoor football game between the Canton Bulldogs and the Morris Supremes was held at the indoor

International Amphitheater. It was billed as "Archlight Football." The field measured the regulation forty yards wide, but was five yards short of one hundred yards long. Canton won 19-0. Guy Chamberlin, the talented Staley end, announced a day later that he had signed to play for Canton and would leave the Staleys.

A record crowd was expected for the city title bout. A year earlier, they had split two games. Two contests that had been scheduled earlier for 1921 had been canceled because of weather. A final game against the Cardinals would earn Halas, Sternaman, and the Harleys a big payout, they hoped. Chic and Pete would share right halfback duties.

Poor weather with frigid temperatures that hovered around zero produced a disappointing crowd of only 3,000. There was a notable lack of enthusiasm not only from the fans, but also from the two teams. They seemed to run out of gas. The game ended in a 0-0 tie. One of the few mentions of Harley was his third-quarter pass completion to Stinchcomb that gave the Staleys their best scoring opportunity. They failed to connect and gave up the ball on downs.

After that, all talk of scheduling another game or two to improve the fan base and ticket sales ceased. Offers to play were turned down. The Staley players had had enough football for the season.

It was the last organized football game in Chic Harley's life. He played in a few exhibition games at Ohio State in the early 1920s, but for all practical purposes, his time as a football player was over. The Staleys ran up a record of 9, 1, and 1 in 1921 in a thirteen-team league. It completed the circle of Chic's career, in which he lost only three times in high school, once in college, and once professionally. By attracting fans and income, Chic had made a huge contribution to the Staleys and set the stage for professional football not only in Chicago, but the country. In about a month, the Staleys would change its name to the Chicago Bears in what Bill Harley later asserted was a secret coup by Halas and Sternaman to dump their two other partners from the club. In Chic's nine games in 1921, he rushed seventeen times for eighty-five yards, or an average of five yards per run; ran for the third-highest yards on the team behind Stinchcomb and Sternaman; completed eight of thirteen passes for 120 yards, or 9.23 yards per completion; achieved a team best pass rating of 131.4; and averaged thirty-seven yards per punt, a team high.

For one short but important season, Chic Harley captivated a sports-hungry city and nation willing to embrace a new form of professional entertainment. He was the player Halas and Sternaman knew they had to have to lure large numbers of fans willing to pay good money to buy tickets and programs. Over the course of the season, the marriage between the operators of the Staleys soured, and Chic Harley, the small, soft-spoken man who only wanted to play football and please his friends and family, was made to suffer the most. Halas and Sternaman went on to fame and fortune with the Bears. Bill Harley had his health and lived a long and successful life, retiring to the warm climes of Florida. Chic Harley was left to struggle with a life of pain and emptiness. This, despite all he had done for others.

Sue Bears For "Chick" Harley's Breakdown

Chicago, Dec. 5 — Charging that Chic Harley, former Ohio State football star and All-American halfback, was virtually driven into a mental collapse through the action of the present owners of the Bears, Chicago professional football team, William Harley, former business manager of the Staley football team, has brought an action in the Superior Court in behalf of himself and his brother to recover one-half of the receipts of the present Bears' season.

CHARGES PLOT.

Harley contends that George Halas and Dutch Sternaman, end and halfback, respectively, and managers of the Bears, were so anxious to terminate an agreement of partnership which they had with him and his famous brother, Chic, that they permitted a situation to arise on the Bears team, at that time known as the Staleys, which broke Chic Harley's heart and made it easier for the Halas and Sternaman to break their own contract with the Harley brothers.

UNDER HANDICAP.

It is contended that Chic Harley was never permitted to run from punt formation, a thing for which he was famous; that the opposing line was permitted to crash through and upset him every time he was sent back for a kick, and that everything possible was done to belittle his abilities which had been sounded throughout the country following his college career.

FORCED TO LEAVE FIELD.

His showing was at all times exceedingly poor as a result of this, William Harley alleges, and finally, when he was called on before 10,000 persons in a game with Buffalo, amid great applause, none of the playing backs would give way to him and he had to run back to the bench.

FINAL BLOW.

This, William Harley asserts, was the final blow that broke Chic Harley's heart and spirit, and soon afterward he suffered a complete breakdown and is now in a sanitarium.

Having disposed of Harley, whose presence was the principal reason for including William Harley in the management of the Bears, or the Staleys, as they were then called, Harley alleges that the name of the team was changed; that he was never consulted upon any matter of management, and was gradually eased out of the club, which has this year been a tremendous money maker.

HELPED GET FRANCHISE.

He gives dates and instances in which Halas and Sternaman slowly brought about his ousting and asserts that in a final move Halas and Sternaman succeeded in getting Chris O'Brien of the Cardinals to sign their application for a franchise. This was necessary in order to permit them to take over the club and get rid of Harley, it appears, and in exchange for this favor they promised to play the Cardinals on Thanksgiving Day. This was the game played on Thanksgiving after O'Brien had used every possible means to keep Halas and Sternaman from getting out of their agreement.

The Harley brothers, in a hearing in equity, seek to force a full accounting of the Bears' season and the allotment of their share of the proceeds as partners.

Story in Decatur, Illinois Review newspaper reports that lawsuit had been filed by Bill and Chic Harley against George Halas and Dutch Sternaman.

CHAPTER 10
The Lawsuit

On a strikingly cold Chicago morning in January 1922, Chic Harley boarded a train bound for Columbus accompanied by his fifty-nine-year-old father, Charles. Chic had been unable to shake what he felt was the acute mistreatment by fellow Staleys and two of his business partners. Severe depression had set in as he stewed about his decision five months earlier to turn professional and about the subsequent season that had just ended. He suffered greatly both physically and mentally in order to please his brother and business partners, and earn a paycheck that meant nothing to him.

George Halas's intuition and sharp mind in recognizing the need to sign Chic Harley proved a remarkable business move. The team had a nearly flawless record, winning the American Football League championship with a 9, 1, and 1 record. So successful were the Staleys under Halas, Dutch Sternaman, and the Harley brothers in 1921 that the team, and professional football, attracted a large base of new fans and lots of money for the pockets of the four young partners.

For Chic, however, the strain had been brewing possibly as early as 1919, when he had been subjected to abusive treatment in the army. The November 1919 defeat in his final collegiate football game had been traumatic. He had failed to earn a degree at Ohio State, had turned down numerous attractive managerial offers, and had not been able to hold onto even the most mediocre of jobs. He also knew that his decision to turn pro had disappointed Coach Wilce and others. The refusal of a teammate to leave the football field when Chic was ordered onto the gridiron before a throng of 12,000 Harley admirers was the last straw for the introverted Chic. Charles and Mattie knew something had to be done for their youngest son before it was too late.

Long before the two Harley men stepped onto the train in downtown Chicago to head east, trouble had been cooking with the Staley management. As it became evident that the Staley team under Halas, Sternaman, and the Harley brothers would be highly profitable, there was discussion of expansion into other towns. But as dreams of further financial reward crept into their minds, so did a thirst for more, which eventually led to total estrangement. No one outside the four partners really knew all the details of why their partnership eventually dissolved. Exactly when it ceased to exist is also a matter of dispute. Halas and Sternaman claimed that the four divided up nearly all of the remaining proceeds of the 1921 season on February 16, 1922. Bill Harley maintained that he knew nothing of the shattering of the business relationship at that time. He contended that it wasn't until September 10, 1922, in a telephone conversation with Halas, that he officially knew of the breakup. Until then, Bill said, he kept busy trying to secure other franchises in other towns—including Chicago—on behalf of the partnership. Expansion in the fertile field of professional football made sense to him, and supposedly for Halas, where they could attract new fans in other markets and sell lots of tickets, programs, and advertising. One of those other franchises, which Harley obtained at the urging of Halas, was for a team in Toledo, Ohio. The now renamed National Football League granted Harley the franchise at its August 22, 1922, meeting in Dayton, Ohio. Seven months earlier at the winter meeting in Canton, Ohio, Halas and Dutch were granted a new franchise to play pro football in Chicago. They named the team the Bears. Bill Harley later said it was his belief, after receiving reassurances from Halas, that the Bears—really the Staleys, he thought—were the property of the four partners. Halas and Sternaman knew differently, but they said nothing to Bill or Chic, who by then was in a hospital. Bill Harley continued making plans to secure more franchises for the group throughout 1922, long after the January 28 league meeting in Canton. About two weeks after the Toledo franchise was granted in late August, Harley called Halas at his home and said, "Now that we've got the franchise, what about the players? What are we going to do with it?" He was hoping that Pete Stinchcomb would play and manage the new Toledo team because he would be nearer to his home in Columbus, which was important to Pete. That thought, however, was quickly dashed when Halas made an amazing statement to Harley that September evening: "My hands are clean," said Halas, as Bill Harley later described. Halas explained that he and Dutch now had a new franchise team of their own named the Bears, and they wanted nothing to do with the Toledo franchise. The partnership no longer existed, he said. "Wait a minute," a stunned Harley shot back. "Click" went the phone as Halas hung up. Bill was stunned. Could it be true? Were he and Chic no longer part owners of the Staleys, which were now called the Bears? What about Toledo? *How could this be?* he thought. Had Halas and Dutch lost their minds?

As the partners' relationship headed for a complete meltdown, treatment for Chic Harley commenced as he settled into the psychiatric clinic in Ohio's capital city. Dr. Eugene Carver, whose Columbus sanitarium had provided early care for the former football star, reported many years later, "In 1921, early in the course of Charles (Chic) Harley's illness, he was referred to me for observation for several days. The result of this observation was that a diagnosis of dementia praecox was made in his case and that he probably would never recover sufficiently to become a useful individual. The various reports I have received from time to time have only served to substantiate the above finding."

Years later, the diagnosis was changed to "schizophrenic reaction," a condition that involves hallucinations and overall inability to live a normal life. That was the path Chic was heading down in late 1921 as he, amazingly, continued to perform well for the Staley football team. Almost certainly the illness that was slowly consuming him was noticeable after the Staleys' first game on October 2, 1921. Though no known records exist that describe his personal behavior either on or off the field, the fact that he ran, punted, and passed well until his last day as a professional football player on December 18 is evidence of his remarkable skill and determination.

Two notable episodes in Chic's life, both related to football, were later blamed by family members as primary contributors to his mental collapse. While it cannot be said that they made him schizophrenic, they may have cracked open the door enough to allow the illness to take hold. Modern psychiatry generally attributes mental illness to hereditary factors more than anything else, and records indicate that mental illness affected a few of Chic's distant relatives.

The first episode was the only loss he experienced as a college football player, on November 22, 1919, as the Ohio State team was on the verge of winning its third straight college conference championship and third straight undefeated season. Chic cried uncontrollably for hours after the 9-7 loss to Illinois, emerging from the locker room at about midnight, only at the continuous urging of teammates and friends. Not only did the team lose that game, but it was Chic's last football contest for Ohio State. So hard was Chic on himself that he blamed the loss on his inability to come through when needed—something he had always been able to do.

The second episode had its genesis on November 6, 1921, during the Staleys' fifth game of the season, against Detroit. In that contest, Chic suffered three broken ribs, which left him in great pain, mostly bedridden for most of the next three weeks, and unable to play the next three games. When he returned to the lineup for the season's biggest game—to determine first place— it turned into a devastating experience for him. According to a 1938 medical report, Chic "was sent in to relieve another player.

The other player refused to leave the field and patient returned to the bench, which was very embarrassing to him. According to the family, this episode preyed upon his mind and caused him great anxiety. After that he thought that all the team was against him. He seemed to close up and crawl into a shell." The report notes that "the family believes this was the precipitating cause of the breakdown." In addition to the emotional scars, Chic carried the physical scars of the broken ribs to the end of his life.

In 1922, as the Harleys' business relationship with Halas and Sternaman continued its slide, so did the mental well-being of Chic. On January 28, 1922, as Bill, Halas, and Sternaman attended the professional football league's annual meeting in Canton, Chic "was having a complete breakdown." Bill involved himself as much as he could with his brother's care, but by early fall, he felt there was no recourse but to fight the wrong that had been done to him and his brother. Told by Halas in the fateful September 10 telephone conversation that there was no place for him or Chic, Bill filed a lawsuit, with Chic as co-complainant, on December 2, 1922, in Cook County Superior Court. The Harleys charged that Halas and Sternaman conspired to freeze them out of their rightful ownership of the football team, despite Chic's major contribution to the squad's success in 1921 at a time that a destructive illness was slowly consuming his mind. The conspiracy of Halas and Sternaman, added the complainants, was also directed against Bill, the only one who a year and a half earlier could deliver to the Staleys what Halas and Dutch desperately wanted—the key to what turned out to be a near perfect football season: Chic, Pete Stinchcomb, and John Taylor. The Chicago *Herald-Examiner* shed further light on the Harleys' action, stating that the Bears management "permitted a situation to arise on the Bear team . . . which broke Chic Harley's heart." The Chicago *Tribune* reported, "The suit contends that Chic Harley was the unremitting object of attempts to belittle his playing ability, that the Staleys' line gave way in games of 1921 in order to let opposing players spill him, and that he was driven into a state of mental collapse by the 'freeze out' treatment which culminated in the team's refusal to accept his insertion into the second half of the game with Buffalo late in the 1921 season with 10,000 people looking on. For months following the episode, Chic Harley was in a sanitarium." Another newspaper account shed further light on the dispute when it reported on December 5, 1922, that Halas and Sternaman were so anxious to terminate their agreement with Chic and Bill that they allowed things to get out of control, which made it easier "to break their own contract with the Harley brothers."

"It is contended that Chic Harley was never permitted to run from punt formation, a thing for which he was famous; that the opposing line was permitted to crash through and upset him every time he was sent back to kick; and that everything possible was done to belittle his abilities which had been sounded throughout the country following his college career. His showing was at all times exceedingly poor as a result," Bill Harley was reported as saying.

"Having disposed of Harley (Chic), whose presence was the principal reason for including William Harley in the management of the Bears, or the Staleys as they were then called, Harley alleges that the name of the team was changed, that he was never consulted upon any matter of management, and was gradually eased out of the club which has this year been a tremendous moneymaker."

As time has shown, Chic Harley was institutionalized not just for months, but for most of the remaining fifty-two years of his life. The darkness of mental illness would eclipse any chance of future happiness and prosperity.

Harley family members have contended that members of the Staley team, jealous of Chic's fame, part ownership, and high salary, conspired to run him out. What about Halas and Sternaman? There's much belief that they not only knew what was happening, but encouraged it and may even have planned for it to happen. If any or all of this is true concerning Halas and Sternaman, the question is, Why is it true? By all appearances, Chic had lived up to his expectations both as a player and as a drawing card. He captured most of the headlines by running, passing, and punting the team to win after win, especially early in the season. He was slowed only after becoming injured in the fifth game against Detroit. After returning to the lineup, he played well. In fact, he played well up until the final game of the year, despite inaccurate passages in some books about the early days of professional football that indicate that Harley did not finish the season. A biography of Halas released in 2006 reported that Chic's playing career for the Staleys came to an abrupt halt about halfway through when, following a physical examination, it was discovered that he had contracted syphilis. Sensitive Veterans Administration medical records obtained by the grandson (the author of this book) of Chic's sister, Ruth, show conclusively that Chic never had venereal disease, a fact more clearly understood when one realizes that for the extremely shy Chic, speaking to a female in a romantic way was nearly next to impossible. When Ruth's grandson asked the author of the book on Halas where he got the information asserting that Chic had syphilis, he refused to identify the source. He added that unless someone could prove that what he published was wrong, he would continue to assert the venereal disease charge.

Perhaps the Staleys of 1921 would have been a success even without Chic, although the record of the day shows nothing to support that conclusion. The problem may have had more to do with a squad comprised of players who had been stars of their college teams who now had to take a backseat to Chic Harley, who was being paid as much as $1,000 per game. Another possibility is that Halas and Sternaman were having difficulty dealing with Bill Harley and didn't like sharing gate receipts with their two partners. The formation of the National Football League and creation of the Chicago Bears out of the same team that a month earlier had been called the Staleys afforded Halas and Sternaman the opportunity to sever the relationship they had all agreed to in a steamy hotel room in Decatur just six months earlier.

Kicked out as business partners, the Harley brothers moved forward with the lawsuit in an attempt to capture what they believed was rightfully theirs, especially Bill. The Bears team was moving forward under new ownership. Details of the lawsuit and what the Harleys were claiming would take almost three years—to 1925—to reach a conclusion.

What specifically the Harleys were asking for in their lawsuit was not only what they claimed was their fair share of the proceeds that the 1922 team—now named the Chicago Bears—generated, but an opportunity to see the team's books to verify their claim. They said they were entitled to see the books since at no time had the partnership actually been dissolved. Bill asked the court for a full accounting of the team's finances for the 1922 season and that a receiver be appointed to take charge of the partnership's records "and collect whatever money or property may belong to the partnership."

To all four partners who had signed the single-page agreement handwritten by Sternaman on July 18, 1921, the potential profitability of the Staleys became obvious early in the 1921 season. Despite later testimony that the only money remaining at the end of the 1921 season was $7.71, which could be construed as the partners having made little or no money at all, a close look at the year's proceeds and disbursements shows there was much more to the story. By February 16, 1922, each partner had been paid approximately $5,400 from gate receipts and scorecard sales for the 1921 season, a considerable sum of money for four young men in their twenties venturing headlong into the cold world of business. While there's no question that Halas was the leader, the other three played critical roles in helping the team achieve success that season. Sternaman was Halas's right-hand man, a smart friend who was a skilled runner and place kicker on the football field. Bill Harley delivered three talented players who contributed significantly to the team's success not only on the field, but at the gate. He also handled admissions, sales, and marketing. And Chic played very well that season. His good name attracted crowds to Cubs Park—sometimes as many as 12,000, an astonishingly large number for professional football, which at that time was struggling to find a fan base.

The legal case officially commenced on November 14, 1923, when the deposition of Halas was taken in the offices of Superior Court Master William W. Maxwell in downtown Chicago. Representing the Harleys were attorneys Charles J. Trainor and Joseph J. Nagle. Halas and Sternaman were represented by John E. Northrup of the law firm Mayer, Meyer, Austrian & Platt, on the recommendation of William Veeck, president of the Chicago Cubs baseball team, who was making money for the company by leasing the ball park to Halas' Bears.

Over the next two years, more than a dozen witnesses were asked to recollect meetings, conversations, and chance encounters involving the plaintiffs, defendants, Staley Company representatives, Staley team players, the Chicago Cubs president, accountants, and others.

While the Harleys' lawsuit focused on their belief that their partners failed to share or even allow them to know what profits the team earned in 1922, what really was at stake was the future ownership of the team. In Bill Harley's mind, the Staley team he, Chic, Stinchcomb, and Taylor joined in 1921 was the same team renamed the Bears in 1922. The agreement signed on July 18, 1921, had never been formally or informally dissolved, he claimed. No papers existed or were ever signed to relinquish anything. On July 18, all four agreed verbally that the life of their partnership would last for five years, and that when they returned to Chicago in a couple of months, a formal pact that said essentially what the July 18 contract said would be written and signed. With the exception of Chic and one or two other players, the Staleys of 1921 were the Bears of 1922. The name was basically the only thing that changed. The Chicago Bears became a corporation in June 1922 following the January league meeting. The Staley Company had no interest in the team whatsoever at that point. Most significant in Bill Harley's mind was that Halas and Sternaman continued to let him believe that the team they all agreed in 1921 to run and share was still intact and the partnership continued to exist. Perhaps it was naivete on the part of Bill Harley, stupidity, ignorance, or game-playing, but whatever the case, around midseason 1921, the writing was on the wall that the partnership was doomed.

For their part, following the September 10, 1922, telephone call between Bill and George, Halas and Dutch claimed that the Bears were a completely different football team from the champion Staleys. After the 1921 season, they contended, the Decatur company would no longer be involved in professional football. Thus, they said, the Staleys no longer existed, and Halas and Sternaman were free to pursue other avenues of team ownership, which they did on January 28, 1922, when they applied for and received permission to create the Chicago Bears. As minutes from that meeting show, Bill Harley sought permission from the league to also field a team in Chicago in 1922. In court testimony, he said his application was not meant to be in place of Halas and Sternaman's Bears application, but in addition to that request. He said the idea was for him and his partners to apply for a new franchise—named the Decatur Staleys—to play in Chicago beginning in 1922 because the use of the name Staleys ended with the 1921 season. The pursuit of league approval of a team called the Bears was a decision made earlier by the four partners, not just Sternaman and Halas, Bill asserted. If Halas, Sternaman, and the Harleys could own two franchises to play in Chicago—the biggest town in the NFL at the time—they would monopolize the market. And in addition to Chicago, claimed Bill, Halas and Dutch had agreed to apply for other franchises, such as Toledo. Serious discussion took place among the partners and other Staley teammates about seeking permission for new teams to play in Milwaukee, Indianapolis, St. Louis, and Cincinnati. In the end, Harley charged, Sternaman and Halas secretly determined that their road to success did not include him or Chic. In 1922, Chic Harley, in and out of sanitariums and well on his way to total mental collapse, was out of the picture. Without Chic, Bill Harley was now likely only a problem to George and Dutch. They still had the talented Stinchcomb. Taylor left for greener pastures with the Canton Bulldogs.

In order to achieve enough security to unilaterally terminate their partnership agreement, Sternaman and Halas apparently felt that two things were necessary: They needed to make sure that Cubs Park would be available to them for the 1922 season, and they needed a big-name player to draw fans and replace Chic. It was Staley's general manager, George Chamberlain, not Halas, who negotiated the lease to rent Cubs Park in 1921, according to court records. It was Halas, representing the Staley Company, who signed the contract with Veeck to lease the grounds because he lived in Chicago and was available. Halas's willingness to sign the contract and his business acumen impressed Veeck so much that a year later when lease negotiations were under way for the 1922 season, Veeck insisted that Halas and Sternaman be part of the deal. Until then—January 5, 1922, to be exact—the Staley Company, despite earlier assertions that it was no longer interested in owning a professional football team, had a change of mind.

On January 5, 1922, Veeck learned by telegram that George Chamberlain would be calling on him in a few days, two days after another telegram informed him that Staley fully intended to own and operate its professional football team in Chicago. "We expect to place another championship team in the field if anything stronger than last year's and trust that experience of the past two years is such that you wish to continue present arrangement with this company." Staley was asking Veeck to make Cubs Park available for pro football in 1922. When Chamberlain arrived at Veeck's office in the Wrigley Building for their 10 A.M. meeting on January 11, he was greatly surprised to find Halas and Sternaman were also there. During the meeting, Veeck insisted that the two young men be part of any arrangement with Staley. An annoyed Chamberlain corrected Veeck, explaining that Halas and Sternaman, as employees of the A. E. Staley Manufacturing Co., would be returning to Decatur to continue their work. Four days later, however, after returning to Decatur and meeting with Augustus Staley and company leaders, Chamberlain relented: "This matter has become snarled up in a way that will probably throw it into the courts before the season opens and may very possibly result in the breaking up of the present team. When on top of these various, rather pessimistic conditions, we contemplate the considerable increase to which you require in the next contract amounting to approximately $5,000 per year, the sum total gives us pause."

At that point, Chamberlain informed Veeck that he was withdrawing the company's application to use Cubs Park for the 1922 season. Chamberlain and the Staley Company, fully aware of the high cost of fielding a professional team for the 1922 season, saw the writing on the wall. Their two now former employees, with the help of Veeck, had the upper hand. Like many others at the time, Chamberlain was well aware that trouble had been brewing between Halas, Sternaman, and Bill Harley, and concluded that continuing the fight for a pro football franchise was not worth the effort. Six days later, Halas and Sternaman, confident that they were in control, culminated a series of meetings with John L. "Paddy" Driscoll, one of the nation's most famous football stars, who played second fiddle to Chic in 1916, to "enter into an agreement to manage and operate a professional football club for the year beginning in October 1922 and to share equally profits and losses." It was pretty much the same agreement that was entered into in July 1921. The difference this time is that Driscoll was in, and the Harleys, out. George and Dutch, knowing that they soon would be rid of the Harleys and assured that they would be able to play football in the upcoming season at Cubs Park, now had their new star attraction to replace Chic—or so they thought. The problem was that Driscoll, a big name in Chicago from his playing days at Northwestern University, was the property of the rival Chicago Cardinals. He couldn't just jump ship to take over one-third ownership of the other Chicago team without permission from Cardinals owner Chris O'Brien. That wasn't going to happen because O'Brien needed Driscoll to keep his team competitive and to attract fans. O'Brien, upon learning of Driscoll, Halas, and Sternaman's shenanigans, took his case to the NFL board of directors, which ruled that the tampering was improper. In September, Driscoll resigned as a director of Halas and Sternaman's team, sending him back to the Cardinals. Halas and Sternaman were destined to field average teams for the next few years until fellow Illini grad Red Grange arrived on the scene in 1925.

Halas and Sternaman, while acknowledging that the Staleys had earned large sums of money and a rabid following in 1921, contended that Harley declared that same year that he no longer wished to remain a partner. They denied any conspiracy to freeze out the Harleys, adding that a final settlement by the partners was made on February 16, 1922, when each received $1,742.16, which constituted all money that was left in the team's bank accounts minus $7.71 in interest. On the other hand, Bill and a now hospitalized Chic, who did not testify at all during the court proceedings, said that another example of Halas's and Dutch's trickery was that they told hardly anyone on the 1921 Staley team that they were not bound by the league's reserve clause. After all, claimed Bill, if the Bears really were a new NFL team, totally different and separate from the 1921 Staleys, then the players on the '21 team were free to join any other team they could sign on with. They no longer remained the property of the Staleys. No one team had the power to reserve their services for the future season. Instead, Harley said, Dutch and George kept quiet, with one or two exceptions, when asked about the situation. In reality, for all practical purposes, the Bears of 1922 was the same team as the Staleys of 1921. If the sixteen or seventeen players of the 1921 Staleys knew that the Bears was a totally different enterprise, and thus the Staleys would be free to peddle their services elsewhere to higher bidders, the near perfect championship squad of 1921 could very well have been dismantled, thus affecting fan loyalty and profits to Halas and Sternaman. Keeping quiet was good for business.

In his final twenty-five-page report dated December 7, 1925, Master Maxwell, the court officer, found that the parties to the lawsuit "gave contradictory evidence at the hearing." He cited testimony that Bill Harley in the middle of the 1921 season became angry and tore up Halas and Sternaman's contracts after they refused his request to assign all team players to the Staleys team, not signed up individually to Halas and Sternaman or to agent Bill Harley, as had been the case. With that refusal, said the Master, Harley announced that he would take his three players and that Halas and Sternaman could take theirs and they would split up, allowing Harley to form another team. Maxwell also acknowledged as significant Bill Harley's comment that he "would not go into partnership with Sternaman anymore" when he and Halas were discussing the possibility of leasing Cubs Park for 1922. As for the reserve clause issue, Maxwell said because the Staley Company refused to be connected with pro football in 1922, "and by its failure to apply for renewal of a franchise to operate a football club on or after the January 28, 1922, League meeting, the Staley Football Club ceased to exist." Therefore, said Maxwell, "the partnership agreement entered into on July 18, 1922, terminated."

Master found that the reserve clause was void on the dissolution of the Staley club. The clause, therefore, was not enforceable. None of the parties to this suit had any ownership or control over said players as a matter of law, and players' contracts could not be accounted as a partnership asset of the parties of this suit.

Master found that the complainants failed to prove the necessary material allegations of their bill of complaint and at the same time should be dismissed for want of equity.

A down, but not completely out, Bill Harley directed his lawyers to immediately file an appeal of Maxwell's findings, citing the Master's ruling that the league awarded a franchise to Halas and Sternaman on January 28, 1922. Rather, Harley argued, the franchise was granted on January 28 for the benefit of the partnership and it continued until September 10, 1922. Furthermore, he said, Halas and Sternaman falsified their books and statement of earnings for 1922 and secured players for the 1922 Bears season by invoking the reserve clause for those who played with the Staleys in 1921. Harley said that those contracts were paid by the Harleys equally with Halas and Sternaman.

In the end, it was ruled that Chic and Bill Harley had received almost everything that was due them from the 1921 season and had no claim to anything from the 1922 season, with one minor exception. That exception was finally taken care of, from Halas and Sternaman's point of view, on January 4, 1924. That's when Sternaman, testifying in the lawsuit filed more than a year earlier by Bill and Chic, was asked whether he had brought along with him nineteen old Staley jerseys and towels.

"At the present time they are at the Sherman House across the street," replied Sternaman, referring to one of downtown Chicago's most famous hotels.

"I asked him to bring them in," said their lawyer, John Northrup, at which point Sternaman crossed the icy street to retrieve the items. After returning, he announced that he was now ready to cosign the checks dividing up the remaining $7.71 in interest from the 1921 season proceeds. Halas said he was willing to part with one-half of the 1921 Staley team's towels and jerseys in order to finalize the partnership.

Exasperated, Charles Trainor, the Harleys' attorney, said, "It's a rather novel way of dissolving a partnership."

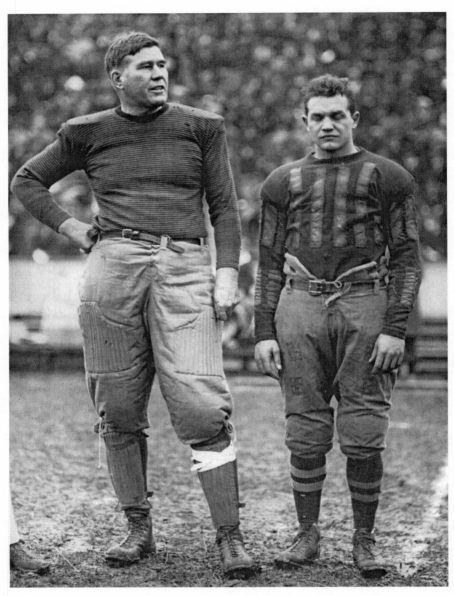

Chic in an early 1920s charity football game at
newly-built Ohio Stadium with Pudge Heffelfinger,
a standout player of his day.

CHAPTER 11
Darkened Days

Months before Halas, Sternaman, and Bill Harley tightened the screws on Chic to play professional football, Chic decided to help wherever he could in the all-out campaign to build a new stadium at Ohio State. It wasn't enough that he had lit the spark that ignited the fire of Buckeye football. There was much more to be done. Wanting to stay involved and help wherever he could, Chic hit the fund-raising circuit.

Just the mention of Chic Harley provoked glowing emotions in people throughout Ohio and the Midwest. His mere presence at chamber of commerce meetings, Rotary club gatherings, and dozens of other social settings throughout Ohio attracted and captivated large crowds. Football fans were electrified at the prospect of actually meeting the great Harley. When word spread that he was going to be in town, curious and excited Ohioans turned out in droves. There, the shy Chic mustered the courage to shake hands, smile, and talk about plans to build the great stadium. On matters unrelated to himself about which he was passionate, Chic could speak freely and inspiringly. When the subject of his football heroics came up, as it always did, he would force a half smile, step back, and deflect praise.

Eventually at these gatherings, Chic would get to the main reason for his visit: to ask for donations to construct what later would become known as "The House That Harley Built." His personal appearances raised tens of thousands of dollars or more—the exact amount isn't known. His enthusiastic support and work after his playing days generated strong interest from hundreds of thousands of alumni and others who might otherwise have paid fleeting attention to the stadium project. His efforts were eclipsed only by the extraordinary excitement he had aroused from his first game as a collegian in 1916 to his final game in November 1919.

While university professor Thomas French is appropriately credited as the visionary whose mind and perseverance led to the building of Ohio State's "Horseshoe," it was Chic Harley who made that dream come true. His emergence was perfectly timed with the zeal of French, university President William Thompson, and dozens of other faculty members to elevate State's sports program to the highest plateau of prominence in the nation. Following his run, Chic did not disappear into the world of business or move permanently out of state as many other college grads do. His heart remained in Columbus. And when called upon to help in a different manner, away from the dirt and grind of the gridiron, he responded magnificently, helping greatly to reach the $1 million goal that would result in the construction of Ohio Stadium.

By mid-1921, the fundraising campaign had been successfully completed and construction on the 62,000-seat arena had begun. Massive steel beams were rising on the flat Ohio landscape along the tranquil Olentangy River on ground that for years had served as farmland for Ohio State's school of agriculture. Meanwhile, Chic reported to the Decatur Staleys training camp to prepare for the forthcoming football season, one that ended as a tragic debacle for him.

The approach of the new year, 1922, did not inspire thoughts of a fresh start. Chic's distress evolved into high anxiety and paranoiac behavior. Realizing something was seriously wrong, the Harley family summoned the services of a Columbus psychiatrist, Dr. Earl E. Gaver. For several days,

190

Gaver observed Chic and documented his behavior and personality traits. Those observations provided Chic's family and friends with the first pronouncement of very serious trouble: dementia praecox, later known as schizophrenia, a severe mental disorder characterized by the inability to distinguish between reality and fantasy, prompted by severe anxiety. It would only get worse, Gaver concluded, primarily because there was no known cure and what few drugs and treatments existed were inadequate. Writing about the diagnosis later, Gaver said Chic "probably would never recover sufficiently to become a useful individual." Some of the manifestations, he said, were impaired reasoning and judgment, emotional indifference, loss of will power, apathy, and asocial behavior. Said Gaver, "His mental trouble is a slowly progressive one. The course of the disease is one of years. A time does come, however, when it is almost impossible to . . . adjust to outside life and [institutionalization] becomes necessary."

In Columbus, Ohio State Athletic Director Lynn St. John, who had been Chic's baseball, basketball, and assistant football coach, took personal interest in the situation. Once again, St. John stepped forward to help Chic, just as he had in 1919, when Chic suffered humiliating abuse by his army officers. St. John and other Ohio friends familiar with the situation that had unfolded at Camp Kelly in San Antonio had lobbied to turn Chic's court-martial into an honorable discharge. For the rest of Saint's life (he died in 1950 at age seventy-four), he cared for Chic like a loving father.

By late January 1922, rumors were spreading that Chic had been admitted to a sanitarium for rest, therapy, and freedom from the stresses—real or imagined—he was under. His close friend Karl Finn, a sports reporter in Columbus during Chic's playing days, denied that Chic was in a sanitarium, according to the *Journal*, saying instead that he was hoping to return to Ohio State in a few days to reenroll. At the time, Finn was on his way to start a new job as football coach at the University of Kansas, the same job Chic had turned down the previous year. On January 17, the Chicago *Tribune* reported that Charles and Walter Harley had recently taken Chic to a sanitarium in Ishpeming, Michigan. He was suffering from a "partial nervous breakdown," the story said, adding hope that "rest will banish the trouble."

By all indications, Chic stayed at the Michigan sanitarium for only a short time before his parents took him to Columbus in the hope that the atmosphere of the university and town might improve his condition. But in Columbus, despite efforts of friends, university officials, and many others, his troubles persisted. He was "under the care of local specialists in nervous diseases" but did not show improvement because, a newspaper reported, Chic "would not follow the prescribed treatment." At times, he behaved normally, carrying on quiet conversations with people he felt comfortable with. He went to sleep at a normal hour, awoke, bathed, brushed his teeth, and lived a seemingly normal existence. But at other times, Chic's behavior was described as morbid; modern-day terminology would include dejected and gloomy. Being surrounded by thousands of admirers provided only partial relief. At one point in 1922, new hope sprouted up: a sanitarium in Asheville, North Carolina, was said to offer the kind of professional help he so desperately needed.

In an amazing show of love and admiration, the community raised $10,000 for Chic's treatment in Asheville. St. John recruited Ray Pennell, Chic's lifelong friend and classmate, to make sure the journey to North Carolina went smoothly. By early April, Harley had been admitted to the sanitarium and Pennell was on his way back to Columbus by train. Everyone felt that Asheville was the right place for Chic. There, they hoped, he would at least improve, if not fully recover.

Upon learning that Chic was in a sanitarium, Karl Finn, now settled at the University of Kansas, wrote him a letter at the instigation of Louise Havens, Chic's one and only love during his high school and college years. Around 1919, Chic had given Louise his varsity "O" pin, a gesture that in those days signified "engaged to be engaged." It was a beautiful diamond piece engraved on the back with the letters "CWH"—Charles William Harley—and "VOA"—Varsity "O" Association. Louise was pretty, outgoing, happy, and personable. During Columbus's hot, humid summers, she and Chic had enjoyed each other's company at Franklin Park pool, where Chic worked as a lifeguard and Louise practiced her swimming and diving skills. Now, distraught about Chic's condition, she asked Finn to write Chic to bring him some comfort and hope.

Finn's amazing letter expresses warm-hearted encouragement from a true friend. The thrust of his message to Chic is that his friends back in Columbus—especially Louise—are pulling for him to get better and come through the same way he did in so many football games. He writes:

I can imagine you playing around in the beautiful summer atmosphere, perfecting your golf strokes, improving your hitting eye and catching some large fish. The buds are coming out now and spring 'has came,' as they say, for which I am glad. In spring everything seems so beautiful. You know I philosophize a good deal in letters, so look out. But anyhow in the spring my feelings are like the trees and the young blades of grass. My feelings grow and everything seems so much more hopeful than when it is raining and there is snow on the ground. I can imagine that you feel much better about everything since you are away from Columbus and in North Carolina, which from all reports should be the greatest place on earth for climate. That is, if we eliminate California after they did that to us in football.

Finn is referring to the 1921 Rose Bowl, in which Ohio State lost to the University of California. During his brief time in Lawrence, Kansas, says Finn, whenever he tells people he is from Ohio State, they bring up the subject of Chic Harley.

You would surely be sore at me for boosting you so, but then it is all done in the best of spirit, I assure you. I told some of the Phi Gams that we had the Harley Chapter at Ohio State and they seemed to appreciate the fact that it was a good name for the organization. .

193

. .Louise reports that you are getting along splendidly and if you disappoint her you don't amount to much. She says you have promised to fight hard, and after all, life is a good big fight from start to finish and I know you will keep the promise to her. You know, Chic, I never realized that Louise was such a fine girl until I heard her tell about you in this letter. You were fortunate to be such a fine football player but the most fortunate thing in your life has been Louise.

You will come through. You will, old boy. In these days we get to talk about girls, co-eds and others, and we come to the conclusion that they are all pretty bad, all very much alike, except that some are wise and others are foolish. Then you see one like Louise and your ideas all change. You realize that girls are very wonderful and that compared to all of them all men are very undeserving. I'm sure you feel that way about Louise, especially since she has been so wonderful to you lately, and she tells me just as wonderful things about you as she tells to you. It isn't put on or imagined in her case, she is simply the best possible sort of person and will do anything in the world for you, and you must do everything possible for her. I know she is sure you are. I am sure you are too, but keep it in your mind constantly.

At this point, Finn goes back to the 1916 football finale against Illinois, one of the most memorable games in Ohio State history and the contest that gave Chic his first national recognition. With the score tied and only seconds left on the clock, Chic had scored a touchdown and kicked the extra point, winning the game and the conference title for Ohio State. Finn continues:

I feel toward you now like I did at Illinois back in 1916. I knew you would score and kick that old goal and you did. I know now you will score, just for Louise if not for your own sake, because you have the goods, and after all, there is only one Chic and he has never failed to deliver yet, so why should he start now? I am a long way from Columbus and a longer way from Asheville, but I am fighting for the touchdown and the goal. Make it now, if you can, but make it anyhow. Every time I think of those old games I get a thrill and

*I am expecting another soon when you finish down there in Asheville
and come to Columbus and I can beat you playing golf, that is, if you
don't get too good down there.*

*Don't forget, Chic, your old friend in Kansas is for you and knows
that you are going to come through all right. You have to deliver for
all of us, especially Louise. If I was selfish I would say for me, too,
but I won't, but I feel it anyhow.*

Karl Finn's letter, written from Kansas, reflected the true,
personal relationship thousands of Ohioans felt with Chic
Harley. While athletics, in particular, football, opened the door
for people everywhere to become knowledgeable about the
sportsman Harley, what they were left with after getting to
know Chic—even a little bit—was something much deeper
and personal. They saw in Chic a very human, down-to-earth
man, tremendously sensitive and gentle, who with his crooked
smile and high cheekbones was magnetic. On the football field,
diamond, track, and basketball court, Harley was a ferocious,
clean, and confident competitor. Off the field, he exemplified
the best in human behavior. He was caring and kind, loving
and generous. He put others before himself.

Despite the warm temperatures and gentle breezes, Chic's
stay in Asheville was short-lived. Within two weeks, much to
everyone's surprise, he was in Columbus, having made his way
back by automobile, train, and foot. His only possessions the
day he arrived in Columbus, grimy-faced and worn-looking,
were the ragged clothes he was wearing. When asked by a friend
why he left Asheville to return to Columbus, Chic answered,
"Because this is where I belong."

For about a month, Chic stayed in Columbus, looked after
by friends and, of course, a more alarmed St. John. His father
wrote to Saint expressing his gratitude for helping Chic. But
any hopes that Chic might improve by being back in Columbus
quickly evaporated, and it was clear that something else needed
to be done. In a letter to Charles Harley on June 7, Saint wrote
that Chic "does not look well and is acting strange." It was

obvious that Chic needed medical care. Efforts were stepped up to persuade Chic that hospitalization was a necessity. Chic reluctantly acquiesced.

On June 10, Saint informed Mr. Harley that "Chic voluntarily agreed to a temporary stay at the Dayton State Hospital under the care of Dr. Baber, who has taken a definite interest in his case. Some of the boys drove him down there and left him. Their request at the time was that he should be left entirely alone for 30 days, that he might receive letters, but it is contrary to their wishes to have visitors."

In July, Charles wrote to Saint to express the family's distress at not being able to see their son and brother. "Family felt it best to leave Chic alone so they have not written him," said Charles, but their anxiety was grueling. By late July, Saint felt that family members should now communicate with Chic through letters. He was more concerned than ever about Chic because he had shown no signs of improvement since being admitted to the hospital.

With Chic's voluntary commitment to Dayton about to expire, the Harleys, Saint, and friends were unsure of what to do next. The press and public were becoming more curious about the famous athlete. Nothing had been explained publicly about Chic's mental condition, with the exception of a few newspaper articles that contained little information of any substance. Those who knew Chic tried to keep a lid on details, fearing that the stigma of mental illness would cripple his reputation for life. Undoubtedly, some people were concerned that Ohio State's reputation could somehow become tarnished as well.

Contrary to Saint's fears that Chic had not improved, an evaluation of the prized patient by the hospital presented a much different picture. "He has progressed splendidly in the last three weeks since he has been put on straw baling," wrote Dr. E. M. Baehr, referring to a strenuous form of physical labor. "He seems to enjoy it and looks better than he has at any time since Asheville." Baehr went on to suggest that Chic be transferred to a state institution in Trenton, New Jersey, which could accept him around September 5.

A letter of August 21 to, of all people, William Havens, Louise's brother, describes in detail the prospect of moving Chic to New Jersey. The letter was from a friend of Havens' in Trenton. Exactly why Havens was involved in Chic's relocation is unclear, although by this time, the Havens family was very concerned about the mental condition of the man who might marry Louise. After leaving the Dayton hospital in August, Chic returned to Columbus and lived in various places, including the Phi Gamma Delta house near campus and in a small rooming house. He frequently sought out Louise, and she, him. However, when he began arriving unannounced at the Havens home at 11 and 11:30 at night, the family became uneasy and then fearful. At one point, Louise's father told Chic that he did not want him to see his daughter or to call her on the telephone. Chic responded that he would see her any time he desired. That's when the Havens began to take steps to have Chic returned to Dayton.

By early September, Chic was back in Dayton, having been strongly advised by everyone concerned, especially the Havens family, that he needed continued help. Coach Wilce, who was preparing to take Chic to the institution in New Jersey, was surprised to learn that Harley was back in Dayton for another sixty-day period and was making excellent progress. In Columbus, the excitement of another football season was taking hold, with team practices and classes now in full swing. Besides the start of a new year, the buzz on campus was the anticipated opening of the new 62,000-seat Ohio Stadium. Wrap-up work was progressing. The steel skeleton had been covered with concrete. The massive bell towers at the far south end of the horseshoe-shaped arena still needed shaping. But for the most part, the project was completed and ready for its official dedication on October 21, 1922, the day of the game against archrival Michigan.

Readers might have noticed a small article in the sports section of many Midwestern newspapers on September 16 that touched upon the imminent opening of Ohio Stadium. That particular story, however, was not so much about the new arena, but about old Ohio Field, which was in the process of being closed down for good. The article reported that Ohio Field engineer Clyde T. Morris made an unusual discovery when removing the goalposts that had been in place on the field since 1897:

> *When the old goal post at the south end of Ohio Field was taken down, Mr. Morris found that the posts had sunk 3 inches in the ground and instead of being 10 feet above the ground, the cross bar cleared the ground by only 9 feet, 9 inches. It will never be known when the goal posts settled in, but if it did so three years ago, Bob Fletcher's kick in 1919 which gave Illinois a 9 to 7 win over Ohio State in the last minute of play would have never cleared the bar had it been the regulation height.*

The discovery marked the last time that old Ohio Field made news. In the field's thirty-year history, Ohio State—the school—had grown from a small Midwestern college with a small and undistinguished sports program to a national power, most notably in football. The Buckeyes had won 162 contests on that field, lost seventy-nine, and tied twenty. It scored 4,619 points; opponents scored 2,203. From now on, the center of sports at Ohio State was the new horseshoe, a magnificent coliseum that prior to 1916 was merely a dream. Harley more than anyone else made that dream come true in just six short years. Ohio State, Columbus, the state of Ohio, and college football would never be the same. The engineer's discovery under Ohio Field's goalposts provided another in a long line of eerie what-ifs concerning Chic Harley. If the uprights in 1919 had been at regulation height, it's possible that Chic's final game at Ohio State would have been victorious, capping a perfect three years.

Chic Harley's sixty-day voluntary commitment to Dayton Hospital, which began in mid-September, was short-lived. Anxious to attend the official dedication of the new stadium, he persuaded a nurse and one of the hospital's male employees to take him to the game. Back in the familiar surroundings of Columbus, Chic and his caretakers walked into the gleaming, awesome amphitheater, the green grass of the gridiron aglow, and stands and aisles filled with 72,000 fans dressed in scarlet, gray, maize, and blue. Michigan won the contest 19-0, but nothing could dampen the spirits of the Buckeye faithful that day. Not only was the new stadium officially open, but Chic was back, if only for a short time.

Throughout the game, Harley seemed like his old self, enjoying the contest and the hundreds of greetings from admirers. But something was still wrong, despite outward appearances. How could Chic have made any significant recovery after only a month at Dayton? Saint could tell that Chic wasn't taking care of himself. He wasn't eating well, and a gradual decline was fairly obvious. Talk sprang up about an extended trip to Wyoming, where Chic could take in fresh air and sunshine and engage in some good old-fashioned hard work. This time, Russell Paul, a basketball teammate of Chic's at State, offered to accompany his friend for the long train ride. But Chic would hear none of it. He did not want to leave the familiar surroundings of Columbus and Chicago.

Friends and family were becoming desperate, and options, more limited. Chic knew he was not well and deep inside was aware that he needed what was probably long-term treatment. But the prospect of lengthy confinement triggered rebellion. He hated the idea of severing attachments in Columbus. His friends—and even the two Dayton staff members who escorted him to the Ohio State-Michigan football game—helped arrange employment for Chic in Columbus once his voluntary confinement ended. Officials from the university agreed to employ Chic on the campus grounds performing maintenance chores. That job lasted only a short time because Chic felt the work was belittling for an Ohio State All-American. Of course, no matter what the work, it was obvious that he could not hold down a job. But friends kept trying. A short time later, Chic was selling coal for home and business heating, but before long, he stopped showing up for work. Later, Lazarus clothing store, the biggest and best-known retail shop in Columbus where he had worked on a part-time basis before, sought to capitalize on Chic's fame by hiring him to mingle with the students and customers and encourage them to buy clothes. But when Chic's interest fizzled out, so did the job. Chic was on a slippery slope into the depths of apathy and indifference.

By late October, the Havens family, unnerved and sometimes frightened by Chic's change in personality, decided to take matters into their own hands. With Bill Havens the primary organizer and with the help of several others, a plan was hatched to force him back to Dayton Hospital.

On December 2, 1922—the same day Bill Harley was filing his lawsuit against George Halas and Dutch Sternaman—the Ohio State campus was abuzz with the excitement over the first ever Grid-Grad football game, a Saturday afternoon exhibition contest in the new stadium that pitted a team of former Ohio State athletes against faculty members. Most of the 10,000 students were stirred up at the prospect of coaches and faculty members getting a whipping. Chic Harley was asked to serve as one of the officials of the game—an invitation he couldn't pass up.

The early December day was cold. Chic, clad only in his varsity O sweater, shivered and finally asked to be excused by the end of the third quarter. Unbeknownst to Chic, two physicians, Dr. R. C. Tarbell and Dr. R. A. Kidd, were in the stands not watching the game, but watching Harley. Most likely they had been recruited by Havens and the others to observe Chic's demeanor and actions. Later, court documents prepared by Franklin County Sheriff Oliver J. Baxter showed that final arrangements to have Chic committed to Dayton Hospital had been made at about 11 A.M. that day, mainly by Bill Havens.

After the Grid-Grad game, students and faculty headed over to Hennick's Restaurant on High Street, a lively campus hangout filled with chatter, games, barstools, and tables.

Inside, Chic was enjoying the company of his many friends. At about 5:30, Havens, a student named "Tee" Young, and Sheriff Baxter arrived at Hennick's by car. Havens volunteered to go inside and bring Chic out while the other two waited in the car. A few minutes later, Chic and Havens exited Hennick's and got into the car. Chic was told that they were going to the Columbus Athletic Club for dinner. But at Third Avenue and Neil Street—about two blocks away—Chic became suspicious and tried to leave the car. Baxter, Young, and Havens persuaded Chic to stay in the car and drove to his rooming house. There, Baxter told Chic that he was going to accompany him to Dayton Hospital.

"What for?" asked Harley. Baxter replied that a warrant had been issued to take Chic to Dayton, where he could get medical help. "You get your belongings, and we will be on our way," directed the sheriff in a calm manner.

Seemingly resigned to returning to Dayton, Harley asked to go upstairs to gather his belongings. Baxter agreed. A moment later, Baxter heard an upstairs window open and saw Harley jumping from the second floor of the house into the back yard. It didn't take Baxter long to corner Chic. Deputy Sheriff Jim Burns was called for backup, and during the thirty-minute wait for Burns, Chic was persuaded to go peacefully back to Dayton. After he gathered up some clothing, the four men drove to the Phi Gamma Delta fraternity house, where Chic retrieved more clothing. At no time during the one-hour drive to Dayton did Harley resist. In fact, as the car motored along the two-lane highway, Chic explained many intricate football plays he had been involved in as a collegian. Baxter said that Harley showed no signs of an unsound mind. At Dayton Hospital, Chic was greeted by several attendants in a friendly manner and proceeded to his assigned room without any problem.

The legal maneuver to put Harley away was engineered primarily by Havens, who solicited the help of Ned Giesy to file commitment papers with the Franklin County probate court. Giesy, an Ohio State student, signed documents affirming his belief that Chic Harley was insane and dangerous to the community. Giesy also said that Harley is violent and has a history of attacking others. No known documentation exists to support that statement. Papers also state that Chic's maternal grandmother and an uncle had displayed emotional instability, suggesting that Chic's problem was hereditary.

Within two weeks, Chic had escaped from the Dayton Hospital and made his way back to Chicago. Once again he had managed to elude the care that so many had worked hard to get for him. In a letter to Saint, Chic's brother Walter explained that Chic had gone to their brother Bill's house, not Walter's or his parents', because he feared that authorities from Dayton would be waiting to take him back. Chic told Walter that he eloped from the hospital because he could not bear the thought of spending Christmas away from the family.

For the next year, Chic stayed in Chicago with his parents and siblings on Chicago's northwest side. His days were empty. While he talked about getting a job, he never did. Occasionally, Bill hired him to help at Mills Stadium, setting up bleachers and preparing ball fields for play. But after a few days, Chic stopped showing up, saying he wasn't feeling well. An exasperated Bill didn't know what to do.

The public was mostly unaware of Chic's situation, apart from whispers in and around Columbus. Sports reporters continued to rave about Harley's impact on college football, three years after his playing days. Grantland Rice, the legendary sports columnist for the New York *Tribune*, declared that Harley was one of the six greatest backs of all time. A story in the Ohio State *Journal* on December 31 declared Harley one of the best halfbacks developed in America in the last twelve seasons.

Chic's forced confinement at Dayton became a major issue in late summer 1924, when Bill Harley, still involved in the lawsuit over ownership and proceeds of the Chicago Bears, filed another lawsuit. Now Bill formally challenged the determination made in December 1922 that Chic was insane, hiring the same attorneys who were representing them in the

Chicago lawsuit to act on his behalf in Columbus. The basis of their case was that Chic had never been brought into probate court to face his accusers and that at the time, he was not a legal resident of Franklin County and Ohio, but of Chicago. Furthermore, the two psychiatrists who observed Chic during the Grid-Grad game did only that—observe. There was no detailed examination, yet they signed the commitment papers. "We think there is no question but that this court has authority to expunge this record and to lift the shadow from Harley's name," they argued.

Even Chic took the stand, testifying that on December 2, 1922, he was living in Ohio, but only temporarily. He wasn't sure whether his legal residence was Chicago or Columbus. The attorneys maintained that Chic was a legal resident of Illinois because his parents resided there, and thus, the Franklin County probate court had no jurisdiction over the matter.

After hearing testimony and considering various documents and letters, Probate Judge Homer Z. Bostwick issued his ruling. In it he said it was the desire of the Havens in December 1922 to have Chic committed to Dayton in part because he had been a patient there before. Records showed that Chic had escaped from the hospital shortly before Christmas to be home with his family but then returned on January 10, 1923, when he was formally discharged. Bostwick expressed puzzlement that it took Bill Harley twenty months from the time Chic was taken to Dayton to challenge the ruling that he was insane. In Bostwick's opinion, Chic was a resident of Ohio on December 2, 1922, and nothing was ever said to the contrary until much later. In his concluding statement, Judge Bostwick reached the crux of the matter:

The patient was in the hands of friends. True friends—those who had seen him climb to the very zenith of athletic honors. Sympathetic friends who were ready to cooperate with the county and medical witnesses to cause no unnecessary notoriety, but quietly and speedily procure the hospital treatment deemed essential. In fact, to save the distinguished patient from all humiliation, and rescue him, if possible, from mental disease, which then seemed surely to be fastened upon him. Counsel for the patient has failed to convince the court that the patient is entitled to the relief sought. The court had jurisdiction in the premises. The inquest was legal and proper. No fraud of any kind or nature was practiced on the patient, and none attempted. It was just a case of kind friends doing what they thought best for one of their number. The hospital treatment received by the patient probably benefited him greatly.

With Judge Bostwick's ruling, the family had no choice but to accept the declaration that Chic was insane and do everything possible to help him cope with the illness. Chic was unhappy with the ruling. He was fully aware of the stigma that had been cast upon him, which further fueled his deep-seated beliefs that he was disliked and that many of his friends were against him. Newspapers began to carry reports of Chic's mental collapse that included details of his stays in mental institutions. One report compared Harley's career and football talent with Red Grange's, citing their many spectacular plays, and regretted Chic's decline into dementia praecox. This was devastating to Chic.

At times, Chic's conduct was normal; at other times, he was deeply depressed and seen crying. Often he would walk in the neighborhood, look up at the sky, and declare that the world was coming to an end. His mother sometimes found him kneeling, weeping for no apparent reason. He lost interest in his personal appearance. When he felt like talking, he said that people were out to harm him. Sometimes he went about the house pulling down the shades so no one outside could see him. He bought a new car and offered to take family members for a ride. Sometimes he drove very carefully; at other times, recklessly. If asked to slow down, he sped up; if told to drive faster, he slowed to a crawl.

By 1933, things were worse. Chic was often found outdoors praying on his knees. On one of those occasions, he became buried in deep snow. Over the next two years, Chic continued to decline. He felt someone was going to take him away. He lashed out verbally at his mother or one of his sisters but never physically harmed anyone. He expressed great love for his many nieces and nephews. He never showed suicidal or homicidal tendencies, although on a few occasions he pulled out his hair. Still, said official records, Chic maintained a keen memory and could clearly remember events that occurred twenty years earlier at Ohio State. In fact, many times, if engaged in conversation, he gave no hint of being mentally disturbed.

By 1935, after more than a decade of trying to nurture Chic at home, in between confinements in hospitals and sanitariums, it was clear that he needed continuous professional care in an institution. The family patriarch, Charles Harley, had suffered a stroke and died in 1930. Mattie was in her late sixties. Major decisions were now left to Bill and Walter. The final straw came when the neighbors complained that Chic had been tapping on their windows and looking inside.

In early December 1935, the family again called upon Dr. Earl Gaver of Columbus, who met with Walter, Bill, and Chic at the Sherman House hotel in downtown Chicago for about three hours. Being among friends, Chic's inhibitions were released, and he talked and acted much more freely than he would have under different circumstances. In a letter to St. John, Gaver said, "My observations at this conference showed to me that Chic had deteriorated mentally to a considerable extent since my last contact with him. This was not surprising to me as it conforms with the usual course of dementia praecox. This mental enfeeblement is the chief underlying characteristic of the above mental disorder." Gaver concluded that Chic would be safer and get along better in a state institution than in a private hospital.

Despite the dark cloud of Chic's illness, the years between 1925 and 1935 contained a few happy times.

In 1925, Harley was invited to play on the Varsity "O" team for the Grid-Grad game, along with Stinchcomb,

Howard Yerges, Charlie Seddon, and Swede Sorenson. On the opposing side were star players from other schools and past and present OSU coaches who were willing to lace up their cleats. The roster included John Vorys, the Columbus native and boyhood friend of Chic's who attended Yale University and later was elected to the U.S. House of Representatives from the Columbus district. As boys, Chic and John belonged to a neighborhood boxing club that would regularly meet in a neighborhood barn. More than once, Harley had sent the tough Vorys rocketing backward into and sometimes through the gray wooden panels.

A Columbus daily observed that "it will be Chic's first game in the stadium—the monument that his efforts built, but in which he never had a chance to play. One of the interesting features of the Downtown Coaches lineup will be the presence of four professional wrestlers, Clete Kaufman, Cliff Binckley, George Walker, and Ector. All are in perfect condition and will not be at all ignorant of football as it ought to be played for all claim to have played the game before."

Slightly more than 5,000 people attended the charity contest, which kicked off at 2:30 P.M. on November 24, 1925. The admission price was $1. As a sportswriter described the game, "The spectators were treated to clownish acts, burlesques of the real game. They laughed uproariously at the antics of some. Harley appeared in the contest. And he was up to his old tricks. He circled the ends, his cleated feet girded past the tackles, his punts were par excellence, and his defensive work brought back many keen memories of the good old days." The Varsity team walloped the Coaches 32-0.

"How does it feel to be back in the harness, Chic?" one reporter asked. "It is my hobby," he replied, "and you know how it feels to pursue your hobby. It is the same way with me. I like it. That's all." Newspaper photos the next day showed a slightly aging Chic next to his smiling friend and teammate Pete Stinchcomb, both in brown, tight-fitting leather helmets. Chic wore jersey number 46.

A triumphant celebration followed the student/grad victory. When police corporal Ivan Gilhooey raced to investigate a report (later proved false) that celebrants were attempting to set fire to a fraternity house, he became the target of an attack by students who tossed eggs and tomatoes at him, some landing squarely on his face.

For a few years in the 1920s, Ohio State would host all-star charity football games around Thanksgiving. Almost from the beginning, the event became known as Harley Day, with Chic on several occasions gleefully participating.

Another escape from the demons that haunted Chic occurred around 1930, when the family decided to get away from the city and drove north for a week's vacation in Door County, Wisconsin. Door County, with its cozy towns of Sturgeon Bay, Ephraim, Sister Bay, and Egg Harbor, is a quiet, pristine peninsula where visitors can sit back, relax, and momentarily let their troubles drift away. The Harley clan packed every inch of the Durante sedan convertible—surprisingly, owned by Chic—and headed north for the seven-hour drive over some very rough, rural roads. Suitcases and bags were strapped to the back of the car and on running boards. Every few hours, the passengers stopped to get some exercise, fill up with gas, and use the facilities. Then they'd be off again.

The Harley family was not immune from the terrible effects of the Great Depression, when millions of Americans found themselves struggling to put food on the table and lead some semblance of a normal life. Over time, as many as seventeen Harleys lived together (at 6456 Oxford Avenue or 6761 Olmstead Avenue in the Edison Park neighborhood) on Chicago's far north side because there was not enough money to live separately. Mattie was undeniably the matriarch until her death in 1947. By her side during these tough times were most of her children—Chic; Ruth and Sig Wessell and their son, Richard; Bill and his wife, Agnes; Walter; Marie; Irene and her husband, Cliff Bowling; and their assorted offspring. Everyone struggled to survive and to cope with Chic's illness. Still, those days were happy in the sense that everyone was together despite the financial hardships and stresses. Whatever money was made went into a family fund to pay for food and utilities.

The only family member with a good job was Cliff Bowling, an engineer with the Mississippi Valley Structural Steel Co. in Chicago. In April 1932, Bowling's boss, H. H. Cosely, wrote to his friend Lynn St. John in Columbus, on behalf of Bowling, about Bowling's idea for a new type of internal combustion gas engine. Could St. John refer him to an engineering professor to see if the engine had any commercial promise? Saint said he would do what he could, but nothing ever came of Bowling's project.

Also helpful were regular visits by representatives of Ohio State University who showed up as a reminder that the people of Ohio had not forgotten Chic. In addition to looking into Chic's well-being, the visitor regularly delivered a check in the amount of at least $100—a precious sum for the Harleys at that time.

Further financial help had been established in April 1927 by a committee of the OSU athletic board. The three-person panel, which included Saint, agreed to "employ" Chic as a year-round assistant coach in football and baseball at a salary of $600 per year. The funding was to come from the Varsity "O" Alumni Association. Eventually, the sum doubled to $1,200 per year. In addition, the athletic board would assume management of the annual Varsity "O"-Downtown Coaches football game, with the goal of raising the fund to $10,000. Money deposited in a special account would be available to pay Chic a "salary" and provide whatever he needed whenever. It was an extremely generous gesture on the part of the university—undoubtedly Saint John was the primary instigator. Chic, of course, was never employed. The money was to help pay his expenses whenever the need arose. Ohio State would continue to look in on Chic and provide financial help for the rest of his life.

With Dr. Gaver's diagnosis and his strong recommendation that Chic be admitted to a state institution, the Harley family made the final excruciating decision to commit Chic to professional and continuous care. Shortly after Gaver's meeting with Walter, Chic, and Bill in December 1935, Chic was taken to Hines Veterans Administration Hospital in Chicago. Its location five miles west of the Harley household would make it easy for the family to visit Chic and monitor his situation. The mammoth facility was filled with World War I veterans, many of who required constant care for the rest of their lives. Chic's nearly two years in the Army and honorable discharge made him eligible for veterans benefits.

For the next thirty-four months, Chic Harley spent much of his time at Hines VA. Every doctor who examined Chic, whether at Hines or Dayton, agreed that he was suffering from the incurable disease dementia praecox. In later years, the name of the disorder changed to schizophrenic reaction, but the basic meaning remained. A man who only fifteen years earlier was on top of the American athletic scene, revered by thousands, poised to conquer the world, had lost much of his ability to reason and function normally. The only recourse was placement in a stress-free environment. Hope for recovery was almost nonexistent. He was believed to be totally and permanently disabled.

Administration building of Danville VA Hospital where Chic was admitted to in 1938 which he called home for the rest of his life.

Official medical report of examination of Chic made upon his arrival in Danville shows that a test for syphilis was "negative".

CHAPTER 12
The Move to Danville

Beaten psychologically and exhausted physically, Mattie Harley by the fall of 1938 had resigned herself to a painful truth: Hines Veterans Hospital was not providing her deeply disturbed son with the adequate constant care he needed. While convenient, it was more of a detriment to Chic's well-being. The hospital's proximity to home kept Chic near to his mother and siblings, but in doing so, it was a distraction. Chic hated to be away from his large family, most of who lived together in a cramped bungalow in Edison Park on Chicago's northwest side, a neighborhood of row after row of small brick houses crowded together along narrow streets. Patches of grass and blotches of dirt filled in the small front yards. In the background was the constant rattle of commuter and freight trains.

For quite some time, Mattie had sensed that the care Chic was getting at Hines was inadequate, but like any caring mother, she held out hope that things would get better. They did not. As difficult as it was to accept, Mattie knew that the seventeen-year struggle to help her youngest son recover—or at least show any sign of improvement—wasn't working. Something else had to be done. It was time for Chic's guilt-ridden mother to let go. After weeks of pleading with her other children to

211

get their youngest brother the round-the-clock care he so desperately needed away from Chicago, the painful decision was finally made to move forward. Slowly and with great care, Mattie affixed her shaky signature—"Mrs. Mattie Harley"—on the formal authorization for Chic's hospitalization and treatment. The date was October 14, 1938.

The necessary steps had now been taken to move Chic from Hines to the Veterans Administration Hospital in downstate Danville, a blue-collar community 120 miles south of Chicago near the border with Indiana. The largest city in Vermilion County, Danville in the 1930s was an island of bustling activity in an ocean of flat farmland. Its population of around 36,000 had not changed for years. Its years as a downstate industrial center had passed. Coal mines provided jobs. One of the area's busiest places then was Danville Junction, where four railroad tracks entered town from four different directions. Teddy Roosevelt, William McKinley, and Booker T. Washington had stopped in Danville for rest and water. Abe Lincoln practiced law here from 1841 to 1859 and departed Illinois for Washington, D.C., on February 11, 1861, telling a crowd of well-wishers in Danville, "If I have blessings at my disposal, Old Vermilion will come in for a bountiful share." In later years, actors Gene Hackman, Dick and Jerry Van Dyke, Bobby Short, Donald O'Connor, and Helen Morgan would call Danville home.

No member of the Harley family rode with Chic to Danville when his journey south began on Saturday, October 15. No one could bear to do so, least of all Mattie and Ruth. They said their tearful good-byes in Chicago.

Two attendants from Hines boarded the steam train with Chic in downtown Chicago's Union Station in the early evening. Chic was his usual quiet self and understandably somber as he stepped aboard, one attendant in front of him, the other, behind. Soon, the familiar sound of hissing steam signaled that it was time to go. Chic was heading to a new and strange home far from the familiar comforts of Edison Park and family. He knew he was sick and aware that something was wrong with his mind.

What specifically was wrong, he had no idea. Chic said very little for the entire trip as the steam train pulled into and out of small towns along the way, picking up passengers and siphoning water from round wooden tanks alongside the steel tracks to feed the thirsty locomotive. Each ticket cost $3.70. Chic had an extra dollar for a meal. He was forty-three years old now. Gray strands of his once thick, dark brown hair began to crowd around his temples. His transfer papers listed his occupation as laborer and his faith, Protestant.

By nine o'clock that night, Chic was in Danville. A short car ride transported him up a winding rode to the imposing administration building, with its white pillars and arched entranceways. There he was checked in. A few minutes later, he was in an unfamiliar and frightening setting, where he knew no one. The attendants who accompanied him had vanished into the night and headed back to Chicago. Chic was led to a massive ward, where long rows of narrow, white beds were set up, most of them occupied by veterans with a variety of physical and psychological infirmities. Chic asked himself if he really belonged in such a place. Because of their service in the armed forces, the 400 or so patients at the Danville VA were entitled to medical care, courtesy of a grateful U.S. government. Scared, Chic quietly and slowly entered the large, unfamiliar room, stopping at the assigned bed a hospital attendant pointed out to him. He had only a few meager belongings in his suitcase. Chic crawled into bed, and after what seemed like hours of tossing and turning, he finally fell asleep.

As 1938 passed into 1939, Chic slowly settled in, though it was rough going. He cherished the visits from his old pals from Columbus. On a few occasions, OSU football coaches and even the team would drop by to say hello while on their way to Champaign-Urbana for a football game. In 1938, Coach Francis Schmidt conducted a team practice on the lawn of the VA Hospital as Chic, St. John, and thousands of patients looked on. With Danville located on the road between Columbus and the University of Illinois, the visits from friends increased with time, especially during football season, when Ohio State played the Illini. The best-known Columbus sportswriters of the day— Johnny Jones of the *Dispatch*, Lew Byrer of the *Journal*, and Russ Needham of the *Citizen*—stopped by every year or two. Jones and Needham were Chic's boyhood chums, and Jones was State's top yell-master—cheerleader—in the few years before 1920. The personable Jones, in later years, often organized trips to bring Chic to Columbus for homecoming games, team reunions, and his September 15 birthday celebrations. Nationwide, Bill Corum of the *Journal-American* in New York City and popular syndicated sportswriters like Grantland Rice and Ring Lardner would write thousands of admiring words about Harley and what he meant to football, aspiring athletes, and institutions of higher learning. The name Harley had stirred hope in young men and women who were outstanding in sports and academics but never dreaming of the opportunity to attend college: If this shy, small, quiet individual could excel, why couldn't they?

In 1939, two decades after Chic last played for Ohio State, Byrer in one of his columns asked readers to submit their recollections of Harley in 200 words or less. Byrer cited an earlier story by Corum in which he asked people to compare Harley with Red Grange, the Illini's "Galloping Ghost" of the mid-1920s. One response, said Byrer, was "from the gentleman from Champaign, Ill., the Iceman's [Grange's] stomping ground, who asked for one more thrill from football—and that thrill was One More Harley."

Of the 400 letters Byrer received, the number of Harley admirers outnumbered Grange's by a thin margin. Grange was a collegian who played at a time when radio coverage of sporting events was just beginning to blossom. With the benefit of this new electronic medium—post-Harley—Grange's fame spread far and wide and well beyond his three years with the University of Illinois. The day after he played his last college game, the pride of Wheaton, Illinois, signed a contract to play professional football for George Halas and the Chicago Bears at a salary of $100,000 per year. The business deal proved to be a gold mine for

Halas and his partner, Dutch Sternaman. With Grange, the barn-storming Bears attracted huge crowds at some of the country's biggest stadiums. For a while, they played three or four games in a single week to take advantage of the craze and demand for tickets. Grange played pro ball for several more years before retiring to a comfortable life in his suburban Chicago home.

One letter Byrer received stood out. It was from a man who lived in Chicago from 1922 to 1925 who said he knew Grange and felt he was the greatest player he ever saw . . . with the exception of Chic Harley.

"All of Columbus loved Chic," recalled the writer. "They don't talk much about Chic anymore, but people still write in his name for mayor and governor. And I mean seriously, and his picture hangs in hundreds of homes, offices, clubs, and hotel lobbies. He has remained in the hearts of the football fans of the Ohio Valley for 21 years—and always will—their All American of Americans. He was positively the greatest and yet so little is said of him when the greats are discussed."

The writer signed his letter, "Crimson Coach from Toledo."

In November 1936, during Chic's time at Hines VA, he managed to attend a reunion of the team of 1916 on the twentieth anniversary of Ohio State's first conference championship. It was the team's first reunion. The university *Monthly* hailed Chic as "greatest of them all." It added that he looked gray and gaunt with illness, but his "shy, wide smile is still the uncertain boyish grin of his college days." On a Friday night, nineteen of the twenty-seven-member squad sat down to a steak dinner. Saint was the official host.

"They lived and relived those colorful, vivid days," the *Monthly* reported. They toasted Howard Yerges, their diminutive quarterback; they hailed behemoth "Minnie" Lapp, and at halftime of the Saturday game against Michigan, they were applauded by the crowd. Sixty thousand people were in the stands, considered one of the smallest crowds in the last several years. At half time, Jesse Owens was introduced, having won four gold medals at the Olympic games in Berlin just two months earlier.

215

Owens was presented with a silver sterling set and best wishes from the university. After the game, Saint asked members of the 1916 team to meet at Hennick's for a "coke" before heading over to the swanky Deshler-Wallick Hotel for the formal dinner. Chic was with his teammates throughout, remaining quiet and appreciative.

After Chic's first thorough clinical examination in Danville, doctors wrote a report, based partly on family sources. It said that Chic was one of eight children, that his father had died in 1930 at age sixty-eight of "heart trouble," and that Chic was a good boy, never getting into trouble with teachers or schoolmates. He was nicknamed "Noisy" because he was very quiet. He spent his time after school and during the summer playing with the neighborhood boys. It was during those early, formative years that he was introduced to the game of football. In high school, Chic said he liked girls, but was never in love except for short periods during school life (probably meaning high school). Throughout his prep years, he excelled in athletics, competing at the highest levels in baseball, football, and track. In one high school baseball contest, after a fight erupted on the playing field, Chic was accidentally knocked in the head with a baseball bat and lay unconscious for three days. Later, some people theorized that this injury may have contributed to his mental illness.

Throughout his years at Ohio State, Harley spent summers employed as a lifeguard. He kept company with the same girl, Louise Havens, all during high school and college. She was popular, and the couple spent many warm summer days at the pool enjoying a close personal bond that began during their years at East High School. "He occasionally went out with other girls," said the report, "but that girl (Louise) was the only girl in whom he ever showed an interest. Even after Chic became ill, the girl wanted to marry him and told the family so, but they refused to allow veteran to marry her because of his mental condition."

Aware that he had growing psychological problems in the early 1920s, Chic told doctors that he considered them periodic nervous breakdowns that led to his placement in sanitariums.

After his one season of professional football, he sold coal in Columbus for a short time. In 1923, he was confined to bed for a month with influenza.

In another report, written at about the same time, family members told VA doctors that Chic suffered convulsions at the age of three, around the time his sister Helen died. And according to brother Bill, said the report, it was Chic's belief in 1921 that some of his teammates on the Staleys were out to hurt him because he had gained so much fame as a collegian, was a one-fourth owner of the team, and undoubtedly earned a higher salary. Bill shared this belief. "As a result, he received many injuries in the games he played," said the official medical report. "He seemed to close up and crawl into a shell."

Within a day of his admittance to Danville, Chic resigned himself to his fate. "I guess I belong in a mental hospital," he told doctors. "I'm restless and nervous. I don't feel so well." He would sit quietly in the ward and say nothing unless spoken to. Often he would be spotted standing in a corner alone in his thoughts. "He frequently smiles and his appearance was neat and clean and he was well aware of current events," said one report. "He liked to talk football and in one conversation named Notre Dame's Four Horsemen without any difficulty."

By mid-December 1938, Harley was given simple outdoor duties, which interested him little. Over the next two months, his mental condition worsened as he became more reclusive. He was frequently seen kneeling and praying and would admit to hearing voices, a symptom of schizophrenia. By late February 1939, Chic was going outside without permission, either quietly slipping away or suddenly bolting from the cafeteria line. Such occurrences forced the hospital to transfer him to an "eloper ward," where doors were locked tightly to secure patients who were prone to disappearing. That didn't prevent Chic from trying to leave whenever the opportunity arose. For the next several years, Chic would try again and again to run away from the hospital after being transferred out of the eloper ward. He was always quickly found unharmed and returned. He told an attendant that he intended to run away to the World's Fair in New York and that no one is going to stop him. Though he never carried out his threat, his mental and physical condition continued to decline. He complained of being homesick and wanting to be with his family—something the hospital and family agreed would not happen until the time was right. He was severely distraught.

In those days, medical treatments for Chic's illness were inadequate. They included small doses of mineral oil along with outdoor activity, which he enjoyed, and attempts to engage him in conversation, which he shied away from. Doctors tried to interest him in a hobby, which he warmed up to after a few years. Records show that he was given elixir bromides and sodium amytol, common treatments then. The drugs he really needed weren't developed until after 1945. Had they been available, Chic may have been able to lead a fairly normal life.

Throughout the first half of the 1940s, Harley's prognosis remained bleak. He was thought to have little chance of any sustained improvement; the disease might eventually take his life. Spurts of improvement, such as interest in engaging in activities like the hospital's print shop, were rare.

As the years went by, Ohio State's interest in the welfare of its greatest athlete continued unabated, although only a few people were aware that Chic's condition was so serious. As Saint neared retirement, his top aide, Henry Taylor, assumed the responsibility of keeping contact with Chic and the hospital and monitoring his well-being and what little progress there was. Taylor reported his findings to family members and friends in Ohio anxious to know how Chic was doing. Members of the Adonis Club organized campaigns to send Chic Christmas cards. Taylor arranged for the Harley family to visit Chic at the Wolford Hotel in Danville by working with the manager to provide a holiday dinner and even a small Christmas tree in a private room. The university would cover all expenses. By this time, visits from family members, especially Ruth, were more frequent.

At one point in the early 1940s, a transfer from Danville to a more modern, private hospital in Kearny, New Jersey, was being

considered. Taylor took an interest in this possibility and corre-
sponded with the hospital to describe Chic's background and
condition, but that plan was abandoned.

The next four years saw little change and no noticeable
improvement for Chic, even though the world around him was
forever changed. In December 1944, the Ohio State *Monthly*
carried a brief report of the death of Fritz Holtkamp, the
talented Buckeye center who played alongside Harley in 1916.
In his college days, Holtkamp was a popular sportswriter for
the *Dispatch* who went by the pen name "Wahoo." He remained
among the most loyal of Harley admirers until the day he died.
After graduating from Ohio State in 1920, Holtkamp became a
football coach at Mississippi State and later at Western Reserve
University in Cleveland, where he also was involved in the
construction business. He enlisted in the Navy during World War
II and was assigned to a base in the South Pacific. Holtkamp died
at age fifty-five, as the war against Japan raged. The *Monthly* did
not list cause of death.

The twenty-fifth anniversary of the 1916 Buckeye team in
the fall of 1941 was a major event in Columbus celebrated by
tens of thousands of Ohio State fans and alums. The university produced a hardcover book filled with reminiscences of the
championship team and its perfect 7 and 0 record capped off
by Harley's last-minute touchdown and extra point in the mud
of Champaign. On the cover of the book was one of the best
portraits ever produced of Chic, his handsome face displaying
a shy confidence, a dimple in his chin, and his wavy brown hair.
Below the picture are the letters CHIC flanked by the years 1916
and 1941. Inside, the four-stanza poem "O Come Let's Sing
Ohio's Praise, And Songs to Alma Mater Raise," by Marion L.
Renick, fills a page. It's a stirring tribute to the 1916 championship team and Harley, in particular:

*Hearts thrilling once more at the memory of that slight figure slipping
away from the tangled teams on the gridiron and scampering over the
goal line . . . Cheers echoing to the blue October skies . . . Yea Chic!*

Yea Chic!... Joy in our hearts when we and the world and the boy with the wistful, crooked smile were young together ... Joy that death alone can still.

Writing about the reunion, *Dispatch* columnist Russ Needham described the team's locker room in the old Athletic House as "a rickety converted dwelling with its two shower baths and lockers in the earth floor basement. Visiting teams dressed in the old gym that later became known as the armory." He continued:

If ever an individual made an indelible imprint on a community, that individual was Chic Harley. Without him, Ohio State would doubtless, in the course of time, become a big school. It would have had a stadium and all the things that go with it. Not as early as it did by any means, but it would have come in time. But Columbus would not have been the same. That Columbus is known far and wide for its singular devotion to Ohio State football springs directly from its prior fascination for the captivating little 150 pounder produced by its own East High School.

A few years later, yet another honor for Chic was under way in Columbus. His close friend Leo Yassenoff, a successful Columbus businessman and Ohio State grad, had commissioned a life-size relief figure of Chic for the façade of the new University Theater he owned at 1980 N. High Street. Yassenoff dedicated the theater—his seventh—to Chic and to future Ohio State football players. The figure of Chic on the outside wall showed him helmet-less and outstretched after punting a football. When the building was dedicated on Monday, March 24, 1947, approximately 10,000 people showed up, including Mattie, Ruth, Bill, and Walter Harley; Saint; Johnny Jones; three-time Buckeye All-American and head football Coach Wesley Fesler; Mayor James A. Rhodes; and Gov. Thomas J. Herbert, who knew Chic from college and the army. Teammates also on hand were Pete Stinchcomb, Gordy Rhodes, Shifty Bolen, Charlie Seddon, and Chic's assistant coach, Red Trautman. Coach Wilce couldn't attend due to illness. Together, Stinchcomb, Fesler, and Herbert unveiled the art piece. That day the theater was playing *The Al*

Jolson Story, along with a film about Harley's football career. Chic could not make the trip from Danville.

"This building may last for 100 years, but the spirit of Harley will last forever," Mayor Rhodes told the throng of shivering spectators. Rhodes suggested that September 15 be permanently proclaimed "Harley Day" in Columbus. Moments later, St. John explained that a Harley Scholarship had recently been established at the school that will provide financial assistance to future Ohio State students and athletes. Johnny Jones came up with the scholarship idea. "A great impetus was given to the Harley Scholarship Fund" with the ceremony that day, reported local newspapers. Coach Fesler, who as a football player earned All-American honors three years, and was a Phi Beta Kappa, was later quoted as saying that Chic Harley was his hero as he was growing up in Youngstown, Ohio, a vibrant industrial town on the state's far eastern border. "And he still is."

Mattie, described in one newspaper as Chic's "sweet-faced" mother, who looked tired and drawn, told the crowd, "All I wish to say at this time is this is the happiest moment in my life."

With the Axis powers defeated and Europe in ruins, the end of another era approached. Lynn St. John announced his retirement as of summer 1947, after thirty-four years as Ohio State athletic director. In his nearly three and a half decades at Ohio State, Saint had coached many in football, baseball, and track. He had joined Ohio State the same year John Wilce did in 1913, and together, with Harley, they completely turned around a floundering sports program, making it one of the most admired and successful in the nation. Wilce had left football coaching in 1928 and thereafter taught at OSU's College of Medicine. Always a close friend and protective figure for Harley, Saint was excited about visiting his prized pupil in Danville later that year on the day before the Ohio State-Illinois game in Champaign. That day the two greeted each other warmly and spent several hours recalling their years together. Later, admirers of the two men liked to say that "Chic took Ohio State football into the big time, and the Saint has kept it there."

221

Through June 30, 1947, university records show, athletics at Ohio State, in particular, football, had seen a major financial boost. Football receipts for that fiscal year totaled $465,149—$85,149 more than the previous season. Athletic department investments had soared to nearly $700,000 and the program had more than $79,000 in the bank. Thirty years earlier, total athletic department receipts were $53,811.27, with football leading the way. By 2008, the athletic department's budget exceeded $100 million. The Harley Trust Fund in 1947 stood at $10,646.78. A month later, the money was transferred into a newly created fund called the Charles W. Harley Memorial Fund. Its proceeds would go to the health and welfare of Chic as long as he lived. Any money left following his death would support scholarships for outstanding undergraduate male athletes at Ohio State.

The year 1948 began uneventfully during the bitterly cold and snowy months of January and February, but it proved to be one of the most significant years in Chic Harley's life. It was a year of personal loss, followed by a period of hope, and by November, a triumphant return to Columbus.

1916 **CHIC** 1941

November 15, 1941 Buckeye football program cover
marks the 25th anniversary of Ohio State's first Western
Conference championship by paying tribute to it most
revered player, Chic Harley.

*Having suffered from mental illness for the previous 14 years,
Chic returned to Ohio State for a football contest in 1936
when he met up with his friend and mentor Lynn Saint John.*

CHAPTER 13
Triumphant Return

Unable to shake the slow, debilitating disease that had sapped her energy and will to live, Mattie Trunnell Harley died of congestive heart failure on March 1, 1948, at Presbyterian Hospital in Chicago. She had been living with Ruth and Sig Wessell in their home in Des Plaines, a northwest suburb of Chicago that was beginning to see tremendous postwar growth, largely because it was located next to Douglas Air Field, later to become O'Hare International Airport. The Wessells had a large, neat two-story frame house nestled on a quiet street just a block from the Des Plaines River. Their only son, Richard, also lived in Des Plaines and was the publisher of the local newspaper. He and his young wife, Mary Jane, had saved the money they earned during the war to buy the newspaper they dreamed of publishing. Mattie's days of worrying about her youngest boy were now over. She had seen much joy and more than her fair share of sorrow in her eighty-two years and six months, having been preceded in death by her husband, Charles, and two of her eight children. Surviving were her three sons and three daughters: Walter, Bill, Chic, Irene, Marie, and Ruth; nine grandchildren; six great-grandchildren; and a sister, Carrie Saunders.

By summer 1948, Chic and his family were facing a monumental decision. Through the miracle of modern medicine,

Chic might have a fighting chance to crawl out, at least partially, of the shell that had encased him for the past twenty-six years. The main question was whether to risk the treatment.

Ten years earlier, the first public mention of the new treatment appeared in *Time* magazine. Soon after, Guy H. Williams, superintendent of the Cleveland State Hospital, described the procedure to Henry Taylor, Saint's assistant in Columbus. It had seen some success among schizophrenic patients, he said. The treatment, insulin shock therapy, called for a regular series of insulin injections over several months.

Wrote Williams to Taylor:

We have used insulin in some other types of mental conditions with some favorable results and some unfavorable. Inasmuch as I would like to grow enthusiastic about this, I do not believe that we have any grounds for so doing. Would that we could find something that would not only help our old friend Chic, but thousands of other cases. But, as yet, we have not discovered that much desired agent. There is one thing, my dear friend, that so many folks forget. Each case of schizophrenia represents a distinct personality change, and in my humble opinion each case must be so treated.

For the next decade, the idea of treating Chic in that manner lay forgotten. But by summer 1948, with advances in the treatment and a new doctor interested in Chic's case, everyone was in favor of moving ahead. Chic wholeheartedly agreed and was anxious to get started. The prognosis was guarded primarily because Chic had been ill for so long. The successes had been seen in younger patients who had been suffering for just a few years. But the Harley family reasoned that even though his chances for improvement were iffy, the opportunity was one they could not pass up.

By early July, Dr. George Rowland, manager of the Danville VA hospital, informed OSU's new assistant athletic director, Oscar Thomas, that the facility had recently doubled its insulin therapy capacity and could take on Chic if permission were granted.

Rowland wrote:

Chic was one of those to whom we had hoped to give this treatment. Preliminary studies on him began a number of weeks ago. Chic has expressed a desire to have the treatment and we believe it would be worthwhile to give him this opportunity. It should be clearly understood that chronic cases frequently do not respond, but aside from the minimal physical risk, the treatment can do no harm. In a small percentage of cases, even of very long standing, very satisfactory results may be obtained. The other specific methods of treatment, such as electroshock and brain surgery, could not be expected to produce any favorable change in your friend's illness.

The insulin injections began on July 21 and continued over the next two months, a total of more than forty treatments. Each procedure began at 7 A.M. and ended at noon. During those five hours, Chic was in a coma, which left him weak but none the worse for wear.

Wrote Ruth to Thomas on August 2:

The doctor seems to think they will help Chic. It all sounds wonderful, and each night I pray Chic can stand the treatments and hope they will help him. One of my mother's last wishes was that we do all we can for him. I hope I can grant her wish. The doctor suggested we visit him often and write often, too. He needs the moral support. Now I wonder if word could be passed along to Chic's friends to write him. I'm going down this week. I haven't seen him since the treatments were started and feel quite worried until I see him.

Ruth arrived in Danville with her son, Richard; her brother Bill; and Bill's oldest son, Vernon. "I packed a lunch, and we went out on the picnic grounds, played shuffle board together, and walked," reported Ruth. "Really had a good time. Mentally, he was wonderful. He said he receives a Columbus newspaper daily and enjoys it."

Harley's neuropsychiatric examination report dated February 1, 1949, describes Chic's shock therapy in great detail. It ended on September 24, 1948, and resulted officially in forty-three treatments, thirty-three of which produced deep comas.

Chic was always cooperative. During treatment, progressive improvement was noted. He took interest in all the activities provided for shock patients and was agreeable as well as sociable with the other patients receiving treatments. His physical condition likewise improved. During these treatments he was often visited by his brother and sister, who indicated their desire to have Chic moved out of the hospital when treatments are finished.

Having not only withstood the insulin shock therapy, but shown signs of remarkable improvement, Chic was granted a ninety-day pass by doctors to stay with Bill in Chicago. His furlough began on October 14, 1948, ten years to the day that he had been transferred to Danville from Hines.

When a much-improved Chic greeted Bill in Chicago, the two decided not to waste any time. The very next day, Saturday, October 16, they hopped in Bill's car and headed south toward Bloomington, Indiana, where the Buckeyes were to face off with the Hoosiers for a Big Ten conference showdown. Chic's interest in football by now had been rekindled, and the six-hour drive to southern Indiana, both he and Bill believed, would provide some well-deserved pleasure.

The morning of game day, the brothers first drove to the Canyon Inn, a resort hideaway about fifteen miles from Bloomington, where the Ohio team was sequestered. As players were packing their gear for the short transfer to Bloomington, heads turned and mouths gaped open when Chic and Bill entered the room. Dressed in a long overcoat and a brown fedora with its front brim turned upward, a smiling Chic approached every player with his right hand outstretched in friendship. He was there to wish the team well. The sixty burly players and coaches were awestruck by the unannounced and gracious visit.

Chic's surprising appearance "so electrified the team that they smeared Indiana's famed running team that gained 13 net yards running the whole game," reported the December 15 Ohio State *Monthly*. While not a smear in a scoring sense, the Buckeyes' effort marred the Hoosiers' homecoming weekend. After the contest, Chic walked to the victors' locker room, offering congratulations as loud, appreciative players swarmed around with praise and pats on the back. A few hours later, Chic, unable to contain himself, visited the team one last time as it was celebrating its victory in a private dining room in Bloomington.

"I just want one more look at the fine boys," he told Coach Fesler.

Over the next few weeks leading up to Ohio State's November 20 homecoming clash with Michigan, Chic and Bill attended games against Illinois and Northwestern. By season's end, the Buckeyes' record stood at 6 and 3—far better than 1947's last-place conference showing.

One Indian summer night, Ruth wrote a heartfelt letter to Oscar Thomas from her home in Des Plaines.

"Thank you for those hours of happiness," Ruth wrote, referring to the grand reception Chic had received during a recent visit to Columbus. She continued:

I never saw Chic display so much enjoyment and happiness since he's been ill, and it afforded me just as much pleasure as it did Chic. I couldn't help but think how much that would have meant to Mother. I hope and pray that it [trial visit with Bill] will work out satisfactorily, but I can't reconcile myself that he's not home here. I've always longed and hoped for the day that I could bring him home, for Chic was part of our home for so many years. But now that Mother's gone, things are so different and perhaps it's better that way. But I can't but feel our home is home to Chic. My only thoughts now are for Chic's welfare and I pray this will be the turning point in his life.

With word having reached Columbus and all of Ohio by late summer that Chic Harley's mental and physical health had turned for the better, his many admirers and friends sensed

229

that the time had arrived to bring their most famous son home. While sportswriter Bob Hooey and others had hoped to organize a huge party in honor of Chic in September—"one he will remember for a long time"—there hadn't been time to put all the pieces into place. Instead, they decided to stage it during the biggest game of the season, against Michigan on November 20.

All of Columbus and the Ohio State campus were abuzz late in the afternoon of Friday, November 19. While the game against Michigan was still twenty hours away, downtown Columbus was abuzz with activity as people scurried up and down along stretches of High Street to find a good spot to watch the parade. About a mile away, more than a thousand people crammed inside Union Station's waiting room. Another forty or so stood a football field distance away on a railroad platform, waiting anxiously for the slow-moving train to come to a complete stop. The weather was nasty. Temperatures hovered in the high thirties. A steady, unrelenting rain soaked shoppers, pedestrians, and those waiting patiently for the parade. A stiff, biting breeze made conditions even worse. Sheltered from the elements were thousands more people perched at open windows inside office buildings that lined the parade route from Union Station to the capitol building.

The streamliner from Chicago finally clunked to a halt. Behind the locomotive, passengers began to exit half a dozen cars. About forty people who had come to greet their friend, most of them in overcoats and hats, inched forward. Suddenly, a slight, graying, middle-aged man carefully stepped across the space between two train cars and then onto the three steps leading down to the platform. At first nothing was said. Even the train engine seemed silent. Their emotions stirred, and their eyes misting, the greeters continued their slight forward movement as the man who some had named "The Immortal" looked up.

"Then a characteristic shy, wonderful smile broke over the little guy's face," wrote the Ohio State *Monthly*. Chic Harley had come home.

230

Swarming around Harley was a reception committee: Allen Thurman, captain of the 1912 East High School team; Congressman John Vorys, captain of East High's last city championship team in 1914; Frank Gullum, Chic's first high school football coach; Dr. Palmer Cordray, Chic's coach in his last two years of high school; John Wilce; Pete Stinchcomb; Leo Yassenoff; and OSU teammate Farky Farcasin. Mrs. John Vorys placed a carnation in the buttonhole of Chic's gray tweed coat, and several women planted kisses on the embarrassed football great.

"Say a few words," barked a radio announcer, planting a microphone an inch or two from Chic's face. "Hello, Joe," said Chic almost immediately as he spotted Joe Mulbarger, one of his closest high school friends and 1914 teammate he'd shared punting chores with. Forgetting the radio interview, Chic draped his arm around Mulbarger in a rare sign of affection. The turnout of forty of his dearest friends quickly caught up with Chic as his mouth quivered and his eyes filled with tears.

Others in the welcoming crowd included university Vice President Harlan Hatcher, later president of the University of Michigan; Ohio Governor Herbert; and Mayor Rhodes. Gradually making their way upstairs, Chic and his entourage— brothers Bill and Walter, sister Ruth, nephew Richard and his wife, Mary Jane, and other family members, along with police officers—slipped into Union Station's giant waiting room. A thunderous cheer rose from the thousand admirers lucky enough to find space in the cavernous area. Chic once again momentarily lost his composure before the large, passionate crowd. He walked slowly along a pathway cordoned off by smiling Columbus police officers, through an exit, and into a waiting convertible. Despite the steady rainfall, the decision was made to lower the roof so all of Columbus could catch a glimpse of the man whom sportswriter Hooey had named "The One and Only." Chic took a seat in the back with the governor and mayor. Vehicles behind them carried family and former teammates, followed by twenty homecoming floats. As cars and floats swung into formation to kick off the parade, a police and fire communications truck blared "Across the Field." With sirens wailing, the parade made its way south on High Street toward the state capitol.

On one of Columbus's worst weather days of the year, a crowd estimated at 75,000 to 100,000 lined the city's most famous street, gawking and cheering as Harley passed by, smiling and waving. From office buildings above, ticker tape floated to the ground, some of it landing on a smiling Chic. "It was without question the greatest tribute ever accorded to any Columbus sports figure," said the *Monthly*.

"The faces of fans lining both sides of the street displayed mixed emotions as Harley's car passed," reported the Ohio State *Journal* a day later. "Youngsters watched in open-eyed wonderment at the turnout for the man who had been just a name to them. Others who must have been around during Harley's dazzling days on old Ohio Field smiled and a few wiped tears as they obviously recalled moments from the great games in which Harley ran and passed his way into the hearts of Buckeye fans."

It was almost dark when the convertible, its windshield wipers continuing their rhythmic back-and-forth, reached the end of the parade route at the capitol steps across from the Neil House hotel. As the auto braked, several thousand fans jumped off the curb and rushed toward the automobile to catch a glimpse of Chic. "It was an unbelievable show of affection like the opening of floodgates," said Richard Wessell years later. "Then magically," reported the *Monthly*, "the black clouds were pierced by the sun. Like a theater spotlight focusing on the star of a great performance just ended, the bright rays dispelled the gloom. And immediately, a brilliant rainbow appeared overhead—scarlet and gray predominating." Across High Street, the landmark clock read 5:35 P.M.

For the next forty-eight hours, Chic Harley was the center of attention in Columbus. Thousands of alumni expressed their feelings for Chic for what he had done for the state, community, and school, and for what he had personally endured over the past two and a half decades. On several occasions, Chic openly wept, only to regain his composure within moments. Repeatedly, he declared that he was undeserving of all the attention.

"He was unquestionably his old self, far along the comeback trail and recovered from the nervous, depressive ailment that had kept him a semi-invalid for nearly two decades," said the *Monthly*.

In several radio interviews over the whirlwind weekend, Chic expressed his happiness at being back. When asked to recapture some of the moments in Ohio State's first-ever win over Michigan, in 1919, he responded, "I don't remember any exact plays in that game. But I remember we beat 'em!"

On Friday evening, Chic was the guest of the football varsity team and later attended a mammoth student rally. On game day, accompanied by close friends and family, the man whom John Wilce called the "perfect player" settled into his seat in section 18A, row 28, seat 30 of Ohio Stadium, also known as "The House That Harley Built." In a special halftime tribute to Chic, the band performed a choreographed number that reenacted his kicking the winning extra point in the 1916 contest against Illinois that secured the Buckeyes' first conference title. In another number, in the center of the field, the band formed the letters OHIO, and then made a gap in the two O's to form C's, changing OHIO to CHIC.

The powerful Wolverines won the game 19-0. While disappointing, the outcome was tempered by the emotional celebration for Chic, whose heroics three decades earlier had done so much to perpetuate the great school rivalry.

On Sunday morning, Chic was back on campus as the guest of honor at the annual Football Captain's Breakfast. Throughout the exciting weekend, Ohio media reported in great detail on Chic's visit and his many contributions to the school, community, and sport of football. Chet Long, commentator for local radio station WBNS, said, "I have seen many fair-weather crowds that numbered less. . . . The demonstration [parade] was almost unbelievable. Certainly, Chic Harley holds a prominent place in the heart of Columbus and all central Ohio."

Wrote Bob Hooey in his column: "If you never saw him run with a football, we can't describe it to you. It wasn't like Thorpe or Grange or Harmon or anyone else. It was a kind of a cross between music and cannon fire, and it brought your heart up under your ears. In the hardest fought gridiron battles, Harley usually would get away and score the winning touchdown. . . . His fame grew so great and spread so far that people came to look upon him as a wizard."

In answer to the question of whether Harley would be as great today as he was thirty years earlier, Lew Byrer of the *Citizen* wrote: "He would be even greater today because he would be used as a specialist, purely as a ball carrier. He might be called upon to punt or place kick occasionally. But mostly, he'd be just a ball carrier. He might pass occasionally. The blocking, tackling and other bruising bodily contact work would be assigned to someone else. When called upon, he'd be fresh and have his full flashing speed at its best."

Byrer also recalled spelling Chic's name "Chick" in 1919 and the berating he took. "When the paper came out Charlie Baxter and the late Harry Keys descended upon me with fire in their eyes," wrote Byrer. "Baxter had written about Chic during his high school years. Harry, then a *Citizen* artist, had drawn many cartoons and pictures of him. 'Look,' Harry said, as he sketched CHIC on a piece of drawing cardboard. Then he took his pencil and drew two lines making the two Cs into Os and the word OHIO."

Finally, *Dispatch* columnist Russ Needham wrote, "Chic was an inspirational player like few who've ever lived. His teammates had unlimited confidence in him, and knew he'd bring them through. It's nice to know Chic has come through that long illness, that the shy smile still is there."

After the Captain's Breakfast, as former team leaders left to return to their homes and businesses across the country, Chic approached Hooey and asked a favor: "Please thank everybody for the fine time I had here. I enjoyed meeting all the fellows. I know more people in Columbus than I do Chicago, and I'll miss them when I go back. It was so nice to have that parade for me. I am not deserving of that."

"Those words of Chic—'I am not deserving of that'— will never be forgotten," wrote Hooey a few days later. "They were typical Chic Harley, the most modest of the modests."

Crowd estimated at between 75,000 and 100,000 converge on open convertible in downtown Columbus, despite rainy weather, to greet Harley 10 years after being admitted to Danville, Illinois Veterans Administration Hospital.

Harley family members and some of Chic's closet friends at March 1947 dedication of the University Theater across from Ohio State campus. The relief figure in background still reminds Buckeye faithful of Harley even though today it is partially covered. At left are Harley family members including Ruth Wessell (far left), Chic's sister. Approximately 10,000 people attended the ceremony.

Chic Harley teammate and good friend Pete Stinchcomb (left), and Bob Kline, a member of the committee arranging 1948 welcome for Harley, hang picture of Chic on the wall of Mayor John Rhodes office.

Front page of Columbus Journal dated November 20, 1948,
tells of Chic's triumphant return to Ohio State.

Chic waves to drenched crowd along parade route. In back
seat, from left, are his older brother Bill, Ohio Gov. Thomas
Herbert, and Columbus Mayor James Rhodes.

With an admiring Jack Wilce at his side, Chic displays framed certificate he received during College Hall of Fame ceremonies during halftime of Ohio State-Michigan State game on November 8, 1953 in Columbus.

CHAPTER 14
Hall of Fame

With the ending of 1948—preceded by nearly three decades of despair—a revitalized, healthier, and happier Chic Harley had emerged, much to the surprise and elation of everyone. He now took a genuine interest in his surroundings, life in general, and the people who loved him, and he loved them. Still as quiet as ever, Chic was able and willing to carry on short, yet meaningful, conversations with friends and family—a huge improvement from the dark days of the 1930s. He liked to keep up on current events by reading newspapers, especially the Sports section. While in Danville, he looked forward to welcoming a regular stream of visitors from Columbus and Chicago, and whenever Ruth or Bill asked him whether he would like to visit the university to take in a football game and see friends, he wouldn't hesitate to say yes.

When not at the Danville VA Hospital, Chic almost always was staying at either Ruth or Bill's home in Chicago. Following Chic's triumphant return to Columbus, Bill reported to doctors and social workers at Danville that his youngest brother was getting along fine living at his home and staying busy by performing chores around the house. Bill was so elated with his brother's progress that he asked for and received permission to extend Chic's stay with him until the middle of 1949. With Bill's house serving as a base, Chic would frequently spend long stretches of time with Ruth and Sig, who lived only about fifteen miles away.

The magnificent progress Chic had made since his insulin therapy had by the fall of 1950 slowed to a disappointing crawl and was even showing faint signs of regressing, much to the consternation of Ruth and Bill. In October, Bill reported that his brother's adjustment to life outside the Danville facility had become more difficult. A few months later, Ruth told Bill that she wanted Chic to stay at her large home in Des Plaines indefinitely. That arrangement lasted for a while, until Sig made it clear that he was tired of having to entertain and house so many Harleys in a home with so many available bedrooms. With that, he announced that he and Ruth were moving to a much smaller home across town. Now it was Bill's turn to take Chic back. All of that back-and-forth could not have been helpful to Chic's state of mind. Ruth by now was sure that Chic needed to return to Danville for better medical care and treatment that neither she nor Bill could provide. Bill, however, saw it differently, and petitioned doctors at the VA hospital to allow Chic to stay with him for several more months. Despite Ruth's assertions to the contrary, the hospital staff agreed, and from that point, the musical chairs between Bill's and Ruth's homes picked up where it had left off.

In a December 11, 1951, memorandum, Danville hospital social worker Genevieve Young noted that Ruth had been complaining that Chic's veteran's allowance from the hospital was still being forwarded to Bill in Chicago even though Chic by then had been back at her house for several months. "He receives no benefit from it," wrote Ruth.

By 1952, Bill Harley, now sixty-three years old, was carefully weighing his future and whether he wanted to remain in Chicago or look for employment and a new start in life elsewhere. That fall he accepted an offer to manage an apartment complex in Daytona Beach, Florida. His decision to leave for warmer climes left Ruth as the only Harley sibling willing to watch over Chic. Walter, in Chicago, offered little or no help, and Irene and Marie lived out of state. Ruth, faced with Sig's insistence that Chic's visits to their home be limited, desperately sought help from other family members with little success. Marie, living in Pittsburgh at the time, agreed to make room for Chic for a month's period of time. Ruth was happy to have the offer of help. The plan, however, fell apart when Chic refused to go. He would not leave Illinois. He insisted on remaining close to Ruth even if that meant returning permanently to Danville. Throughout much of 1952 and well into 1953, Chic was back at the VA hospital, taking frequent trips to Chicago to see Ruth. In April 1953, Chic insisted on traveling to Des Plaines for the thirty-first birthday of his nephew, Richard Wessell, Ruth's only child.

Uncertainty over the absence of Chic's army pension funds had eaten away at Ruth since late 1951, when she noticed that he was not getting the $100 per month stipend that was rightfully his. By May 1953, Ruth took her worries about the disappearance of Chic's pension funds and his deteriorating mental condition to the VA hospital. Nervous and tearful, on May 13, she drove herself the 130 miles to Danville to explain her concerns in a face-to-face meeting that was also an opportunity to see Chic. There, Ruth explained that for the last several days, she had been in constant worry and panic over the condition of her brother, fearing she would find him in terrible mental condition. She explained that during Chic's previous extended two-year stay with Bill, Chic had been allowed to visit her only a few times and never on holidays. And on those rare occasions when Bill would permit Chic to travel to Des Plaines from Chicago, Chic was always unaccompanied and without any spending money. Ruth told doctors that after the war, Bill's financial condition worsened. Bill's entrepreneurial spirit led to his opening a small restaurant in Des Plaines he named The Chic Harley Café. That enterprise was short-lived when Bill's sons reneged on helping him run the operation, said medical reports. Ruth further told hospital doctors that when Bill moved to Florida, he one day announced out of the blue to Ruth that Chic was now her responsibility. That's when he sent Chic packing for Ruth and Sig's home in Des Plaines. Bill made no prior arrangements and gave Chic no money, Ruth said. By that time, Ruth and Sig had moved out of their eleven-room house in Des Plaines into a tiny three-room, undeveloped home that until recently had been a garage. There was hardly enough room for Sig and Ruth there, let alone Chic. Bill's actions in suddenly announcing that he would no longer care for his brother and sending Chic away stirred a resentfulness in Ruth and Sig that lasted for many years. They nevertheless took in Chic, finding a small corner of the home where he could sleep. In time, Chic settled into a routine, ate well, and took much better personal care of himself than if he were at Danville.

While the matter of where Chic would stay when not in Danville was resolved, the story of what was happening to his army pension checks was still a mystery to Ruth. It's not that Ruth and Sig wanted the money to pay for their personal bills. The money was Chic's, and they felt that it could be used to buy him food and clothing and for other basic necessities, hospital reports stated. Unable to determine on her own where the money was going, Ruth finally took matters into her own hands. She asked the hospital to change Chic's address from Bill's home in Chicago, where he lived until he moved to Florida, to her home in Des Plaines. Within days, Bill was on the phone with Ruth, demanding an explanation. Their conversation ended in an argument over a new overcoat for Chic.

Not long after that, Bill one day suddenly appeared at Ruth's home and announced that he wanted to take Chic out for a day of fun and relaxation. Ruth, still upset with Bill, nonetheless agreed, believing the day out would be good for Chic. Chic kissed Ruth good-bye and said he would see her the following day. Three days later, there was no sign of Chic or Bill. No phone call had been made; no telegram had arrived. Nothing. Ruth went into a panic, fearing the worst. Unable to locate Bill and having nowhere else to go, she called the Danville VA hospital to see if they had any idea as to her brothers' whereabouts. After Ruth explained her story, she was told by the hospital that Chic had been returned to the hospital by Bill a couple of days earlier. First startled, then angry, Ruth replied that Chic's behavior and condition did not warrant his return to the Danville hospital. She said he had been doing just fine living with her. He was sociable and happy and had shown no signs of psychotic behavior in recent weeks. Why would Bill have done such a thing? Why did he say he was going to take Chic out for a day of fun when, in reality, his intentions, it seemed, were to take him back to Danville? Why did he not say anything? Then the light clicked on in Ruth's head: the pension checks.

Danville social worker Genevieve Young told Ruth what she had learned when Bill brought Chic back to the hospital a few days earlier. Bill, explained Mrs. Young, said he resented Ruth for "having my son taken away from me when he was a baby." The son Bill was alluding to was his firstborn child, Vernon. Ruth was aghast at such a comment made by Bill, explaining to Mrs. Young that she as a young woman and her mother, Mattie, took care of Vernon when Bill's first wife became paralyzed after giving birth. When she died three years later, they continued caring for Vernon with Bill's blessing and gratitude. When Bill remarried, Vernon was returned to live with his father and stepmother. It was a reunion that lasted only three weeks because Vernon cried constantly because he missed his grandmother. After those three difficult weeks, Bill decided to return Vernon to Mattie and Ruth. Vernon never again lived with his father and stepmother. Ruth faulted Bill for lacking patience and sending away his firstborn son after only three weeks. His comment made to Mrs. Young seemed to come out of nowhere, Ruth thought, and involved an episode that occurred more than thirty years earlier.

As for the other Harley siblings, Irene in California was willing to find room for Chic, but for only a short period of time at the insistence of her husband. Marie again said she was willing to care for Chic in Pittsburgh, but only for a month—no longer. Older brother Walter, in Chicago, "shows practically no interest in Chic's welfare," said a VA report. Ruth would have liked nothing better than to have Chic stay with her indefinitely, but Sig had strong misgivings. Ruth told hospital authorities that she was holding out hope for Chic to return to Des Plaines once expansion of their small home was completed. Mrs. Young summed up the situation in her official report:

The social worker is definitely sure that Mrs. Wessell would always be willing to accept Chic in her home if her husband were agreeable and it is quite possible that Mr. Wessell would be agreeable if he were considered in such planning. He definitely resented Bill's "dumping" the veteran on them when they were living in overcrowded conditions. The social worker is also quite definite in her feeling that Mrs. Wessell's only interest in Chic's pension funds is for the payment of his board and room, adequate clothing and spending money for Chic and the fact that he derives some enjoyment from the money. The social worker does not have such an impression as far as the brother, Bill, is concerned.

Ruth fully embraced a suggestion made by Mrs. Young to appoint a conservator to handle Chic's pension funds, though she anticipated an angry reaction from Bill.

The report said:

But her [Ruth's] present feeling in the situation is that she does not care [about Bill's reaction], that she does not want to write her brother [Bill], neither does she want to see him. She states that she is entirely indifferent in her feelings toward him because of the way he has handled Chic and returned him to the hospital without her knowledge.

Back at the VA Hospital, Chic was doing well, despite all the family turmoil around him. He was conversing with other patients, working on special projects, and participating in numerous activities. "He is neat and clean and his appearance normal," said a hospital report. "He is oriented to time and place. He has a good attention span."

In 1951, efforts to establish a shrine for the nation's greatest college football players had picked up steam. By fall, selection of America's greatest players for induction into the newly established College Football Hall of Fame was well under way. The site of the nation's new sports shrine was going to be at Rutgers University in New Brunswick, New Jersey, where the first official college football game had been staged eighty-two years earlier.

On November 4, 1951, newspapers reported that thirty-two players and twenty-one coaches had been selected as charter inductees. Among those selected were nine of the eleven men chosen by the country's top sportswriters and sportscasters in 1950 for an Associated Press All American Team for the first half of the twentieth century. In that 1950 poll, Chic Harley and Jim Thorpe were named America's two best half-backs (right and left) by journalists who had actually seen them and their contemporaries play. Red Grange, who played just a few years after Harley and Thorpe, was named to the second team in that same poll. Grange in 2008 was proclaimed the greatest college football player ever in a poll by ESPN television network. Those who picked Grange had never seen him, Thorpe, or Harley play.

Among the charter members of the Hall of Fame were Chic, Thorpe, Grange, George Gipp, Walter Eckersall, Pudge Heffelfinger, Bronko Nakurski, Ned Mahan, Sammy Baugh, and Nile Kinnick. Among the coaches honored were Walter Camp, Knute Rockne, Fielding Yost, Robert Zuppke, and Amos Alonzo Stagg. The colleges they represented were directed to organize and conduct their own induction ceremonies in games of their choosing during the 1953 season.

By mid-summer 1953, officials at Ohio State had determined that Chic's induction into the first class of the National Football Hall of Fame would occur at halftime on November 7, 1953, during the game against Michigan State. George E. Little, executive secretary of the Hall of Fame, sent a one-page letter to the school outlining instructions for the ceremony. He said that during the ceremony, Chic would be presented with a framed honor that would read:

Charles William Harley, Ohio State University, All American, 1916, 1917, 1919 has been granted the highest honor of the National Football Hall of Fame in recognition of his outstanding playing ability as demonstrated in intercollegiate competition, his sportsmanship, integrity, character, and contribution to the sport of football, this certificate bears witness that his name shall forever be honored in the National Football Hall of Fame, November 3, 1951, New Brunswick, N.J.

With Little's instructions in hand, Coach Wilce, Chic's many friends, the college community, the city of Columbus, and the state of Ohio sprang into action.

"THE GREAT CHIC HARLEY, OUR BOY, HAS BEEN ELECTED TO THE NATIONAL FOOTBALL HALL OF FAME," wrote Wilce in a letter to all living members of Ohio State's football teams of 1916, 1917, and 1919. "To us, this is a magnificent natural. We of Ohio State think that no one deserves such honor more than Chic. Your presence is essential to serve as a member of the Hall of Fame Chic Harley Court of Honor. MY PERSONAL HEARTY HOPE IS THAT YOU WILL COME BACK FOR THIS BIG ONE."

A seven-man Committee on Arrangements was formed, with Wilce as chairman. Membership included Leo Yassenoff, C. J. "Farky" Farcasin, Floyd S. Stahl, George. R. Staten, Wilbur E. Snypp, and Ohio State Athletic Director Richard C. Larkins. The halftime ceremony would last twenty-five minutes, and the Honor Court would consist of Harley teammates and Ohio State All-Americans. There would be a decorated stadium box at midfield for Chic, family members, and close friends. Wilce would present the award. A program of "Harley stories" would be published. Well-known local author and writer Snypp would be in charge of publicity.

When the big day arrived, 82,328 fans crammed into the great horseshoe. At halftime, the school's colorful marching band and public address announcer presented a choreographed show on the field called "The Chic Harley Story." As the band played "Long, Long Ago," forming a huge "1916" on the field, the announcer described how the then small university came into national prominence when sophomore Harley led the football team to its first conference title. Next, part of the band formed the shape of a football while another section formed the shape of a football shoe that moved swiftly toward the ball and kicked it to signify Chic's 1916 point after touchdown boot that sealed Ohio State's 7-6 victory over powerful Illinois. The band then played "You've Got to Be a Football Hero" as the announcer's voice boomed throughout the gigantic stadium describing how Chic changed his shoe in that pivotal game thirty-seven years earlier that provided the opening for the emergence of what has become one of America's leading athletic and scholastic institutions of higher learning.

Then, as the band rhythmically moved into position while playing "Beautiful Ohio March," it formed the letters O-H-I-O. Suddenly, the two O's became C's, changing OHIO into CHIC. The throng in the stadium went wild. Chic, standing just off the football gridiron, smiled broadly. Tears welled up in Ruth's eyes as she sat in the special field box.

"During the playing days of Chic Harley, a song was written by the student football manager, Bill Dougherty," continued the announcer. "Ohio State fans began singing 'Fight the Team Across the Field' as they have been doing ever since."

Finally, the band formed two O's with an arc between them that provided the perfect setting for the award ceremony to begin. As the band played "My Hero," the large Court of Honor, which comprised about thirty people, slowly moved onto the field.

Wearing a warm gray overcoat, a striped tie, and a dark brown fedora, its tip turned slightly downward, Chic Harley looked out of place as he and the Honor Court walked toward midfield. The entourage of famed Ohio State players formed a protective semicircle around Chic, who by then weighed less than 140 pounds. Everyone wore a heavy coat as a guard from the biting, chilly weather. A half dozen newspaper photographers crouched in front of the Honor Court ready to snap away at just the right moment.

In the stands in front of Chic and the honor guard, Ohio Gov. Frank Lausche sat next to school President Howard L. Bevis and Bevis's guest, Gregg M. Sinclair, president of the University of Hawaii. Perched on folding chairs in the special box were Ruth and Bill. Walter had died four months earlier in Chicago. The stadium press box high above the stands was also full to capacity. Before the game and ceremony, Western Union predicted it would tie the all-time record of 120,000 words sent out in one football game, equal to the 1935 game against Notre Dame. With every one of the $3.50 to $5 seats sold, a large number of Columbus boys tried to sneak into the giant arena. One young man got caught by the seat of his pants on a steel upright that encircled the stadium. A grinning police officer helped him down and said, "Next time, let's don't be so obvious." Another enterprising boy tried to enter the stadium by traipsing in with the Michigan State Marching Band, holding a sheet of music. When a security guard stopped him, the youth explained, "No, buddy, you got me wrong. I'm helping the band." It didn't work, and the Michigan State trumpet player, who was part of the conspiracy, got his music back.

When the formal ceremony began, Coach Wilce and President Bevis told the story of what Chic Harley meant to Ohio State. Said Bevis:

It takes a lot of people a long time to build a university. Such building, as a matter of fact, is never done; it is a continuing process. This building is done in many ways, and spreads out in many directions—the physical plant, the faculty, the courses and curricula, the extracurricular activities, including athletics. Intercollegiate athletics in this part of the country to put it mildly has a strong hold upon the alumni, and upon the public generally. This occasion is a witness to that. There have been many buildings of this university, and there will be many more. Among the names of the builders in the realm of intercollegiate athletics stand out those of former President George W. Rightmire, who presented the argument that got Ohio State admitted to the Western Conference; of Professor Thomas E. French, generally regarded as the "daddy" of the stadium; of L. S. St. John, director of athletics during the period of major building; and of Chic Harley, whom we honor today.

It is no exaggeration to say that in his way, Chic Harley was one of the builders of the university, and as such he will always be remembered.

248

Moments later, Wilce stepped up to the microphone:

It is difficult to put into few words all that I would like to say for and about Chic Harley on this occasion. He was the answer to a coach's prayer, as an athlete and as a personality. Nature blessed him with the superb coordination, unusual speed, and superior enduring resiliency of a true All-American. He was a rare sportsman and an honestly clean player. Do not think that I try to exaggerate when I say that I do not remember his committing a single personal foul, in spite of a great legitimate fighting spirit. The phrase "ideal competitor" describes his seemingly intuitive ability to rise to heights of achievement in clutch situations. He led to victory at times over obstacles and opposition that would have defeated one of lesser talents or smaller spirit. He was a general specialist because he could do everything in football in a superior way. His all-around abilities made possible outstanding demonstration of a then relatively new open game. It is sometimes forgotten that he also excelled in track, basketball, and particularly in baseball. His natural ability was such that he could have excelled at almost any sport. He had the honest affection of his teammates and quickly earned the admiration and respect of his opponents. Characteristic of his personality was real modesty as to his own ability and achievement. While he was the true individual star of his great teams, to him it was the team that counted, rather than himself.

"Hello everybody," said Chic after slowly approaching the microphone. "I certainly am pleased to be here again." He then turned to Wilce and Bevis, acknowledging their hard work and recognition. "I want to thank the members of my team who made it possible for me to be here. I'm enjoying the game." He then stepped away from the microphone.

The crowd erupted into applause that lasted several minutes. Someone from within the sea of seated football fans in the stands shouted, "Yea, Harley!" Another fan screamed, "We love you, Chic!" The powerful applause was a showcase of respect and admiration for the man who, now age fifty-nine, had put the school and all of its programs—both athletically, in a direct sense, and indirectly, academically—on the map. Clutching his hat

249

firmly in his right hand, Chic bowed his head as 82,000 people sang the school anthem, "Carmen Ohio."

A few weeks before the Hall of Fame ceremony, tributes of Chic poured in. George Little, a Columbus native, reminisced about the high school games he refereed and marveled at Harley's ability. Little added that when he returned from World War I, he noticed hanging on the walls of the famous Southern Hotel in Columbus pictures of President Wilson, General Pershing, and Chic Harley.

Congressman John Vorys said:

Chic and I were teammates in high school. He lived in our home the season I was captain [1913]. I have followed him closely ever since. He was the greatest football player I have ever seen, and I have seen some great ones. He was the most modest celebrity I have ever known, and I have known some great ones. I think the real reason for his undying fame is that fame never spoiled him. In his greatest playing days, he was heroic in victory—and defeat. Sport statistics do not give the real story. It is reflected from the hearts of those who have known him intimately through the years, and to us he is still the "one and only."

Other tributes included:

Robert C. Zuppke, former coach of the University of Illinois:

I remember Chic Harley today as well as I did yesterday, for his name dominated Big Ten football as only a few did before and after his time. He was without doubt the fastest, most capable, and colorful football figure of his day and always will rank tops among football immortals. The Big Four in my 29 years of coaching in the order of their times are Harley, Grange, Berwanger, and Harmon.

William A. "Bill" Dougherty, manager of the 1916 Ohio State team and author of *Fight the Team Across the Field*:

Chic had an intuitive ability to grasp a situation and act on it quickly. Near the end of the Illinois game in 1916, his first Western Conference contest, a forward pass by Chic was called. Seeing his opportunity, he decided not to pass but to run wide. Chic's footprint hit the goal line about one foot from the sideline. Then, with everyone else full of excitement, he calmly kicked the goal, winning over Illinois 7 to 6. On the train trip to that game, the late L. W. St. John had said, "Chic is the finest football player I have ever seen." Saint never changed that opinion, and Chic justified it fully.

U. S. Senator John W. Bricker, president of the Varsity "O" Association in 1916:

It was my privilege to be in school when Chic Harley was playing. His contribution to Ohio State will never be forgotten. Our Western Conference standing, the stadium, and much of the athletic development date from the Harley days. He gave to all of our programs a great impetus. It was my privilege to be president of Varsity O during his heyday and to welcome him into that organization. He was the best among many great football players. He could do anything required to win games and do it better than anyone who opposed him. The memory of his great athletic ability still lingers and will much longer on our campus. He is truly Ohio State's great athletic hero.

The honor accorded Harley by the Ohio State community that day was one of the great highlights of his life. Never during his three years of college ball or his one year as a professional did Chic ever perform before such a large crowd. For one twenty-five-minute period, thirty-four years after he played his heart out in the only college game in which he tasted defeat, Chic Harley once again became one with all of Columbus and all of Ohio. Immediately following the ceremony, he walked over to the special box off the fifty-yard line on the home field side where a proud and beaming Ruth and Bill were waiting.

"I'm enjoying the game," said Chic in response to a fan's greeting. Michigan State won the game 28-13. The Buckeyes were never so happy.

Johnny Jones, the *Dispatch's* famed columnist and one of Chic's closest friends, wrote about his pal the following day: "I have never seen another player like Chic. He is our Grange,

Poe, Thorpe, Gipper, Booth, McMillen." Then Jones reminded readers of a poem by James Thurber, a Columbus native and Harley friend at the height of his playing days who had become an international literary giant. Jones wanted to publish Thurber's revered poem about Chic one more time "to serve as a pep talk not only for the Buckeye team, but as a hypodermic needle for the entire stadium crowd.

"The big crowd will feel this needle and bumps will form in their throats as they rejoice at the final acknowledgement of the greatness of Chic Harley," Jones wrote. "This will be his greatest hour."

Thurber's four-stanza tribute, "When Chic Harley Got Away," at first captures some of the great moments of Ohio State football up to 1916, when Harley arrived on the scene. Those moments, he wrote with rhyme and purpose, were nothing compared to watching Harley. Then the poem ends:

But there'll never be another thing can light up all the day,

Like the glory of the going when Chic Harley got away.

One of Ohio State's all-time football great Wes Fesler (right), who considered Chic Harley his hero, chats with The One And Only during luncheon in Harley's honor on November 20, 1948.

In this undated photo, likely taken in the early to mid-1950s, Chic (left), is seen at table with (from left) Johnny Jones, a lifelong friend of Chic's and popular newspaper columnist, University of Michigan football great Tom Harmon, George Steinbrenner, who went on to become owner of New York Yankees, and former pro football player Fred Gehrke

Chic (second form right) shares light moment with old friends Jack Cannon, Notre Dame All-American, Walter Gerber, former Major League shortstop, and Hank Gowdy (right), ex-big league catcher during function in Columbus on September 30, 1950.

OSU great (from left), Harley, his coach Jack Wilce, and team-mate Swede Sorenson during team reunion.

With several of his teammates by his side on October 30, 1948, Chic meets with longtime friends (from left) Leo Yassenoff, Pete Stinchcomb, John Tarzan Taylor, Mel Shaw, and Milton Yassenoff (in front).

*Chic returns to
Columbus to watch
the Ohio State-Iowa
football game on
November 13, 1955
with his sister
Ruth and Ruth's
husband Sig.*

*Howard "Hopalong" Cassady shakes hands with Chic
during encounter in 1955 when Cassady was awarded
the Heisman Trophy.*

256

In this 40ᵗʰ reunion photo of 1916 Ohio State championship team, Coach John Wilce makes a point as his players Chic Harley, Swede Sorenson and Charlie Seddon look on.

Chic's three surviving sisters (from left) Irene, Marie and Ruth, gathered in Des Plaines, Illinois in this 1960s photo at Ruth's home.

Teammates and friends of Chic signed book presented to Harley during gathering in November 1972. The first to sign was Bill Dougherty, who served as Ohio State's 1916 team manager and wrote the school fight song "Across the Field", which was created in 1915 in honor of Coach Jack Wilce.

Chic with great nephew Stephen Wessell in photo taken in Des Plaines, Illinois around 1951.

258

Richard Wessell, Chic Harley's nephew and son of his favorite sister, Ruth Wessell. It was Mr. Wessell who suggested to former school Athletic Director Andy Geiger the idea of honoring Ohio State's Heisman Trophy winners by retiring their jersey numbers and hanging those numbers in the stadium's outdoor "Ring of Fame". The idea was that once the Heisman winners numbers were retired, Harley's number 47 would also be retired. Harley played nearly 20 years before the Heisman Trophy was created. Many people believe that Harley would have won one, possibly two Heismans, if the honor had been in place during his playing career.

Todd Wessell (left) and Richard Wessell at Chic's gravesite at Union Cemetery in Columbus, located about two miles north of the "horseshoe" stadium.

259

Chic during Ohio State football game in mid 1950s.

CHAPTER 15
Fading Back

With all the accolades, reminiscing, fanfare, media interviews, and newspaper columns of praise having run their course during the uplifting November 1953 Hall of Fame weekend in Columbus, life for Chic Harley quickly eased back into the familiar routine that had become his life. For the previous fifteen years, he had been confined to the Danville VA hospital and its vast grounds, except for periodic visits to Chicago and Ohio and the extended period following the successful shock therapy. In the sixteen years before his arrival at Danville, Chic's life had been a fog of depression and uncertainty that baffled and worried his family and friends. Schizophrenia had consumed well over half of his lifetime by now. There was no hope of recovery and only slight expectation for improvement.

In Danville, Chic engaged in brief periods of activity, such as classes in leathercraft or basketweaving. In all cases, he would quickly lose interest and drop out after only a few weeks. Medical reports chronicled his demeanor as sociable and cooperative, but he remained seclusive and downtrodden. Several IQ tests during his years at the hospital always showed that he had average intelligence. He maintained a neat appearance, a habit that remained important to him for the rest of his life. He also kept physically fit. But, as had been the case for many years, he lacked judgment and rarely engaged in meaningful conversation unless prodded to do so. The medical staff was guarded about pushing him too hard, fearing he might become passively resistant and even more confused.

By the time Chic reached the age of sixty-five, the visits from old friends and his sister Ruth had become continual and even more enjoyable for him. Visitors would spend the day taking Chic on walks about the grounds or for car rides on narrow rural roads lined with cornstalks and soybeans. Many times, they'd lunch at a roadside café and eventually wind up in downtown Danville to do a little shopping. Chic would never buy anything, but he liked to browse.

The train trips north to see Ruth also were becoming more frequent. The ride to Chicago and transferring by bus to Des Plaines, which by 1960 had grown to 35,000 people, no longer intimidated Chic. The journey gave a boost to his confidence, and he was always excited to see his sister and his extended family. The Wessells' home was nestled on a slender, private gravel road lined with handsome houses of different shapes and sizes scattered on half-acre lots. Sig and Ruth's once tiny single-bedroom house had grown into a comfortable three-bedroom home with a large screened-in porch, two-car attached garage, huge kitchen, and wide living room with a fireplace and color TV set. A large picture window offered a pleasant view of the yard where peonies, rose bushes, and marigolds flourished throughout spring and summer. There was plenty of room for visitors, including Richard, Mary Jane, and their family. There now was more than enough room for Chic as well. While there, he often would rest in a cushioned chair on the large patio, occasionally rising to rearrange the outdoor furniture. He also liked to walk the block or so to the quiet residential street, named Elms Terrace, before turning around and heading back to the house.

During Chic's visits, the always attentive Ruth regularly wrote to the hospital to assure them that her brother was doing fine and there was nothing to worry about. From Columbus, Leo Yassenoff, Charlie Seddon, John Wilce, Ben Ratner, Bill Snypp, and others kept in touch with their old friend by corresponding with Ruth. Once or twice every football season, someone suggested celebrating Chic's birthday or reuniting him with friends and teammates. They would contact Ruth to see if Chic was feeling well enough to make the trip. He always was.

"I believe it will turn out to be one of the most pleasurable evenings that Chic and his family could possibly have as well as bringing a tremendous amount of pleasure to those who are sponsoring it," Yassenoff wrote in a letter to Ruth. He and others in Columbus were planning a sixty-sixth birthday party for Chic on September 23, 1960, and they wanted to make sure the guest of honor could attend. Ratner was chairman of the birthday committee, and Paul Ginger would be toastmaster. Both were boyhood chums of Chic's. A column by Johnny Jones reported that 200 people had signed up to attend the celebration at the downtown Deschler Hotel.

The weekend of partying proved to be a great joy for everyone involved. Chic received many gifts, including a bright scarlet and gray Ohio State blanket, an engraved wristwatch, and a football autographed by each member of that season's football team. During halftime of the game against Southern Methodist, the crowd of 85,000 wished him a happy birthday with thunderous applause. Chic rode in the backseat of a convertible with Coach Wilce that circled the football field. When the auto reached the Ohio State bench, the marching band played "Happy Birthday."

"Chic Harley will never be forgotten," wrote Jones in his column named "Now Let Me Tell You." He couldn't resist reminding readers once again of the 1916 game against Illinois that thrust the Ohio State football program—and the entire university—into national prominence.

"It inspired the movement for the stadium," Johnny wrote, adding that Chic was so admired for his clean, skillful play and modest personality that years after that contest, the Illini honored him by transporting him to Champaign by ambulance from the Danville hospital for a special tribute. Speaking to a hushed crowd that included many Illinois football greats of years past, legendary Illini Coach Bob Zuppke said these inspiring words as he looked out over the quiet, respectful gathering: "Ladies and gentlemen, over there is Chic Harley. Red Grange, all you could do was run behind Britton. That fellow over there beat me all the time except once. Grange, Chic Harley is the greatest football player who ever donned a uniform. You couldn't even lace up his shoes. Good luck, Harley."

Despite efforts to stem the relentless tide, Chic showed no signs of noticeable improvement, evidence that a slow relapse was taking place. Repeated attempts by hospital staff to engage him in activities did nothing to spark him out of a state of disinterest. During warm months, he strolled around the tree-shaded hospital grounds. His days of running away had long passed. He now emptied ashtrays and dusted windowsills and furniture. He never complained and was always pleasant. Whenever the opportunity arose to visit Ruth and to attend parties, confirmations, and graduations of Richard and Mary Jane's youngsters, he immediately accepted.

Ruth's worry about her brother's condition and his future continued unabated as she dreaded the possibility that somehow the hospital would decide to move him to a private facility. In 1960, after decades of anxiousness, stewing, and torment about her brother, Ruth's health suffered a major setback. During a visit to Danville to see Chic, Ruth suffered a heart attack. She spent the next seven weeks recovering at Danville's largest hospital. The years of worry and stress about Chic had finally caught up with her. Heart problems plagued her for the rest of her life.

On the morning of May 20, 1963, while reading the sports section of the Chicago *Tribune*, Chic's eyes moved over to a small article near the bottom of the page. The story reported the death of Dr. J. W. Wilce in Columbus. The two men Chic had looked up to more than anyone else during his years at Ohio State, Wilce and Lynn St. John, were now both gone. They had done everything in their power to help him in the tragic years after 1922 and to perpetuate the memory of what he had accomplished for the school and sport. That task was now left up to others. Chic took the news hard, mourning alone, with a nurse occasionally looking in on him. The closest family member was 130 miles away. No one could fully appreciate how important Wilce and St. John had been in Chic's life. At Chic's request, through social worker Genevieve Young, Ruth conveyed his sympathy to Mrs. Wilce.

The passing of John Wilce ended the remarkable life of one of college football's true pioneers and mentors. A star fullback at the University of Wisconsin, he was hired in 1913 by Saint, Ohio State's new athletic director. In 1916, the pair of newcomers took their own personal energy and intelligence, the raw talent of Harley, and the skill and unselfish teamwork of the Buckeye players to forge the genesis of one of America's greatest sports dynasties. From those early years, there was no turning back once St. John and Wilce had arrived on the scene. In the decades that followed, Ohio State became one of the most prestigious centers of higher learning, combining scholarly excellence and athletics. Wilce's even-tempered, calculated, controlled demeanor was a perfect match with the quiet, shy, and sensitive Harley and the cerebral St. John. After fifteen years, Wilce ended his coaching career in 1928 to pursue the one passion that eclipsed football for him: the study of medicine. In 1934, he was appointed director of the university's Health Services and later joined Stagg, Rockne, Yost, Zuppke, and others as a member of the College Football Hall of Fame. The American Football Coaches Association honored him with its Amos Alonzo Stagg Award for "perpetuating the example and influence of the great coach in football." A portrait of Wilce, financed through contributions from many of his players, was commissioned in 1938 and dedicated after the game against Michigan State that season. It would hang in the arena that later would be named after his friend and boss, Lynn St. John. Nearby at the time, as if keeping an eye on things, were similar portraits of both Saint and Thomas E. French, the professor credited with the vision and drive that led to the construction of "The House That Harley Built."

The year 1963 brought another period of worry and despair for Ruth. One day in early September, seemingly out of nowhere, a social worker in Danville informed her by telephone that the decision had been made to discharge Chic from the hospital. The caller was not Genevieve Young, who had known Ruth and Chic for years, but a new staff member, who explained that the decision to release Chic resulted from a new VA policy to gradually return certain patients to mainstream society. It was irrelevant that Chic had not been a problem for years at Danville and was a model patient, well-liked, and always quiet. His mental capacity had nevertheless remained at the level where he would never be able to function on his own.

Ruth agonized at the thought of Chic's leaving the one place outside of her own home where he was safe and satisfied. Sig was opposed to Chic's moving into their home, and Ruth knew that her shaky personal health wouldn't permit her to take care of both Chic and Sig on a daily basis. Ruth immediately fired off a letter to the hospital begging them to reconsider:

This to my mind would be the biggest mistake, for Chic isn't mentally fit to be on his own. I went all through this three years ago and suffered a heart attack while in Danville worrying about it all. I beg of you to try to help me to keep Chic at the hospital which is home to him and I feel it would be a big mistake to think of taking him away from everything that means home to him. I feel it would be an injustice to him. There are so many reasons why he should stay here.

The prompt response Ruth received from Howard B. Spain, caseworker supervisor, explained that the VA had embarked on a program to eliminate as much "custodial care" of veterans as possible and to focus on serving as active treatment centers for those suffering severe illnesses.

"It is the old tendency for the public to regard our type of hospital as an Old Soldiers Home that we are now urged to try to overcome," wrote Spain, adding that he was nevertheless sympathetic to Ruth's concerns. Surprisingly, her emotional pleadings worked, despite the VA's strong desire to move in a different direction. The decision to release Chic was reversed. He could stay in Danville, wrote Spain.

Chic's only surviving brother, Bill, died in late January 1964. As young men, the two brothers played sports together, especially baseball on Chicago's north side. Six years older than Chic, Bill was his antithesis. Endowed with a strong personality, he was ambitious, personable, and smart, especially in the business side of athletics. In summer 1921, they became business partners when Chic reluctantly caved in to tremendous pressure to play professional football. Like everyone else, Bill knew Chic was the best football player in America at the time. Combining his own business acumen with Chic's talent, Bill believed, was the ticket to fame and riches. In time, the hospital staff concluded that some members of the Harley family—especially Bill—tended to take advantage of Chic's fame as a football star. Whenever Chic was invited to Columbus for a reunion or honors, Bill liked to accompany him, soaking up the attention bestowed not only on his quiet brother but also on himself. There's no doubt, however, that Bill cared very deeply for his brother.

Ruth got another jolt on April 20, 1965, when, for the third time in five years, she was told that the hospital wanted to move Chic to a private facility, perhaps in the Chicago area. This time, they said, it was Chic who asked for the change. Frantic, Ruth wrote back:

I have gone through this twice before as you know, and I feel I can't take it all again. . . . Surely you couldn't judge his asking [for the change] enough reason to consider doing this? You don't really believe he is capable of making such a decision himself? This has been his home for nearly 30 years. He needs supervision. I have had him home enough to know he does not make decisions on his own. He needs to be with others. He needs what he has had all these years. If this had been done years ago, perhaps he could have adjusted his life, but now at 71 years old? Why can't he live the rest of his life as is? I had the care of Chic many years before he came to the hospital and have had him home many weeks and months since he entered the hospital. I have had the heartaches and responsibilities, so he is a big part of my life. It took a long time for me to adjust to giving him up, but in time I realized how wonderful it was he had a place to be and after a long time, he became adjusted and this is like home to him. Surely there is a place for him. I positively don't approve of putting him in a nursing home or a foster home. Each night I pray that he will never get worse mentally. Physically, one expects poorer health as one gets older, but mentally, I pray he never gets worse. If it were possible I would care for him, but my health won't allow it. I brought one heart attack while in Danville after receiving the first letter in regards to discharging Chic and I was in a hospital for seven weeks. Now this is the third time I am going through this. So please, keep him where he is. I am willing to do all I can other than agree with you.

The hospital staff once again submitted to Ruth's wishes, reluctantly agreeing that the time had passed for any major changes in Chic's life. "In view of your own feelings about the matter, we can continue to keep him in the hospital," wrote a staff member in late April. "I was sorry to learn that the letter was upsetting to you." It was the last time Ruth had to face the real possibility that Chic would have to move.

As the warm, humid months of July and August scorched the Illinois prairie, Chic spent hours outdoors enjoying bicycle rides of three to four miles a day. He walked up to half a mile a day on a hospital treadmill and toned himself up by rowing as many as fifty strokes at a time on a special workout machine.

"Patient was most cooperative and friendly. Conversation was relevant and coherent. Seemed quite shy," a hospital evaluation of Chic reported.

In late October, Ruth wrote to the hospital to express her happiness and appreciation about the appearance of her favorite brother, who had just ended another week's stay at her home. "I just couldn't believe he could be as good as he was," she wrote. "Whatever you did for him proved wonders. I can't remember when he looked as well both mentally and physically."

Chic's condition continued to improve as he approached his seventy-second birthday in late summer 1966. He now was riding five miles a day on an exercise bike and was unusually talkative with the hospital staff, especially on the subject of sports. He especially liked to joke with them about the University of Illinois teams since his loyalty was with Ohio State.

"Your visits mean a great deal to him and I am sure any discontinuation of contact with you would be quite disturbing to him," wrote the hospital's chief of staff Dr. M. B. Ardis to Ruth. Any thought of Ruth ending or even curtailing her visits to Danville never entered her mind. In fact, Ruth was all for increasing them, even though by the spring of 1966, at ages sixty-seven and sixty-nine, she and her husband had settled into senior lifestyles.

Ruth had retained her youthful good looks, though her light brown hair was now snow white. She spent her days taking care of their big home, which included a cozy den, where Chic slept when he visited. All meals were eaten in the large kitchen. In the hallway that connected the living room with the kitchen were a grandmother's clock that chimed every fifteen minutes and a framed photograph of Chic on the Ohio State gridiron, famously posing with hands on hips. The Wessells now had an in-ground pool right next to their patio—a perfect setting for their six grandchildren to frolic, and friends and relatives to be entertained. Chic spent many hours and days resting and puttering around. At the driveway entrance, hanging from a coach lamp next to a white picket fence, a sign welcomed visitors to "Deep Comfort the Wessells."

By fall 1966, as the fiftieth anniversary of the 1916 championship approached, Ohio State supporters and players from that era planned a reunion celebration. Several members of the 1916 team had passed on by then—Shifty Bolen, the Courtney brothers, Kelly Van Dyne, and Howard Yerges. There remained a corps of about fifteen players who were healthy enough and willing to meet at the Ohio Stater Hotel for an evening of fun and reminiscing. Chic was one of them, as were the feisty Charlie Seddon, song man Bill Dougherty, Swede Sorenson, and Bob Karch.

A year later, the championship team of 1917 also held its fiftieth reunion at the Ohio Stater. The dozen or so teammates who attended sat at a long dinner table on the night of

Friday, November 10, homecoming weekend. Many of the aging former players brought their wives, children, and grandchildren. Accompanying Chic were Ruth, Sig, Richard, and two of his children. Ruth later said that Chic was the best he had been in years during the 1917 reunion, something that had brought her much happiness. A year later, Chic returned to the Ohio State campus when the school honored him at the annual Captain's Homecoming Breakfast prior to the Saturday afternoon football game against Michigan. The memory of Chic remained alive and well in the Columbus and Ohio State community.

Not all of Chic's admirers were athletes. One of them was Ruth's close friend Edrie Tomlinson of Columbus, whose husband, John, had been confined to the Chillicothe VA hospital since the mid-1940s. Edrie eked out a living as a bank teller in Columbus while caring for her husband as best she could. When the opportunity arose, she enjoyed taking road trips with her sister. Over the years, Edrie frequently called Ruth, not only for herself, but on behalf of many others back in Ohio.

In January 1967, Edrie asked Ruth about the possibility of visiting Chic, and Ruth wholeheartedly approved. When Edrie wrote to the Danville hospital for permission, she assured doctors that she was quite used to visiting veterans facilities.

Over the next several years, Edrie and her sister often drove 200 miles west to Danville to visit with the man still regarded as Ohio's most famous football player and to pass along cards and letters of encouragement and personal gifts from the people back home. They also brought photographs, slides, and home movies from their various trips, which Chic enjoyed immensely. There were movies of trips to the Grand Canyon, to the New York World's Fair, and to the Great Lakes region. On one occasion, Edrie followed through on a promise to bring a homemade German chocolate cake.

Back home in Columbus after one of her visits to Danville, Edrie wrote to the hospital. "The privilege you granted us of having him with us for the day and evening both days meant more to us than we can ever tell you. I always leave Danville with a warm glow around my heart and especially this time as we had time for the things we wanted to do." On September 4, 1967, she wrote, "So we who love him, not just for fame, but for his own sweet self, take the trip whenever possible, and hope we are able to give him as much joy as he gives us. That bright smile is ample reward for crossing half of Ohio, all of Indiana, and a little in Illinois!"

For the 1967 homecoming weekend in Columbus, Edrie invited Sig, Ruth, and Chic to her home, after which she wrote, "We had a wonderful time and everyone is still talking about how well Chic was. He really is a grand person and we love him devotedly."

The year 1969 brought much sorrow and loss for Chic. His lifelong friend, sweetheart, and one-time fiancée, Louise, died on January 21 in Columbus after several years of confinement to a wheelchair, the victim of painful and unrelenting arthritis. She was seventy-two. Survivors were her husband, Russel Paul, and three children. Fifty years earlier, Chic and Louise had considered marriage, but with the onset of mental illness becoming clearer in Chic's case, Louise's family—and eventually Louise herself—felt that marriage with her high school and college sweetheart would never happen. Devastated at first, she eventually found happiness, while Chic's life went in the opposite direction. Louise, Chic, and Russel remained close friends for the rest of their lives.

Inevitable health problems started taking their toll on Ruth as 1968 came to a close. Chicago's freezing, blustery, and frequently bleak winters had always been hard on her. She easily contracted colds, and hardly a season went by without a bout of influenza that laid her up for weeks at a time. But she always recovered and resumed her regular routine as a homemaker and caretaker of Sig and Chic, mother to Richard, and loving grandmother. When Chic arrived for his visits, Ruth always had time to tend to his every need. "I always worry about Chic. In case he should become seriously ill, I'd want to know," Ruth confided in a follow-up letter to the VA staff.

Even in the early morning of July 12, 1969, one could tell by the humidity in the air and the forecast of sweltering temperatures that difficulty lay ahead. Summertime in Chicago is always torrid. Relief comes only from a quick rainstorm or an air conditioner—for those people fortunate enough to own one in the 1960s. Ruth and Sig had no air conditioning then. Rain was not in the forecast.

That day was the last of Ruth's life. Now at age seventy, the long-term effects of heart disease, worry, and stress proved to be too much. Arising early to see off a grandchild who had spent the night, Ruth made the beds and was preparing to drive the short distance to a local shopping center when she suffered a cerebral hemorrhage. Sig, her husband for nearly five decades, was home. He could not revive her. She never regained consciousness and succumbed at about noon at a nearby hospital.

For years Sig had wanted to move to Florida and tried without success to persuade Ruth to make the move. She could not cut the ties to her home and family, in particular, Chic. But by early 1969, Ruth agreed to move for part of the year to their favorite place in Sarasota, Florida, a quiet upscale community on the Gulf Coast about forty miles south of Tampa. They bought a new condominium on Longboat Key, planning to spend the winters away from the terrible cold and the likelihood of sickness. Ruth insisted that they retain their permanent residency in Des Plaines. She died before they could make the move.

"My dear friend and Chic Harley's sister died this month," wrote Edrie to the staff of Danville hospital on July 31. "So her sudden death was a terrible shock. I do hope Chic is all right. I really don't know what he will do without Ruth."

Chic arrived in Des Plaines on July 15, having traveled the three hours by car from Danville, accompanied by his thoughts, as the small farm towns and dirt roads flashed by. At that moment, the world was transfixed on one of the most remarkable events in history: the first landing of a man on the moon. Newspapers and TV stations were full of exciting coverage. But in a small corner of Des Plaines, there was anything but euphoria. The person closest to Chic, who had taken care of him for most of his life, who worried over him and attended to nearly every one of his needs, was now gone. Chic was never more alone than now. At the funeral home a day later, Chic wiped away the tears that flowed from under his wire-rimmed glasses. Two months shy of his seventy-fifth birthday, he was neatly dressed in a gray suit and blue tie. The last time they had seen each other was a month earlier. Ruth had asked the hospital for permission for Chic to visit her home just before she passed away. "He hasn't been here since Christmas, which seems to be a long time," she wrote.

Upon his return to Danville on July 24, a sorrowful Chic tried his best to cope with his loss. It was a long and painful process, but one he managed to handle.

With Ruth gone and Sig spending more time in Florida, Richard and Mary Jane readily accepted the responsibility of monitoring Chic's well-being and providing family care when he resumed his trips north. Shortly after Ruth's death, Mary Jane assured the hospital they wished to remain in close touch with Chic and have him at their home for his birthday celebration on September 15. A few weeks earlier, Edrie and her sister had visited with Chic in Danville, describing him as sad and a little more frail than normal. Richard drove to Danville to pick up his uncle and bring him back to the Wessell household for the celebration. Edrie and a group of friends telephoned Chic and sang "Happy Birthday." Later Edrie said, "He talked most happily with all of us, told us about the birthday cards and gifts he had received, and thanked us so sincerely."

Plans for Ohio State's 100th anniversary in 1970 had been under way for more than a year. The huge campus was a far cry from the school of 6,000 students that Chic Harley entered in 1915. The university invited Chic to the All American Commemorative Banquet, and Richard made plans to take his youngest son, eight-year-old Robert Harley Wessell, and his uncle to the affair after picking up Chic in Danville. At about the same time, Richard inquired about the possibility of moving Chic from Danville to a facility in or near Des Plaines. He told the hospital that he hoped to have a place picked out within ten days. Despite the good intentions, delays and pressing business of Richard's suburban newspaper business stymied any progress. Chic would remain in Danville.

Ohio State's anniversary marked a century of progress for a university that had grown into one of the grandest schools of higher learning in the country. Numerous commemorative events during the yearlong celebration recalled accomplishments and milestones over that time. Individuals who played significant roles in the school's growth and transformation from its days as a sleepy college were recognized, such as former President William Oxley Thompson; Thomas French, a faculty leader during the Harley years; Harlan Hatcher, later president of the University of Michigan; and noted author James Thurber were also recognized. Ohio State grads in sports were lauded: Woody Hayes, 1930s football star and Coach Wes Fesler, basketball player John Havlicek, and golfing great Jack Nicklaus. The weeklong series of activities culminated with a gigantic banquet inside the downtown Deschler-Wallick hotel. At one of the "Reserved" round tables sitting with school President Howard Fawcett were Woody Hayes, Jesse Owens, Chic Harley, Richard Wessell, and two of his sons, Rick and Bob. When the four-time Olympic gold medal winner Owens was introduced, thunderous applause filled the circular arena. Then it was Chic's turn. When his name was announced, a deafening, piercing roar like no other shook the rafters and continued for what seemed like half an hour. The thousands crammed into the banquet hall could barely contain themselves. They had not forgotten. Neither time nor mental illness had succeeded in erasing their love and affection for the humble little man who had performed such colossal feats fifty-four years earlier.

As the 1970s marched on, time was the enemy. The year 1971 began on a note of excitement as Chic, accompanied by a few friends and family members, flew to Pasadena, California, for the New Year's Day Rose Bowl game, pitting Ohio State against Stanford University. It had been fifty years since the Buckeyes' first appearance there, with Chic as the team's running back coach. In the 1971 contest, Stanford beat Ohio State 27-17, ending a Buckeye season that until then had been perfect at 9 and 0. Chic shrugged off the loss, preferring instead to be thankful that he could make the trip and see the colorful Tournament of Roses Parade before the game.

The year 1971 brought more sad news with the inevitable passing of old friends. One of Chic's best pals and most ardent admirers, *Dispatch* columnist Johnny Jones, died in mid-March. Probably Chic's biggest booster and cheerleader at games and rallies, Jones later entertained Columbus and the rest of Ohio with his popular newspaper column. Dressed in his famous white sweater and trousers, Jones made a college career of leading cheers and chants at football games on old Ohio Field. In later years, he would be called upon to lead cheers at banquets and other events where Chic was the guest of honor. As Columbus's most famous sportswriter, Jones used up buckets of ink writing about his favorite player.

"Sure, that's fine," Chic had told Jones years earlier when asked for his thoughts about having his likeness on the façade of the new Varsity Theater. "But why monuments to the living heroes? How about monuments to the dead?" said Chic, naming several of his teammates from decades earlier. "I don't rate what they did. I am alive." It was a story Jones liked to tell over and over.

Five months later, Leo Yassenoff, who owned the Varsity and insisted featuring Chic's likeness prominently, also passed away. "Chic is going to be desolate, I'm afraid," wrote Edrie. "Would you say a word to him, helping him understand how Leo had suffered so much and only his iron will kept him going as long as he did?" Yassenoff loved Chic like a brother, and from the time they were in college to the day Leo died, there was nothing he wouldn't do for him.

"Leo was a great person, builder, philanthropist, and supporter of the university and one of Chic's best friends," added Edrie. A social worker in Danville observed that Chic often remarked that so many of his friends have died, but "I have tried to point out to him he still has many friends left who are interested in his welfare and with whom he has so much in common."

A few months later, on January 20, 1972, Sig passed away in Des Plaines after suffering a heart attack in his sleep. He was seventy-four.

With the arrival of spring in 1974, Chic, now 79 1/2, was battling increasingly serious health problems. His tight hand-shake had weakened; the smile that had lit up rooms and hearts was subdued. He spent more time in bed resting, biding his time. By mid-April, he had developed a serious case of pneumonia, which he was unable to shake, despite the best efforts of VA physicians and intravenous doses of antibiotics. Sensing that death was near, his only surviving sibling, Irene, of Monrovia, California, wrote to the Danville VA on April 16, authorizing her nephew Richard as the official next of kin to "make the neces-sary decisions regarding my brother's health and treatment." A day earlier, newspaper reporters had begun calling Danville to ask about Chic's condition. Word had reached Columbus that he was very ill and might not recover.

Chic died peacefully at 5:15 A.M. Sunday, April 21, 1974, in a ward of the Danville VA hospital. Bronchopneumonia was the official cause of death. He also suffered from heart disease. His only personal effects were a Norelco electric razor, college foot-ball book, framed athletic certificates, and some clothing. His funds, which consisted primarily of his military pension, totaled $3,088.81. They were released to Irene.

On the day Chic died, he weighed 125 pounds, had grayish white hair, and was considered fairly well-nourished. He was listed as eighty years old, though his eightieth birthday was still five months away.

News of his passing spread rapidly throughout the nation, especially in Chicago, Columbus, and all of Ohio. Accolades poured in to the university as newspapers published banner front-page stories with large photos of him during his playing days. Close college friend Charlie Seddon, who coached football at the universities of Tennessee and Texas and at OSU, said Harley and Thorpe were the best football players he had ever seen.

"He was a great inspiration," said Jack "Farky" Farcasin, Chic's substitute in 1919. "We were nobody in football. Then he came in the picture. He built the tremendous hysteria you see today. He got everybody riled up when they raised the money for a new stadium in just a year."

Former Ohio Gov. and U.S. Sen. John Bricker, a catcher with the Ohio State baseball team in 1915-16, said Red Grange "was a great runner, maybe even as good as Chic, but he couldn't do all the things that Harley could do." It was Bricker who initiated Harley into the school's Varsity "O" Club in 1916. "He was the greatest football player I ever saw in my life," Bricker would reminisce.

Dr. William Kannapel, Danville VA's director of medicine at the time of Chic's death, said that his condition would have had a good chance to be treated successfully had he been afflicted later in life or born some years later. With the medical advances of the 1950s, Chic's life could have been relatively normal.

"But in 1921, there was little that could be done," said Kannapel. The combination of the 1921 football game, where Chic felt belittled and embarrassed, the crushing defeat in his final game as a collegian, and his history of withdrawal since childhood were likely triggers of his emotional breakdown, Dr. Kannapel added. Numerous tests never showed a medical reason for Chic's illness. The entire problem was psychological.

A crowd of about 100 people gathered at the Presbyterian Church in Columbus on April 26, 1974. Six members of that season's Ohio State football team had been designated pallbearers: Archie Griffin, Arnie Jones, Pete Cusik, Neal Colzie, Steve Myers, and Kurt Schumacher. There were another thirty-five honorary pallbearers, mainly former teammates, local sportswriters, and dignitaries. Also in attendance was Rex Kern, an Ohio native who quarterbacked Ohio State football teams from the national title championship in 1968 to 1970. Those who couldn't stand during the half-hour service sat in the lobby of the chapel. A minister spoke for a few minutes, and a high school teammate reminisced about their youthful years. At the end, the church organist played "Carmen Ohio" as men removed their hats and those present solemnly sang the words. Moments before the casket was closed, Kern placed on Chic's lapel his diamond Varsity "O" pin.

"There were not many tears," wrote a Columbus sportswriter. "The honorary pallbearers posed for pictures in front of the hearse. It looked like the documenting of a historical event. Perhaps it was."

The long procession of cars led by a black hearse bearing Chic's casket left the church and traveled north on Olentangy Road. The motorcade slowed to a crawl as it passed the huge concrete edifice of Ohio Stadium—"The House That Harley Built"—for one last glance along the swirling, chilly waters of the Olentangy River. A moment later, the vehicles quickened their pace and within five minutes had entered the front gates of Union Cemetery and stopped at the gravesite, about two blocks from the front iron gate. The long line of cars backed up out onto Olentangy Road. The only sounds were the rolling tires of three dozen vehicles easing to a halt, the thumping of doors closing, and the shuffling of shoes toward Chic's final resting spot.

As the pallbearers removed the casket and people got out of their cars, newspaper photographers and video cameramen gathered around to record the scene. With a crowd of about fifty huddled around the modest gravesite, the minister read from the *Book of Common Prayer*: "Ashes to ashes, dust to dust." A few moments later, it was over. Hands were shaken, hats placed back on heads, and pleasantries exchanged.

"The final chapter of the Chic Harley story was finished," said a newspaper story.

Within a few short years after the death of Chic Harley, many more of those who had stood next to him on the gridiron and become close personal friends also passed from the scene. Pete Stinchcomb died a year before Chic. The only Harley sibling still alive was Irene. Nephew Richard died in 2003, and Mary Jane, in 2004.

The light that had dazzled the football world in 1916 and burned for nearly sixty years had dimmed to a mere flicker by the mid-1970s. As the few remaining survivors of the early great years of Ohio State football finally passed on, the memory of what had occurred and who was responsible among a cadre of great sportsmen had faded nearly beyond recognition. There was no longer serious talk about naming Ohio Stadium Harley Stadium, which for many years had been a foregone conclusion. A proposal made in the 1920s when construction on the new stadium was under way that the main road leading up to the front of the coliseum be named after Harley disappeared with the murkiness of aging memories. Ohio State has named streets, arenas, dormitories, and classroom buildings after its many greats, but nothing in memory of Chic Harley, with the exception of a large rock at the school entrance on High Street, which signifies the site of old Ohio Field.

The comet called Harley that for decades shone brilliantly above Ohio and the nation had become a distant twinkle. Whether it would completely fade from the heavens was something only time could tell.

Columbus newspapers often published sketches of Chic in their Sports sections. This one published in the fall of 1916 depicts the Western Conference trying to get the attention of Eastern football authorities to recognize that Harley should be named an All-American, which he was.

By the end of the 1916 championship season for Ohio State, the call for building a new, much larger football stadium had reached a fever pitch due primarily to the excitement generated by Harley. Within three years a full-blown campaign to raise the $1 million—mainly from small contributions by grateful fans—was underway and in 1922, the famed "horseshoe" had opened. Today, after several renovations and expansions, the stadium still stands with a seating capacity of more than 101,000 making it one of the largest arenas in the world.

Epilogue

"When he dies, I am sure Ohio Stadium will be called Harley Stadium. It is too bad to wait till one passes away to be properly honored."

—Letter from Leo Yassenoff
to President John Kennedy,
November 18, 1963

It was chilly and very damp the early morning of Saturday, October 30, 2004. Circling low over the city of Columbus, Ohio, were swirling dark clouds pushed along their way by a swift autumn breeze. The forecast was rain. *No way,* I thought, *was Mother Nature going to cooperate on this very important day.* Rising early from my hotel room bed, I knocked on the adjacent doors of my brothers' and sisters' rooms and asked if anyone wanted me to purchase rain-protective coverings at a nearby convenience store. Without a moment's hesitation, everyone said yes. Thus began my quest for six ponchos.

The Penn State football team was in town to take on Ohio State in a highly anticipated Big Ten conference football battle. The famed Ohio State "horseshoe" stadium would be filled to its 105,000 capacity. Sitting in a drenching, cold rain shoulder-to-shoulder with so many people was not a pleasant thought.

What made this day's game different from any other ever staged at Ohio State did not involve the two teams battling on the white-striped green gridiron. The real show would be at halftime.

In each of the previous five seasons, Ohio State had hosted a halftime ceremony during one of its biggest conference games of the year to retire the jersey numbers of its five Heisman Trophy winners. Two-time recipient Archie Griffin's number 45 was first retired, followed by Les Horvath, Vic Janowicz, Hopalong Cassady, and Eddie George. On this day, when the temperatures seemed like they would not get much above freezing and the threat of rain loomed in the air, preparations were being made to add another jersey number to the "Ring of Fame" at the enclosed end of the mammoth outdoor arena. The decision had been made by university officials to retire jersey number 47 that day—one of several numbers Charles "Chic" Harley wore throughout his three years at Ohio State. Of the six numbers and names that by the end of the day would hang from the stadium rafters, Harley would be the only one who had not won a Heisman Trophy. He played nearly twenty years before the Heisman honor was created. If it had been in existence when Chic played, many people believe he would have won at least one, perhaps two, proclaiming him the best college football player in the land.

"You know how I started the program of retiring the numbers of our Heisman winners?" Ohio State Athletic Director Andy Geiger asked me in August 2004 as we sat in a couple of dark, cushioned chairs in his office.

"No, I have no idea," I responded.

"Your Dad came up with the idea," said Geiger, referring to Richard Wessell, the late nephew of Chic Harley. "He suggested that we retire the Heisman winners first, and when that was done, Chic's number would be retired. I think he had something in mind, don't you?"

By the time the first half of the Penn State game had ended, the skies above the "horseshoe" had turned a stunning blue and the temperature had reached a pleasant sixty degrees. It was an amazing turnaround. The dark green of the football field presented a stark contrast to the blazing scarlet attire worn by tens of thousands of Ohio State fans who filled the stadium. The public address announcer then told the crowd that the honor now being showered upon Chic Harley is one long overdue.

It took Ohio State eighty-five years—and an idea spawned by an out-of-stater (Harley's nephew)—to adequately recognize perhaps the most influential figure in the school's history. By 2004, Chic Harley had been deceased for thirty years. Nearly everyone who had seen him play was gone as well. What his contemporaries considered a foregone conclusion—the naming of the great football arena Harley Stadium—had become nothing more than a memory known faintly to only a few. Throughout the Ohio State campus, great edifices and byways bear names like Nicklaus Museum, Jesse Owens Plaza, Jesse Owens Athletic Center, Jesse Owens Memorial Stadium, Larkins Hall, Thompson Library, St. John Arena, Taylor Tower, Woody Hayes Drive, and Woody Hayes Athletic Center. The list is endless. What about Chic Harley? There's the retired jersey number and a small plaque that hangs near the stadium entrance that provides some recognition. There's also a boulder, nicknamed the "Harley Rock," that marks the site of old Ohio Field, where he played. To most people who walk by, it's nothing more than an out-of-place stone, unless they read the small inscription.

Why has Ohio State University gone to such exorbitant expense and effort to rightfully recognize many of its standouts, but fallen woefully short in doing the same for Chic Harley? The answer lies hidden somewhere beneath the blanket of time where memories tend to gradually fade. Chic Harley played in an era when there was no radio or TV to record his heroics. No clear movies exist of the famed "Harley Hip Move" and straight-arm. Unlike many modern-day athletes, Chic never boasted. He never complained. He was never concerned about making money or perpetuating his fame. He found enjoyment in spending time with his family and playing the game he loved—football—which he referred to as his hobby. Only a few of the handwritten letters

Chic wrote survive. None offer any insight into his athletic abilities. With all of this, the passage of time, the stigma of mental illness, and false, wild rumors that he had somehow contracted venereal disease, dampened the memory of what he had done to near extinction. Only the university and those who knew and loved him have the power to right that wrong, if they have the will to do so.

Some of the best times of my life were spent in a comfortable single-story home on a sleepy, narrow rural road in Des Plaines, Illinois. The half acre of open land provided more than enough room for me and my siblings, parents, grandparents, aunts, uncles, and cousins to spread our wings. There was a built-in swimming pool, a large screened porch, and a wide patio, where Uncle Chic would spend many summer days absorbing the fresh air, warm sunshine, and affections of his family and friends who would often stop by. The meals my grandmother Ruth made were always full and delicious, especially her raisin cake dessert. We'd all gather around the table to laugh and talk. Uncle Chic was there as well, rarely uttering a word, but always smiling. If he wasn't at peace with himself during these precious moments, he was at least happy in his surroundings.

Hanging on a wall in the small hallway separating the kitchen from the living room was Ruth's favorite picture of her brother. It's of Chic clad in his college football uniform, helmetless, hands on his hips, his head tilted slightly to his right, and a smile of satisfaction on his face.

To us, that picture was his monument. Perhaps some day the school he loved so much will christen an appropriate memorial of its own.

BIBLIOGRAPHY

NEWSPAPERS CONSULTED

Buckeye Sports Bulletin
Chicago American
Chicago Evening Post
Chicago Examiner
Chicago Tribune
Cincinnati Enquirer
Cleveland Plain Dealer
Columbus (Ohio) Citizen
Columbus (Ohio) Dispatch
Columbus (Ohio) Star
Indianapolis Star
Iowa City Press
Journal News, Hamilton, Ohio
Lancaster, Pa. Eagle

Mansfield (Ohio) News-Journal
Ohio State Journal
The Champaign Gazette
The Chicago Daily News
The Citizen –Journal, Columbus, Ohio
The Coshocton (Ohio) Tribune
The Decatur (Illinois) Review
The Lima (Ohio) News
The Milwaukee Daily News
The Ohio State Lantern
The Portsmith Daily Times
The Zanesville (Ohio) Signal
Wisconsin State Journal

MAGAZINES, JOURNALS, PROGRAMS CONSULTED

Athletic World
Biographical Dictionary of American Sports
Colliers Magazine
Columbus Dispatch Magazine
Encyclopedia of Chicago
History of Danville and Vermillion County (Illinois), 2008
Liberty Magazine
Makio

Ohio State Football Programs
Ohio State Monthly
Pro Football Reference.Com
Psychiatrict Quarterly
Staley Journal
The Columbus Citizen Magazine
The Ohio State University Bulletin, 1920-21
The Sundial
Time, The Weekly News Magazine

ORGANIZATIONS CONSULTED

National Alliance on Mental Illness
National Institute of Mental Health
The National Football Hall of Fame, New Brunswick, New Jersey
Phi Gamma Delta Fraternity

PHOTOGRAPHIC ARCHIVAL SOURCES

Bentley Historical Library, University of Michigan
Columbus (Ohio) Dispatch
Connie Paul
Ohio State University Archives
Wessell Family Archives

BOOKS

Brown, Brent, Kiess, Thomas, White, Steve, *One Game Season*, 2007

Davis, Jeff, *The Life and Legacy of George Halas*, McGraw-Hill, 2004

Halas, George, with Morgan, Gwen and Veysey, Arthur, *Halas by Halas*, New York: McGraw-Hill Book Company, 1979

Johnson, Dick, *Columbus Discovers Football*, 1972

Park, Jack, *The Official Ohio State Football Encyclopedia*, Champaign, Illinois, Sports Publishing L.L.C., 2003

Sharpe, Wilton, *Buckeye Madness*, 2005

Synpp, Wilbur, *The Buckeyes A Story of Ohio State Football*, 1974

Thurber, James, *James Thurber His Life and Times*

Watterson, John Sayle, *College Football: History, Spectacle, Controversy*

Whittingham, Richard, The Bears: A 75 Year Celebration, 1994

Wilson, Kenneth L. and Brondfield, Jerry, *The Big Ten*

INTERVIEWS

Bliss, Harry
Farcasin, Jack
Finneran, Joe
Finneran, Russell, Jr., Columbus, Ohio
Finneran, Russell, Sr., Columbus, Ohio, 1974-75
Huffman, Iolas
Johnson, Ernest
Paul, Connie, Columbus, Ohio
Seddon, Charlie
Wessell, Richard, Des Plaines, Illinois

GOVERNMENT RECORDS

Circuit Court Clerk of Cook County
Cook County Marriage Records
Department of Veterans Affairs, Illiana Health Care System
Fayette County (Ohio) Marriage Records
Franklin County (Ohio) Marriage Records
National Park Service
Ohio Historical Society
Ohio State University Archives

Pennsylvania Archives
Probate Court of Cook County
Probate Court, Franklin County, Ohio
Ross County's Government Website
Ross County (Ohio) Federal Census Records
Ross County, Ohio Marriage Records
State of Illinois Medical Certificate of Death
University of Michigan Archives
U.S. Army Military Registration
U.S. Census Data
Vermilion County (Illinois) Death Certificate
Virginia Military District Property Records

VETERAN'S ADMINISTRATION MEDICAL REPORTS

Application For Care and Treatment By Patient's Guardian, Relative, or Responsible
Representative
Funeral Arrangements
Laboratory Examinations
Medical Officers' Statement
Narrative Summary
Neuropsychiatric Examination
Occupational
Operation Records
Physiotherapy
Psychological Study
Rehabilitation Progress
Relative Interview
Report of Neuropsychiatric Examination
Social History
Social Service
Ward Physician's Progress and Treatment
Ward Surgeon's Progress and Treatment Record

ARTICLES

Adkins, Wendy J. Ohio Canals, 1997
Arter, Bill Homes of a Hero, Columbus Vignette, Columbus Dispatch Sunday
    Magazine, 1969
Baker, Sam, The One and Only-Chic, November 1960
Bennett, Henry Holcomb, County of Ross
Butler, Brian, S. The Coffin Corner, The Role of the Road Team in the NFL:
    The Louisville Brecks, 1988
Cannon, Ralph, Harley to Horvath, Esquire, September 1945

Homan, Marv and Hornung, Paul, Ohio State 100 Years of Football. Columbus, 1989

Hooley, Bruce, Greatest Moments in Ohio State Football History, Triumph Books, 1997

Ladd, Keith and Rickman, Greg, The Pullman Strike, kansasheritage.org, 1998

LaLonde, Brent, Legends of the Scarlet & Gray, The Columbus Dispatch, 2005

McCarty, Bernie, The First Buckeye Superstar

Odell, Kerry and Weidemeir, Marc D., Real Shock, Monetary Aftershock: The 1906 San Francisco Earthquake and the Panic of 1907, Claremont Colleges Working Papers, 2001-07

Ohio Public Library Information Network & The Ohio Historical Society, The Evolution of Ohio, Virginia Military District, 1997

Pollard, James E., Pollard's Papers, Ohio State Athletics, 1879-1959. Columbus: Ohio State University Athletic Department, 1959

Sabbatini, Renato, The History of Shock Therapy in Psychiatry

Scheibeck, Irven, Chic Harley 'the one and only,' The Columbus Dispatch Magazine, September 2006

The Buckeye Battle Cry, August 2008

The Ohio State University Marching Band Drum Major, "A Brief History of the Ohio State Drum Major"

The Great 1906 San Francisco Earthquake, United States Geological Survey

Tributes to Chic Harley, October 10, 1953

REPORTS, DIRECTORIES, LETTERS

City of Chicago Directory

Endowment Fund Report, Cornerstones, Ohio State University Treasurer 2001-2002

Gaver, Earl. E., M.D., Dr. Gaver Sanitarium, December 10, 1935

Memorandum of Agreement between Ohio State University Athletic Board and Varsity

"O" Alumni Association, 1927

Minutes from meeting of the Ohio State Athletic Board, November 21, 1939

Sphinx (Ohio State University) Directory

The Ohio State Athletic Department Balance Sheet as of June 30, 1947

The Ohio State University, Office of the University Registrar

Thompson, Williams O., to Chic Harley, November 29, 1916

Wessell, Richard C., Sr., to Andy Greiger, July 5, 2001

Index

Tarbell, Dr. R.C., 200
Taylor, Glenn, 63, 66
Taylor, Henry, 218, 226, 219
Taylor, John "Tarzan,"159, 161, 166, 255, 163, 164, 177, 181, 182
Thomas, Oscar, 226, 227, 229
Thompson, William O., 103, 146, 190, 274
Thorpe, Jim, 62, 91, 159, 165, 166, 234, 245, 252, 277
Thurber, James, 252, 274
Thurman, Allen "Husky," 22, 25, 231
Tinker, Joe, 144
Tomlinson, Edrie, 270, 271, 272, 273, 275
Touer, "Tubby," 26
Trafton, George, 163
Trainor, Charles, J., 181, 187
Trautman, Red., 112, 152, 220
Trunnell, David, 10, 11
Trunnell, Frances, 10
Turner, Irwin, 48

Union Cemetery, 259, 278

Van Dyne, Kelly, 57, 58, 80, 89, 269
Van Dyke, Dick, 212
Van Dyke, Jerry, 212
Veeck, William, 156, 181, 183, 184
Vorys, John, 22, 25, 26, 27, 39, 167, 206, 231, 250

Wahlquist, Larry, 142
Walker, George, 206
Warner, Pop, 75
Wessell, Bob, 274
Wessell, Mary Jane, 1, 2, 3, 225, 231, 262, 264, 273, 279
Wessell, Richard, 1, 2, 3, 207, 225, 227, 231, 232, 241, 259, 262, 264, 270, 271, 273, 274, 276, 279, 282
Wessell, Rick, 274
Wessell, Ruth (see Ruth Harley)
Wessell, Sig, 207, 225, 240, 241, 242, 243, 256, 262, 266, 270, 271, 272, 273, 276
Wessell, Stephen, 258
Weston, "Beak," 120
Wilce, Jack, 39, 47, 48, 72, 73, 75, 80, 85, 87, 93; 110-155, 174, 197, 220, 221, 231, 233, 238, 246, 248-249, 254, 257, 258, 262-265
   31, joins OSU staff
   35, recruiting Chic
   58, tells team to concentrate

246, Hall of Fame role
Wilson, Woodrow, 75, 250
Willaman, Fred, 87, 95, 111, 142
Williams, Guy, 226
Witherington, Paul, 61,
World Columbian Exposition, 15
Wortman, Lt., Art, 99

Yassenoff, Leo, 220, 231, 246, 255, 262, 275, 281
Yassenoff, Milton, 255
Yerges, Howard, 48, 50, 53, 56, 67, 80, 86, 87, 88, 89, 110, 152, 206, 215, 269
Yost, Fielding, 39, 115, 117, 118, 119, 120, 121, 155, 245, 265
Young, Genevieve, 240, 243, 265, 266
Young, Tee, 201

Zupke, Bob, 55, 59, 61, 85, 86, 87, 264, 126, 134, 136, 142, 143, 145, 245, 250, 264, 265

Todd C. Wessell was born in Evanston, Illinois in 1952, the second oldest of six children born to newspaper editors and publishers Richard and Mary Jane Wessell. He graduated from Illinois State University in 1976 and since that time has served in various capacities at the family-owned Journal & Topics Newspapers that serve Chicago's Northwest suburbs. He currently is editor and publisher. During his newspaper career, he has won many awards for distinguished journalism from the National Newspaper Association, Illinois Press Association, Chicago Headline Club, Midwest Travel Writers Association and Society of American Travel Writers.

Until his death in 1974, Charles Harley, known to the Wessells as "Uncle Chic", spent much time with the family visiting with them in their suburban home in Des Plaines during extensive stays away from the Danville, Illinois Veterans Administration Hospital.

Todd Wessell and Carolyn Kessler married in 1975 and are the parents of four children, Thomas, Erin, Katelyn and Daniel.